THE TREE OF THE DOVES

Also by Christopher Merrill

Workbook (poems)

Outcroppings: John McPhee in the West (editor)

Fevers & Tides (poems)

The Forgotten Language: Contemporary Poets and Nature (editor)

From the Faraway Nearby: Georgia O'Keeffe as Icon (editor, with Ellen Bradbury)

The Grass of Another Country: A Journey Through the World of Soccer (nonfiction)

Anxious Moments, prose poems by Aleš Debeljak (translator, with the author)

Watch Fire (poems)

What Will Suffice: Contemporary American Poets on the Art of Poetry (editor, with Christopher Buckley)

The Old Bridge: The Third Balkan War and the Age of the Refugee (nonfiction)

The Forest of Speaking Trees: An Essay on Poetry

Your Final Pleasure: An Essay on Reading

The Four Questions of Melancholy: New and Selected Poems of Tomaž Šalamun (editor)

The Way to the Salt Marsh: A John Hay Reader (editor)

The City and the Child, poems by Aleš Debeljak (translator, with the author)

Only the Nails Remain: Scenes from the Balkan Wars (nonfiction)

Brilliant Water (poems)

Things of the Hidden God: Journey to the Holy Mountain (nonfiction)

Even Birds Leave the World: Selected Poems of Ji-woo Hwang (translator, with Won-Chung Kim)

Because of the Rain: A Selection of Korean Zen Poems (translator, with Won-Chung Kim)

Scale and Stairs: Selected Poems of Heeduk Ra (translator, with Won-Chung Kim)

7 Poets, 4 Days, 1 Poem (collaborative poem, with Marvin Bell, István László Geher, Ksenia Golubovich, Simone Inguanez, Tomaž Šalamun, and Dean Young)

Translucency: Selected Poems of Chankyung Sung (translator, with Won-Chung Kim)

THE TREE OF THE DOVES

CEREMONY, EXPEDITION, WAR

CHRISTOPHER MERRILL

milkweed
editions

Published 2011 by Milkweed Editions
Printed in Canada by Friesens Corporation
Cover design by Stewart A. Williams Design
Cover photos by (from top) Nikada, Knighterrant, Rafal Olkis
Author photo by Ram Devineni
Interior design by Connie Kuhnz
The text of this book is set in Warnock Pro.
11 12 13 14 15   5 4 3 2 1
First Edition

The poem on p. 210 is from Dan Pagis, "written in pencil in the sealed railway car," in *The Selected Poetry of Dan Pagis*, translated by Stephen Mitchell. © 1989 by Stephen Mitchell. Reprinted by permission of the University of California Press.

Please turn to the back of this book for a list of the sustaining funders of Milkweed Editions.

Library of Congress Cataloging-in-Publication Data

Merrill, Christopher.
    The tree of the doves : ceremony, expedition, war /
    Christopher Merrill. —1st ed.
        p.   cm.
    Includes bibliographical references.
    ISBN 978-1-57131-305-8 (acid-free paper)
    1. Terror—Social aspects.   2. Terror—History.   3. History—
Philosophy.   I. Title.
    HV6431.M463 2011
    363.325—dc23

                                                        2011021332

This book is printed on acid-free paper.

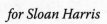

for Sloan Harris

Terror is opportune as is relief from terror.

—*Geoffrey Hill*

THE TREE OF THE DOVES

PROLOGUE

I take my bearings on the Golan Heights, between an Israeli observation post and a UN peacekeeping base. Israel captured this strategic plateau in the Six Days' War in 1967, and through the haze of an autumn afternoon, beyond a line of bunkers and a vineyard, I can see the road to Damascus, forty kilometers away. Beirut is a little farther off, over Mount Hermon—one of the sites traditionally ascribed to the Transfiguration, where Jesus appeared to his disciples in a new light. When Peter, James, and John saw their rabbi in a radiant white robe alongside the prophets Moses and Elijah, they recognized him as the Messiah. Out of a cloud came the voice of God: "This is My beloved Son, in whom I am well pleased. Hear Him!" Jesus told his disciples to keep his metamorphosis secret until after he rose from the grave, then continued his ministry in the communities around the Sea of Galilee, at the base of the Golan Heights. It was there that he revealed his plan to build a church destined to reshape the course of history, first in the Roman Empire and then around the world—a religious movement that became inseparable from politics. It started with Jesus demanding a change of heart from his followers, and twenty centuries later I began to reflect on some of the changes wrought by another revolution in political thinking: the "war on terror" declared by President George W. Bush in the aftermath of the 9/11 attacks on New York City and Washington, DC.

Terror is always with us—a fact borne out by countless examples from daily life: the heart racing on a turbulent flight, the dread felt before the diagnosis is delivered. But a lookout on the Golan is a particularly good place to consider the consequences of living in fear. This is disputed land, in the sights of military planners and observers, politicians and diplomats, clerics and poets; and even on a quiet day it is hard to escape the sensation that all hell could break loose at any moment. Syrian claims on this land, which provides Israel with a crucial supply of fresh water, have for forty years added new threads to a tangled history, which periodically unravels in a spectacular fashion; hence the peacekeepers, more than a thousand strong, who patrol a zone of separation between the two countries, maintaining the cease-fire negotiated after Syria's failed invasion of the southern Golan in the Yom Kippur War of 1973. A Security Council resolution regards the Golan as Israeli-occupied territory; any settlement of the Arab-Israeli conflict, which dates back more than a century, must thus resolve the matter of the Golan, which for the Jewish state forms a critical bulwark against Arab attacks.

The story of living in the presence of fear belongs to the ages. Terror's leading role in the history of the region that gave rise to Judaism, Christianity, and Islam reminds us that much religious discourse is predicated on questions rooted in fear—particularly of the unknown: Where do we come from? Where are we going? What shall we do? Such was the drift of my thinking on the drive up the escarpment, along a narrow, twisting road past fenced-off minefields, olive groves, and Druze villages carved into hillsides. At the sight of a police station surrounded by barbed wire my Arab guide told me that most Druze are waiting for Syria to regain the Golan, either through negotiations or force, although they keep silent about this in public for fear of antagonizing the authorities. Nor, he added, would I learn anything from the only man in the street, a religious elder dressed in a black robe and white turban. He would not breathe a word about his faith or politics to an outsider, my guide explained; members of this small Islamic sect have long since learned to keep their own counsel. On we drove toward the Syrian border.

Now at the lookout the guide points beyond the peace-keeping base to the remains of a Druze village destroyed by retreating Syrian forces, and shakes his head.

"Too much war," he mutters, leading me to the kiosk, where he insists that I try a Druze pita—a wrap filled with *labneh*, a soft, sour cheese, almost a yogurt, sprinkled with *za'atar*, which is a blend of spices including oregano, dried sumac, sesame seeds, and salt.

From here we descend to the Sea of Galilee, past fields of obsidian and scrub, military bases, and an extensive system of rain catchments and reservoirs that drained the wetlands and turned this desert into an agricultural oasis. The three sources of the Jordan River are located on the Golan, whose vineyards ensure that water is regularly turned into wine, and across the river in which Jesus was baptized we stop in Capernaum, so that I can walk in the land of his ministry. There is no time to visit the synagogue in which he preached, or climb the hill above a banana grove to see the church raised on the site on which he delivered the Sermon on the Mount, or board the wooden boat that carries pilgrims across the lake, on which he sailed with his disciples. But I do wander through the Church of the Multiplication of the Loaves and Fishes, the altar of which is built around the stone on which he is said to have laid five loaves of bread and two fishes to feed five thousand, fulfilling Isaiah's prophesy to leave his birthplace in Nazareth and dwell in Capernaum—where "the people who sat in darkness saw a great light, and upon those who sat in the region and shadow of death light has dawned." Three Indian women in bright blue saris fall to their knees to touch the stone, and then I do the same.

Another light had dawned in America when I made the journeys to Malaysia, China and Mongolia, and the Middle East described in this book. After 9/11, the argument ran, threats to the homeland were to be viewed in a new light, through the prism of terrorism—politically motivated violence against civilians, to be precise. Thus the fear of another terrorist attack prompted Congress to pass controversial legislation limiting civil liberties, while offering little resistance to Bush administration decisions to flout its treaty obligations, forge a doctrine of preemptive war, invade and occupy Iraq, ignore the Geneva Convention on the treatment of prisoners of war, and implement a wide-ranging domestic surveillance program—decisions that defied not only legal precedent and common sense but also the values upon which this country was founded. When in the summer of 2007 a nominee for the position of attorney general refused to say in his confirmation hearing that waterboarding (an interrogation technique developed in the Spanish Inquisition, employed in Nazi Germany and North Korea, and prosecuted as a war crime for over a century) was a form of torture, it became clear that something fundamental had changed in our body politic—in our soul, that is.

How and why this came to be will furnish historians, scholars, and writers with material for generations. For my part I wished to take an alternate reading on the Age of Terror, traveling to distant parts of the earth to record some of the ferment marking our days and nights. For it is at such fraught moments in history that civilizations may move in radically different directions. Just as the life and times of Jesus of Nazareth coincided with the first stirrings of revolt against the Roman Empire, so now we are witnessing changes—political and social, technological and environmental—presaging the end of one order and the creation of another: a world that bewilders, frightens, and inspires. And it seemed to me that a description of the conditions at hand—of our predicament, if you will—might begin to clarify who and what we are becoming.

This, then, is a book composed in the key of terror. The vertigo experienced at the edge of a cliff; the involuntary shaking that attends a brush with death; the way that a child clings to her mother when a stranger approaches—terror is a fact of life, which poets and divines have addressed since time immemorial. It is the ground note of much of what is best in humanity—and worst. It is not easily explained away or overcome; and if we celebrate those brave souls who transform their encounters with it into enduring works of literature, art, and music, our destinies are also inscribed by those who seize on it for their own gain. From the Paleolithic cave paintings of wild beasts in Lascaux to Olivier Messiaen's *Quartet for the End of Time* the human ability to translate terror into beauty has been one of our distinguishing features—no less so than the machinations of those who exploit it for political advantage. History turns on an axis of terror.

The Tree of the Doves is my take on that axis. *Ceremony, Expedition, War*: these essays represent three attempts—*essais*, in Montaigne's original conception—to explore some portion of experience, some way of being in the world, through the lens of terror and its sometime corollary, courage. I begin with the proposition that our lives are shaped by ceremonies, expeditions, and wars, the origins of which are rooted at least partly in fear. "Every angel is terrifying," the poet Rainer Maria Rilke wrote in *Duino Elegies*—an insight integral to ceremonies of celebration and praise, of healing and mourning; to expeditions undertaken for pleasure, profit, or the pursuit of meaning; to wars waged justly and unjustly. This dark knowledge informed my itinerary, which took me to three very different parts of the world to explore how individuals and societies are framed by this triad. What follows is an account of impressions and encounters from my travels—geographical, historical, literary, political, and religious.

The performance of a banned ritual in the Malaysian state of Kelantan is the setting for a meditation, in *Ceremony*, on the clash between modernity and tradition in the Islamic world. The events of 9/11 demonstrated that the outcome of the battle for Islam's future will also have important ramifications for the West, and so I was keen to hear from Malaysian artists, writers, and politicians grappling with the issue of Islamic identity. The relationship between Islam and the West, which from the rise of the Muslim caliphate in the seventh century has helped to define both civilizations, has grown more complex in the Age of Terror—a truth made clear in my meetings with those on the front lines of a long war of ideas. What I witnessed in the jungle may or may not be a harbinger of things to come, but it did offer a way to think about a society in transition, a palimpsest in which to read layer upon layer of aesthetic, religious, and political experience.

In *Expedition*, I retrace part of an epic voyage made in 1921 by the French poet-diplomat Saint-John Perse from Beijing to Ulaanbaatar—a symbol, it seems to me, of the human drive to explore, to attempt to grasp life in its entirety, and then to set forth again. In every historical period the clocks are set at different times, figuratively speaking; history unfolds in such distinct rhythms around the world that it is sometimes difficult to imagine that events far removed from one another—the first moon walk, say, and the Cultural Revolution—are concurrent. And nowhere is this more apparent than in China, whose dizzying changes in the modern era often bewilder its inhabitants and observers alike. From his post in Beijing, though, Perse was an astute judge of a society that from a Western perspective was peripheral to the march of history but which in the fullness of time would edge ever closer to the center. All eyes were on Europe then, reeling after the carnage of World War I, and while China's interests had figured into the deliberations of the Paris Peace Conference its fate did not matter to Woodrow Wilson and his colleagues. But the world's most populous country could not be ignored forever. The same is true today. Our attention may now be on the Middle East, which is still sorting out the maps drawn up at Versailles, but we also live in what some call the Chinese Century. Where to look for a guide to navigate us through those puzzling landscapes governed by a different sense of time, of history? A great poet may hold in mind the contradictory rhythms and ideas integral to a global perspective, and Perse's cool-eyed, ceremonial verses, which measure time and distance in a unique fashion, fusing occidental and oriental styles of thought, offer in their music another way to map the present: a new route to the interior of Asia—and of ourselves. It may be wise to heed the words and example of the man who finished off his Nobel lecture with this maxim: "And it is enough for the poet to be the guilty conscience of his time." Saint-John Perse was such a conscience.

The final essay, *War*, recounts my journey in the spring of 2007 to Syria, Jordan, Israel and the West Bank, Greece, Turkey, and Lebanon, when the Middle East seemed poised, yet again, for regional conflagration. In the fifth year of the American occupation of Iraq the Bush administration had adopted a new strategy to end the bloodshed, sending thousands of troops into Baghdad—a surge designed to pacify the insurgency and then to create the conditions in which to reconcile the warring parties in what now appeared to be a failed state. Whether this strategy would work or not was an open question; what *was* clear in the Levant, in the remains of the Ottoman Empire, was that the war was changing everything; the breakup of a political order can paralyze the civilian population, if it does not lead to flight, and spawn terrible angels, many of whom were abroad on my travels. *The Tree of the Doves* is thus also a meditation on empire, specifically the terror at the heart of any imperial project—Persian, Chinese, Roman, Mongolian, British, American. Ceremony, expedition, war: in this trinity of human actions, devised to keep terror at bay, history is forged. And I was privileged to witness some of it.

PART I

CEREMONY

CEREMONY

Her symptoms were vague: aches and pains, a general feeling of despair. Yet the figure she cut in the circle of women
seated on one side of the stage was regal. This was not her first
main puteri (literally, "playing the princess"), a healing ritual
performed in the northeastern Malaysian state of Kelantan despite the proscription, dating from a 1991 decree by Islamic
authorities, against traditional ceremonies. And she betrayed
nothing in her demeanor of the drama about to unfold on this
hot, humid night in the jungle.

After evening prayers, the entire village or *kampong* assembled by the stage, an open-sided tin-roofed shed cleared
of its tools, machinery, and motorcycles. The size of the gathering was the first surprise: hundreds of people of all ages sat
on fallen palm trees or stood in the fringe of forest thicken-
ing the darkness. I had traveled here with Eddin Khoo, the
director of Pusaka, a small organization dedicated to preserving Malaysia's traditional art forms; and while his passion
for indigenous ways of apprehending reality had spurred my
journey it also raised questions in my mind about their true
place in this society. Dislocation, a recurring theme of our
conversation on the long drive from Kuala Lumpur, through
lowland plains and rubber-tree plantations, then jungles
and forests and craggy mountains, to the coastal city of Kota
Bharu, the royal seat of Kelantan, explained some of the appeal of the Pan-Malaysian Islamic Party (PAS), which ruled

this conservative state: it offered a belief system to counter the uncertainties and encroachments of modern life. If I had assumed that PAS's strictures would keep the villagers away, their numbers seemed to vindicate Eddin's efforts to save the banned ceremonies. He had studied, documented, and promoted them for over a decade, defying the Islamists in an inventive fashion—apprenticing himself to a shadow puppeteer; sponsoring *main puteri* shamans and musicians; and training young people in indigenous dance forms. It was not hard to imagine him losing perspective in his enthusiasm for what remained of Malaysia's old ways. He thought himself fortunate thus far to have avoided arrest.

"What we're doing is basically illegal," he said with feeling.

He was a short, fidgety man, half-Chinese, half-Tamil, with a lilting British accent (courtesy of Newcastle University in Newcastle upon Tyne); his pugnacious bearing did not issue from his black belt in kung fu as much as from a lifelong feud with his countrymen. Born during the Sino-Malay race riots of 1969, which left hundreds dead and part of Kuala Lumpur's Chinese population homeless, he decided early on that there was no place for him in his society, and so he became a thoroughgoing Anglophile. He read *David Copperfield* at the age of seven; his parents would trot him out at parties to say the word "conflagration"; asked to name the most important Malaysian writers, he said, "Joseph Conrad, Somerset Maugham, and Anthony Burgess." English on Eddin's tongue had a marvelous ring, all flattened vowels and trilled *r*'s and cackles of delight punctuating his speech as he drove himself to exhaustion in a bid to change his culture through the word. He slept no more than four hours a night—his soporific was watching *World Wrestling Federation* TV shows—and in his insomnia he had devised an ambitious literary agenda. He was tinkering with his first collection of poems; writing books on the Muslim predicament and his shadow puppeteer master; translating literary works from English into Malay. His version of *Moby-Dick* was proceeding by fits and starts; he intended to do all of Shakespeare's plays and publish them under his own imprint.

That was not the end of it. He planned to run in the Kuala Lumpur Marathon—a foolish risk, I thought, for a smoker with high blood pressure. Equally disturbing was his claim to be adept at catching king cobras—a skill acquired in childhood from the family gardener, which might be put to use during the *main puteri*: a swarm of king cobras had invaded the *kampong* earlier in the day; if they returned, the headman planned to spray them with ammonia. It is taboo to kill a king cobra, which for Hindus like Eddin is the incarnation of Shiva, and also unwise, since the scent of the dead snake could attract other snakes. Likewise the sound of the *serunai* (a reed instrument similar to an oboe), Eddin added as we took our seats behind the musicians, on a plank of wood laid on the sand. Not to worry, he said. Rubber tappers had discovered that spitting on a wad of tobacco made a poultice that, if applied to a king cobra bite, might keep you alive until antivenin serum—always in short supply—could be located.

"We have a Malaysian saying," he said. "Fight poison with poison."

The saying has a political dimension. This healing ritual, for example, was taking place against the backdrop of a Muslim insurgency in southern Thailand. Two weeks earlier, on April 28, 2004, rebels had coordinated attacks on ten police stations just over the border from Kelantan. Armed with machetes, the rebels were no match for the Thai military, which killed more than a hundred, many of whom had sought refuge in a mosque. The Thai government accused Malaysia of supporting the insurgency, which some believed was connected to al-Qaeda and Jemaah Islamiyah (the militant organization responsible for the Bali car bombings in October 2002); and while the border was closely monitored (preventing, among other things, a group of traditional Thai dancers from traveling to Eddin's next festival, in Kuala Lumpur), no one thought that the bloodshed was over.

Meanwhile a story had just broken on the television news magazine *60 Minutes* and in a *New Yorker* article by Seymour Hersh of a scandal at Abu Ghraib prison in Iraq, where under the rule of Saddam Hussein thousands of dissidents had been tortured and executed. After the Iraqi strongman was deposed in the US-led invasion, the prison was used to inter suspected insurgents, and now photographs were circulating on the Internet of American military police torturing and abusing the prisoners—images of naked men stacked in a pyramid, punched by a soldier, and cowering before a German shepherd; of a woman with a cigarette dangling from her mouth giving the thumbs-up sign to a hooded prisoner's penis; of corpses laid out on cement floors. The occupation of Iraq had taken a sadistic turn, the revelation of which was met with particular revulsion in the Islamic world; the photograph of a hooded figure standing on a box, with electrodes attached to his arms and genitals, was a fixture in political cartoons and graffiti from Egypt to Malaysia; Iraqis nicknamed the image *The Statue of Liberty.*

Eddin was scrutinizing the patient, as if to place her in his memory. She towered over the women attending to her—her sisters-in-law, Eddin guessed—and her features were as angular as theirs were round; her plaid sarong offset their bright yellows, blues, and greens; when she wrapped an orange scarf around her neck—the only colorful note in her attire—Eddin wondered aloud if her problems stemmed from barrenness. The success of the *main puteri*, he explained, depended upon the shaman discovering the source of her illness; part divination, part theater, this spirit-raising ceremony, usually undertaken as a last resort, would require her to surrender to his ministrations for two nights running, and the resignation etched into her face suggested that she was willing to try almost anything, if it would bring relief. She radiated a kind of fatalism familiar to Eddin.

"The Kelantan sensibility," he said, laying his hand over his heart, "is located entirely in lament, in loss." Tonight we would learn what was missing from this patient's life, in a performance combining animist, Hindu, and Islamic elements. The magical spell woven by the *main puteri,* drawing on the oldest customs of the Malay Peninsula, was precisely what the purifying Islamists campaigned against. Kelantan is predominately Malay—hence Islamic—but its traditional rituals reflect a more complicated heritage of mixing and mingling than PAS acknowledged—a history of foreign influence dating back millennia. Malays descend from a variety of peoples: seafarers who migrated from China thousands of years before Christ, Indian traders who established kingdoms on the coasts, Arab travelers drawn to the Land of Gold, as it was called in Sanskrit records. The sea lanes fostered exchange with diverse cultures, attracting merchants, missionaries, and warriors from near and far, who helped to shape Malay customs, artistic expression, and religious practice—even as the original inhabitants of the peninsula, the indigenous people known as the Orang Osli, retreated into the interior. Thus Indians built Hindu and Buddhist temples for several centuries before Arab traders introduced Islam around 1400, a pattern repeated a century later with the arrival of Christianity, courtesy of Portuguese, Dutch, and then British colonizers; each group left a mark on Malay life; none destroyed its rival cultures; hence elements of each order contributed to the heterogeneous character of modern Malaysia—a history of exchange that some in power wished to eradicate. How would they react to such a large turnout tonight?

The air was still, the crowd rapt in the firelight of coconut husks burning in a sand pit beyond the stage. The faces of the villagers hunched by the trees were intermittently illuminated by flashes of lightning and the headlights of trucks and scooters arriving from neighboring *kampongs*. From the rafters hung jasmine flowers and a tray of sticky yellow rice topped with betel nut, coins, and an egg to attract the spirits; more food was set out on the reed mats covering the floor, along with bowls of ritual water and a pillow. The shaman, in a white shirt and blue vest, sat cross-legged before the musicians—the *serunai* player, ten percussionists arranging a variety of drums and gongs and cymbals, a man with a three-stringed *rebab* or spike fiddle—and recited verses from the Koran, swaying from side to side, a glass of water in one hand and a tray of food in his lap: a feast for the invisible powers of the earth, air, and water. And as he called on ancestral saints and *jins* and teachers to heal the patient, apologizing for any omissions, I did not know which to fear more: the arrival of the police or of the king cobra and her brood.

But the spectacle of the *main puteri* gradually dispelled some of my anxiety. First the shaman blessed the musical instruments with smoke from a burning coconut husk (a Hindu custom); and then, in time to the haunting melody of the *serunai*, which in my imagination carried far into the forest, and the complicated rhythms of one man striking a floor gong and another tapping a drum, he removed his vest and shirt and began to sing with the *rebab* player, who served as the *minduk*—the séance singer and dancer who for the next several hours would summon, interrogate, and appease the spirits from the world beyond the river. The *minduk* bantered with the shaman, coaxing the spirits to join them onstage, to inhabit the shaman, the medium for this elaborate production, who sank into a trance, and one by one the spirits took shape in his words and gestures, revealing different aspects of the patient's personality, history, and character. Now he was whirling from the *minduk* to the musicians, now he was dancing slowly, seductively, around the patient, seated with her legs bent to the side at center stage, under a mobile of bananas, jasmine, rice cakes, bottlebrush, bougainvillea, a pink triangle, and an orange. She watched the shaman with a weary expression. I could not imagine the pain that had led her, or others acting on her behalf, to this very public examination of her soul.

The *minduk* and the shaman were divining what had upset her balance—and thus the harmony of the universe. The success of the ritual depended upon them discovering whether a *hantu*, a malign or unsettled spirit, had taken possession of her. Or had she lost the essence of her soul, her *semangat*? Did her malaise arise from unfulfilled desires? Act by act, the medicine men would summon spirits, populating the stage with a cast of characters from a cosmology rooted in the belief that divinity inheres in everything (in stones and trees, in the distant thunder and the water buffalo grazing by the rice paddies), one of whom might hold the key to healing the woman's soul sickness.

Eddin described what followed as a form of improvisatory poetry, in the manner of ancient Greek bards who employed stock phrases as mnemonic aids and added new verses to each performance: an oral literature long since vanished from Western practice. No doubt its proscription in Kelantan leant it a certain power, in the same way that some poets in the Soviet Bloc held a special place in their countrymen's hearts, answering the strictures and tedium of state-sponsored art with more vital forays into the language. And I likened the shaman's commerce with the spirit world to the modern poet's role as intermediary between the visible and invisible realms of experience. For I subscribed to the Polish poet Czesław Miłosz's notion that poetry "is dictated by a daimonion"; hence the hope "that good spirits, not evil ones, choose us for their instruments." Like shamans, like divines navigating between this world and the next, some poets work on the premise that good and evil spirits are abroad. Who can say which will possess them in the act of writing—and whether a given poem will heal or harm?

Just as a shaman can be a medium for good or ill, so this ritual preserved, for better or worse, the memory of a people who had inhabited the Malay Peninsula through successive waves of invaders and missionaries and traders, adapting ideas and customs from the larger world—Chinese and Indian, Khmer and Siamese, Portuguese and British. *Main puteri* called the crowd to its origins, descending through layers of history, through sultanates and empires and kingdoms, to remind the paddy farmers and their families that in Kelantan, the cradle of Malay civilization, where witchcraft was still alive, there were measures to take if they were felled by one of the black arts.

Thus the *minduk* interrogated the spirits revealing themselves through the shaman to diagnose the cause of the woman's problems, which, Eddin said, seemed to stem from her *angin*, her inner winds. From birth these winds had blown through her, now stronger, now lighter, determining her personality, talents, desires. Like the humors of Greek and Roman theory, as well as medieval European and Muslim thought, the four bodily fluids governing individual temperament and health (black and yellow bile, phlegm and blood), the *angin* constitute for Malays a system of understanding human behavior—the inherited traits and inclinations, which can be expressed or not, depending on a variety of factors, including the environment in which one lives. Indeed the most common condition treated in *main puteri*, anthropologist Carol Laderman notes in her study, *Taming the Wind of Desire: Psychology, Medicine, and Aesthetics in Malay Shamanistic Performance,* is blockage of the inner winds, *sakit berangin,* which tends to afflict artists and musicians, not to mention healers. *Main puteri* is thus a means of reckoning with sicknesses born of the inner winds, which must periodically be freed and refreshed.

It is also a branch of the secret knowledge that mystics have sought through the ages in various religious traditions: the direct experience of worlds beyond the self, made known through poetry and music and dance, often leavened with humor. I admired Eddin for his dedication to preserving the rituals integral to a system of belief that threatened the religious authorities. And in the chanting of the *minduk* I heard echoes of the haunting music and refrain—*Allah, Allah*—that accompanied the whirling dervishes I had seen perform some years before at a sacred music festival in Morocco: men in white gowns, wide black belts, and tall brown hats spun around and around an outdoor stage in the city of Fes, arms raised, heads cocked to one side, the singer seated behind them, leading an ensemble of percussionists. That spring evening had been stifling, and in the press of the crowd I had stood on tiptoes to watch the Sufis turning and turning toward the truth, toward God, following a mystical path that some Islamic clerics deem heretical. It seemed as if my mind and body, numbed by a trans-Atlantic flight and a wearying drive into the interior were no longer my own, and as the dervishes from Damascus whirled on and on I slipped into another realm of being, not quite a trance, though I felt as if I was falling. It was not an unpleasant sensation, and I was experiencing something similar now in the jungle.

A second shaman entered the stage by the circle of women—oblivious, it seemed, to the other performers. Tall and dark, he bore a family resemblance to the *minduk,* and it was with a ceremonial air that he unfolded and donned a blue-and-white-checked sarong, cinching a bright red cloth around his chest with a flourish. The first shaman changed his clothes and left the stage, while the second made a show of greeting Eddin, his patron. The music stopped when this shaman knelt before the musicians and closed his eyes. In a deep, rich voice he praised Allah, he recited verses handed down through the ages, he went into a trance. It turned out that the seductive approach had not gone far enough. For the spirits inhabiting the second shaman were harder, his dancing more robust, calling to mind the gestures of a martial-arts master. Evidently a firmer hand was needed to bring out the conflicting elements in the soul of the patient, the *pesakit*.

"In traditional Malay society," Eddin told me, "there's very little room for the individual. But the stage is a place of liberty, where you can move out of your customary ways of relating to others and acknowledge individuality."

This was the moment when the shaman asked for, and received, permission from the *pesakit*'s husband to touch her, and now he told her that she could go into a trance, if she liked, or jump into the air. Her body went limp, her facial features softening, and her first words from the depths of trance brought forth laughter from the crowd.

"She said she hasn't been felt up in a long time," Eddin explained. "This can be very embarrassing for the husband!"

The shaman pretended to hump her feet for a minute or two before resuming his banter with the *minduk*. He danced in an exalted state, he brushed off the *pesakit*'s request to caress her, he rubbed up against the other shaman. Eddin laughed.

"Whoa," he said, translating the first shaman's words. "He said he wants to fuck her, but he needs some lubricants."

The *pesakit* sat before the *minduk*, and the shaman took up a position behind her, gazing at her long hair. Then he said something that drew a gasp from the crowd.

Eddin turned to me. "This is becoming very interesting," he said.

"It's already very interesting," I replied.

He shook his head. "He just asked her if she's a man."

"What?" I said, incredulous.

"What a crazy country this is," he said.

"Is that common?" I said.

"There are lots of transvestites in the villages," he said.

"No wonder the Islamists disapprove," I said.

The *pesakit* rose uncertainly to her feet, and the shaman began to spin her like a top under the mobile, slowly at first then faster and faster, spurred on by the drums and gongs and cymbals. Nothing that I had witnessed during my travels could have prepared me for the shock that I experienced when the *pesakit* dramatically tore off her scarf and said that she was indeed a man. He leaned toward us, head down, panting.

All your life, the shaman sang in a soothing voice, *you haven't known what to do, where to go, how to dress.* He turned solicitous, almost tender, as if to calm a child in the throes of nightmare, and what he sang went to the heart of the matter. *You're still hungry after you eat, you don't really sleep, and when you bathe you don't get wet.*

With a loud sigh the *pesakit* suddenly collapsed, as though stricken, falling heavily to the floor, and lay his head down in the *minduk's* lap, and closed his eyes. Eddin took note of his gold earrings and bracelets, which glittered in the soft light.

"Gold is *haraam* for Muslim men," he whispered. "Forbidden."

Now the shaman tapped the floor with his fingers, marking time in what became an entrancing rhythm, and sang a lament that seemed to echo from the beginning of time, and now the *pesakit* rose up on his knees to dance, twisting and turning, rolling his head from side to side, shoulders swaying, transported into an exalted state.

For he had crossed the threshold between waking and dreaming, leaving the rest of us on that strange border between daily life and enchantment. What was ordinary had become extraordinary, or vice versa, and the sight of a man in a sarong rocking on his knees like a supplicant, a man who had spent his life pretending to be a woman, was, to say the least, unnerving. Trance is integral to religious practice; also ecstasy. And the knowledge gained by spiritual adventurers in altered states of mind had certainly shaped my life, alerting me, for example, to the poetic possibilities of things glimpsed at the edge of vision—the mineral quality of sunlight after rain, the hieroglyphs that birds inscribe in the sky. But I had never witnessed such complete surrender, such visible evidence of out-of-the-body travel, and the *pesakit*'s gyrations made me wonder if he would return whole. Eddin assured me that the medicine men would not lose control of what happened onstage, but even he seemed astonished by this revelation.

Tonight in this place you are the queen, the shaman sang, wiping sweat from his eyes, and the *pesakit* stared at him. *Don't be afraid.*

There was good reason to be afraid. Homosexuality is forbidden in much of the Islamic world, punishable by death in countries like Iran, Saudi Arabia, and Yemen, and elsewhere by flogging, fines, and prison terms. Indeed the former deputy prime minister of Malaysia, Anwar Ibrahim, was serving a prison sentence for sodomy and corruption, charges that Human Rights Watch and Amnesty International regarded as politically motivated; this week a panel of three judges on the highest court would hear his appeal to have his convictions overturned. This night in the jungle a banned ceremony had elicited a stunning confession, and I suspected that I was not alone in fearing what would become of the *pesakit* now that he had disclosed the secret of his sexuality.

The shaman rendered his diagnosis: the *pesakit* suffered from the thwarting of the wind associated with a young demi-god, *dewa muda*, which makes the afflicted want to be the center of attention, to enjoy all the finery, flattery, and privileges of royalty. *You want to feel grand,* the shaman sang—a recurring problem in Kelantan, Eddin added. And since it is difficult to convince most sufferers to give up their delusions of grandeur *dewa muda* is the most common blockage of the inner winds treated in *main puteri*. But would this ceremony release the malevolent spirit from this tormented man?

A woman in a pink veil left the circle of the *pesakit's* attendants to rinse his hair in a bowl of ablution water, and when she had patted it dry with a towel the shaman asked them to dance with him—the first movement of a communal dance that lasted for close to an hour, the *minduk* and the other shaman joining in, men dancing with men, women with women, the *pesakit* spinning from one partner to another or whirling alone, flinging his hair around and around, still in a trance. A man from the crowd entered from the side of the stage, the drums beat faster, the *serunai* sounded deep in the night. Lightning flashed, people danced in the trees, and in the frenzy the *pesakit* fell to his knees, and rose to dance with the shaman who had caught out the malevolent spirit tormenting him, and fell, and rose again, up and down, up and down, and then crawled toward the *minduk*, the shaman looming at his back, swinging his hips, leering, as if to take him from behind.

It was after midnight when the *minduk* brought the music to an end. He bantered for a while with the shaman, who coaxed the *pesakit* out of his trance and instructed him to stay calm when he went home: he needed all his energy for the next performance. The shaman sang a benediction, the *minduk* crept away on his knees, tossing jasmine over his shoulder to close the stage, and from a nearby house women brought out cups of coffee layered with condensed milk. How to remain calm after *this*?

"Politicians are a terrible people," Anthony Burgess declares in his autobiography, *Little Wilson and Big God*, recalling his service as an education officer during the Malayan Emergency (1948–60), which included a stint in Kota Bharu. He wrote his first novels in Malaya and Brunei, and upon his return to England, his tour cut short by the diagnosis of an inoperable brain tumor, he set out to write enough books to provide for his wife after he was gone. In the year that doctors gave him to live he finished nine novels—and then discovered that he was perfectly healthy, by which time he had learned how to live by his pen. Had an incorrect diagnosis spurred the development of a great novelist? Perhaps. A shaman might have divined that he suffered from a blockage of his *angin*, but Burgess was in all likelihood never treated by a shaman. And no one ever would be again, if the PAS leader tipped to become Kelantan's next deputy prime minister had his way. Husam bin Musa was the sort of politician that Burgess despised.

Eddin and I went to visit Husam the morning after the *main puteri*. In the lobby of his office, in the provincial parliament building in Kota Bharu, a small old man greeted us in a friendly manner—a PAS official whose son was in prison for his ties to Jemaah Islamiyah, the militant group bent on turning Indonesia, Malaysia, the southern Philippines, Singapore, Thailand, Cambodia, and Brunei into an Islamic caliphate, like the dynasties that once ruled much of the Islamic world. It would not be long before three Indonesian members of the group were tried, convicted, and shot for their role in the Bali bombings, which had killed over two hundred people, the majority of them tourists; their bid to scare off Western visitors and investors and thus reduce the island to penury inspired some in Kelantan who also wished to be free of the infidels. Oh, to have listened in on the conversation between the terror- ist's father and the PAS leader.

Husam, tall and lean in his olive Iranian shirt and black pants, struck me as a humorless man, and there was something in his cold black eyes that brought to mind my one encounter with the Serbian military commander, Ratko Mladić, orches- trator of the siege of Sarajevo. On New Year's morning 1993, a filmmaker I was with spotted him in the lobby of a Belgrade hotel, on his way to Geneva to negotiate an end to the fight- ing in Bosnia, and when we asked him about the prospects for peace he fixed his eyes on us, growling that he was in no mood for compromise. His troops occupied two thirds of the republic, and he calculated, rightly, that the Western powers would take no action against him. In fact the war dragged on for thirty more bloody months, culminating in his order to slaughter thousands of Bosnian Muslim men and boys in Srebrenica, before NATO finally intervened, preparing the ground for the Dayton Peace Accords and Mladić's indictment by the International War Crimes Tribunal for genocide and crimes against humanity. But justice remained elusive: Mladić was on the run, rumored to be hiding in Serbia or Montenegro, a hero to some Serbs who saw him as a defender of the homeland, just as some Muslims hailed Osama bin Laden for defending Islam against the West: his outlaw stature grew as long as he remained free. And it was his glare of certainty that I saw in Husam's eyes now. When I asked the PAS leader if his party was providing support to the Islamic insurgents in southern Thailand, he bristled.

"It is very strange," he said. "We never interfere outside our border."

"Never?" I said.

"We believe in argument, not force," he insisted. "If Islam is a true religion, it can win the argument by open debate."

This line of defense he repeated several times, which led me to speculate that if he was not involved in the insurgency he probably knew who was—though a glance from Eddin prompted me to move on to another subject: PAS's setback in the recent elections. Perhaps the theocratic argument has lost its power to persuade? I said, hoping to spark a conversation about the relationship between Islam and democracy, which in the view of al-Qaeda was "a man-made infidel religion," and between Malays (who make up half of Malaysia's population) and their countrymen—aboriginal, Chinese, Indian. It was no secret that Malays had an advantage: Malay was the official language, Islam the state religion, and one political party, the United Malays National Organization (UMNO), had ruled the country in coalition with smaller parties, including PAS, since independence in 1957, in a constitutional arrangement that favored Malays in business, education, and government. Religious and ethnic tensions were built into the system.

It was a point of pride for Husam that Kelantan had avoided bloodshed during the 1969 race riots, PAS having warned the village headmen that they would be held responsible for any fighting. Nonviolence, said Husam, is a basic principle of Islam, a word that means both peace and surrender. And Eddin added that Islam had spread to Southeast Asia by peaceful means, through the preaching of Sufi traders who did not raze the Hindu temples they found in Java, Malacca, and elsewhere, as happened in the early centuries of the Muslim conquest of India; some missionaries had used shadow puppetry (another art form banned by PAS) as a medium of propagation, translating themes from the Hindu epic, the Ramayana, into an Islamic idiom—a process of borrowing and adaptation common to the dissemination of ideas throughout human history.

But if Islam is the peace that comes from surrendering to God, a darker vision of the faith possesses the Western imagination, a legacy of centuries of conflict between Muslims and Europeans; in the aftermath of 9/11, with American forces on the march in Afghanistan and Iraq, it seemed to me that a clearer picture of the world's second largest religion might serve as a foil to the fear and ignorance driving much of the debate in the American media about the relationship between Islam and the West. For the history of Islam, its triumphs and defeats, reforms and counterreforms, is like that of Judaism or Christianity: a study of inspiration, inertia, and the mundane; the record of its responses to changing circumstances, to the work of time and space, resembles that of every human endeavor—sometimes wise, sometimes foolish, always partial.

The history begins one night in 610, in a cave outside Mecca, when Muhammad, an Arab trader deep in prayer, received a call from the angel Gabriel to recite. What shall I recite? he said. Twice again the angel called on him to recite, and twice again he asked what he should say. "Your Lord is the Most Bountiful One, who by the pen taught man what he did not know," said Gabriel—the first in a series of revelations, over more than twenty years, dictated to the trader, memorized by his followers, and eventually written down on palm leaves and stones to form the Koran: that is, the Recital. God's "standing miracle," in Muhammad's words, consists of a hundred and fourteen verses, arranged not chronologically but in order of length, mostly longest to shortest, and Muslims believe that what the prophet recited in trance was the final set of divine instructions revealed to mankind, a perfect transcription of God's word to complete the revelations of Abraham, Moses, and Jesus; hence Jews and Christians are regarded as fellow People of the Book, whom God commands Muslims to respect. For God speaks throughout the Koran, defining the obligations of the faithful and meaning of the faith that united the warring Arab tribes; within a century, Muhammad's followers had conquered the Levant, North Africa, Persia, and Spain, spreading the new religion to the edge of the known world, and it was not long before Islam had gained a foothold in India and Southeast Asia.

Muhammad was an ordinary man—the only miracle that he took credit for was serving as the vessel for God's word—who emptied himself, through prayer, to receive a message preserved on a tablet in heaven, a continual surrender that may bring to mind Saint Paul's account of Jesus emptying himself into human form to bear God's word into the world. For mystical experience begins in emptiness, in humility; and if Islam differs from Christianity in its conception of Jesus, viewing him as a prophet, not the Son of Man, it is worth noting their common mystical source—a spring that periodically refreshes the faith and also waters creative work. The poet's supplication (to the muse, the language, the beloved, God) is a form of prayer, and what Muhammad heard in his night-long vigils brings to mind visions vouchsafed to poets the world over. There is indeed a poetic quality to the Koran, which is not always apparent in translation; hence Muslims are encouraged to recite it in the original Arabic—the divine version. This did not seem to hinder Islam's appeal when Sufi traders introduced it to Southeast Asia.

Eddin liked to describe Islam's penetration of the Malay Peninsula in the fifteenth century as a process of accretion and secretion, the pantheism of Sufi teachings falling in nicely with pre-Islamic beliefs; with the spice trade came an esoteric poetry and music congenial to the Malay sensibility, and Eddin attributed Islam's spread to the syncretism of the Sufis, who incorporated into their practice elements of Persian, Chinese, and Indian thought; their belief in the possibility of a direct encounter with God was of a piece with the play of spirits central to Malay cosmology; hence its broad appeal.

Not until the turn of the twentieth century, Eddin continued, did some Muslims begin to blame the enervation of

Islamic civilization, notably the decline of the Ottoman Empire, on the inwardness, the hedonism, of Sufism. Reformers urged the faithful to use their powers of reason to grapple with the problem of modernity, and Sufis were confined to small communities insulated from the society at large.

There is always tension between the visible forms of faith, its ceremonies and institutions and hierarchies, and the interior journeys undertaken by seekers of the divine. Individuals and societies alike navigate between the demands of the temporal and eternal orders, the things of this world and the next; and while I had touched on the relationship between politics and religion in my last book, an account of my pilgrimages to the center of Eastern Orthodox monasticism, the Holy Mountain of Athos, in northern Greece, I wished now to explore the subject in greater detail, particularly as it related to Islam. The age-old argument among Muslim clerics and intellectuals over the role that religion plays in matters of state had, as far as I could tell, acquired new urgency after 9/11; an infidel could hardly gauge the multifarious ways in which a billion or more Muslims, pious or not, sought to make sense of their time here below, but I hoped to hear echoes of their debates, in mosques and universities and the halls of power, in cafés and *kampongs*, about their obligations to God and society. Husam's answer to the changes wrought by modernity, for instance, was a changeless understanding of his faith.

"You can classify us as moderates," he intoned, "but we believe in fundamentals: that Islam is the solution to everything. We were born before the Taliban and Osama bin Laden, and we can live as brothers."

Not everyone agreed with him, certainly not his Chinese and Indian countrymen, and with more and more Malays rejecting his theocratic vision even in Kelantan, he might have adopted a different tone. But he remained defiant, blaming PAS's electoral losses on UNMO's control of the levers of power, including the judiciary, the security forces, and the media. UNMO had in his mind devised a form of autocratic government as corrupt as any in the Middle East, and Husam seemed to relish the disparity in power between the ruling party and PAS, seeing in it a metaphor for his province.

"Kelantan is so small," he said, "small enough to free itself. Not Malaysia."

I took him to mean that a theocratic ideal could serve as a model for the rest of his country, and I agreed with his idea that change comes from the periphery. This was, after all, one lesson of the Christian anchorites who settled in the Egyptian desert in the fourth century, fleeing cities to devote their lives to God; what they made in solitude, a monastic system of prayer and fasting and the study of scripture, continues to shape Christian thought, including my own. I keep near my desk the sayings of the Desert Fathers, a compendium of wisdom born of their experience of faith; in their desire to live by the teachings of Jesus I recognized a mechanism of reform that may be universal: the center stagnates, corruption sets in, and from the periphery idealists seek to return to their origins—of a faith, a literary heritage, a political tradition. What the Desert Fathers discovered in their devotions was a corrective to the newly Christianized Roman Empire, in which a heretofore religious minority subjected to draconian forms of discrimination had assumed authority; the marriage of church and state made deviation from the ideals of the early church inevitable, as Christian rulers inevitably compromised on issues temporal and eternal; in the desert the religious sought to return to the purity of faith preached by Jesus, cultivating interiority in much the same manner that a later generation of reformers, Sufis disillusioned by the growing worldliness of Islam, tried to recover Muhammad's message of liberty and love, the mystical heart of the faith. In both cases, Christian and Islam, reformers created a healing force.

But some reformers resort to violence, the David and Goliath narrative having inspired oppressed believers since—well, the time of David and Goliath, if not before. This was what led Osama bin Laden to send his men on a suicide mission to New York and Washington, hoping to rid Saudi Arabia, the holy land of Mecca and Medina, of the American military bases established there during the Gulf War. (In this he was successful: the Bush administration closed the bases in 2003.) And it was what prompted a band of Serbian terrorists to assassinate Archduke Franz Ferdinand in Sarajevo in 1914, setting off the Great War. I asked Husam if he thought another world war was in the offing, this time between Islam and the West.

"I don't believe there is a clash of civilizations," he said. "America doesn't have to worry about Malaysia. Our role is to bring people to understand Islam. From the beginning PAS distanced itself from terrorism. That's our contribution to peace."

And the proscription on *main puteri*?

Husam made a halfhearted attempt at humor. "We do not *ban* the traditional dances, we *ben* them," he said, lazily pronouncing the word in the Malay style. "We bend them and blend them, because culture is a dynamic thing for us."

But his idea of bending or blending, Eddin later explained, was to strip from the ceremonies all Hindu, shamanic, and fantastic elements. PAS had even instituted a code of ethics for shadow puppetry, which required the use of lifelike puppets to tell didactic stories. Once onstage, however, the puppet masters would take out their classical puppets and let their *angin* take over, literally throwing the code to the winds.

The dancer bent his fingers all the way back to his wrists and smiled. Eh Chom Eh Kuan, the legendary performer of the Buddhist dance drama known as *manora*, possessed the suppleness of a man half his age. And his smile broadened when the younger of his two wives served us tea in the living room of his house near the Thai border.

"Are Buddhists allowed to have two wives?" I whispered to Eddin.

He grinned. "Only if you are the master of *manora!*"

Eh Chom, who came from a long line of dancers, was Kelantan's last remaining *manora* performer trained in the traditional style—which meant that at the age of nine he was sent to live in a Buddhist temple, and after four years of intensive instruction he was raised as a girl so that he could develop the grace required for the role of *manora,* a bird-woman in the Jataka tradition of tales about the previous births of the Buddha. Professor James Brandon retells her story in *Theatre in Southeast Asia*: how Manora, the youngest of seven daughters of the king of a mythical race of bird people, is bathing one day with her sisters in a mountain lake when a hunter, entranced by her beauty, steals her wings and tail; her sisters fly away, the hunter takes her to the palace of his own king, and there she falls in love with the crown prince. They marry in due course, and when he is sent off to war she is betrayed by a conniving minister, who convinces the king that she is a threat to him and must be put to death. The order is given to burn her alive, and as the flames rise around her she pleads to have her wings and tail returned. Her request is granted—what harm can there be in *that?*— and now, miraculously, she rises above the fire and ascends to the heavens. The prince's triumphant return from war turns to tragedy when he learns that Manora has vanished, and so he sets out to find her, searching for seven years, seven months, and seven days, overcoming many obstacles, until he climbs to the summit of the Himalayas, home of the bird people, where no mortal has ever gone. There he is reunited with Manora, and they live happily ever after. In the last verse of the tale it is revealed that the prince is in fact a previous incarnation of the Buddha.

Manora is the most popular Buddha birth story performed in Southeast Asia, and for centuries all-male troupes played the roles of the bird-woman and the prince. But over time women were trained for the drama, and indeed Eh Chom's second wife played Manora in his troupe, which for more than twenty years had performed for large crowds until PAS deemed the dance antithetical to orthodox Islamic teachings. Now she was embroidering headgear for the second of her two sons, who in two months' time would be initiated into the troupe, carrying on his father's work. Eh Chom's soul would never rest if he died without passing on the tradition, said Eddin, who was documenting every aspect of *manora*—transcribing its repertoire, recording its catalogue of songs, plays, and music, detailing its rituals. *Manora* incorporates elements of Buddhist worship and Malay forms of storytelling and music making—a typical performance features both Thai and Malay dancers; the troupe of young men and women that Eh Chom was training, with Pusaka's support, came from both sides of the border. The strange thing, Eddin added, is that Thais dominated on this side of the border, Malays on the other.

"Boundaries are ludicrous things," he said.

Here the lines blurred between Buddhism and Islam, a mingling of discourses that might have intrigued the Trappist monk and contemplative writer Thomas Merton, whose dialogue with other religions was for me a model of spiritual inquiry; his exploration of the mystical heart of faith fired my own thinking. On the day that I finished reading his autobiography, *The Seven Storey Mountain,* in graduate school, my mind was set aflame with questions of faith. I set out on foot for a nearby canyon in Salt Lake City, where I was living. One of my creative writing professors happened to drive by me, and slowed to say hello. He must have seen something in my expression, for he asked if I was all right. I replied that I was trying to sort out my feelings about a religious vocation, which drew a curious response from him: he advised me not to read the King James Bible, the translation being unfaithful to the original, then drove away. I walked on, resolving to change my life. I began to read more Merton.

His writings became central to me when I abandoned graduate school not long after my encounter with the professor and moved with my wife to New Mexico. It was a critical juncture in our lives: we were the caretakers of an estate at the edge of the Santa Fe National Forest, with no money, health insurance, or prospects. Which is to say: we were free, even if we did not realize it at the time. I wrote in the morning, and in the afternoon I worked in the gardens, split firewood, and cleared the arroyo that irrigated the apple orchards in our canyon. At the end of the day I would hike among the junipers on the mesa rising above the estate, trying to figure out how to survive outside academia—to make a life in poetry, that is. In Merton's versions of the sayings of the Desert Fathers I found a source of wisdom that seemed as fresh as the Zen koans dear to my Buddhist friends—parables and teachings illustrating the insight that poverty is integral to the spiritual life—and while it would be some time before I read Merton's essays on Zen, and longer yet until I discovered his lectures on Sufism, his open-minded search for spiritual vitality convinced me that he was a reliable guide for what turned out to be a journey into the mystical ground of experience common to many religions.

He did not just strengthen the links between poetry and the contemplative life, building on the inheritance of mystical writers through the ages, but reached beyond the walls of his monastery, the Abbey of Gethsemani in Kentucky, to the wider world, lending his voice to the civil rights movement, articulating protests against the war in Vietnam, drawing connections between Buddhism, Christianity, and Islam. He likened the Zen experience of the Void to Christ emptying himself into human form for our salvation, Christian consciousness to Buddhist mindfulness; the "deep ontological awareness" that Buddhists cultivate in meditation was in his mind akin to the awakening that Christians experience in their obedience to God or what Sufis discover at *le point vierge,* the secret place in the soul where God reveals himself. Yet Merton was careful to distinguish between the central tenets of each religious tradition, refusing to blur the differences integral to their practice, and this added another layer of meaning to his work: he saw into the heart of things, which is by its nature multiple, world upon world, and what he kept finding were different versions of the truth, the gift, bestowed upon him by his Christian faith—a new nature. The perfect poverty of a Christian mystic was not so distant from the perfect freedom granted to an enlightened Buddhist or Sufi master. Merton considered Mahatma Gandhi to be the ideal thinker and man of action, someone who used the Bhagavad Gita to dedicate his life to the nonviolent resistance of British rule; the study of Taoism and Buddhism, Hinduism and Sufism, convinced the monk that East and West share "a unity of outlook and purpose, a common spiritual climate."

This was the unity that he sought to explore when in December 1968 he traveled to Bangkok for a monastic conference, stopping en route to visit the exiled Dalai Lama in Dharamsala, in northern India; to see the giant statues of the Buddha in Sri Lanka; to listen to Vedic scholars chanting in Madras and Sufi music in Delhi. In Bangkok, he gave a lecture on Marxism and monasticism, concluding with a Zen saying: "Where do you go from the top of a thirty-foot pole?" Then he returned to his room, where some hours later his body was discovered in the bathtub—electrocuted, apparently, by the frayed cord of an electric fan. His death shocked a world still reeling from the assassinations earlier in the year of Martin Luther King, Jr. and Robert F. Kennedy, for now the spiritual voice of the civil rights and antiwar movements was also gone. Merton had written in his short life over a hundred books and pamphlets, a number of which I read sitting by the woodstove in the converted chicken coop that served as our caretaker's residence, and when I climbed the mesa his words often seemed to guide my footsteps.

Which makes it all the more mysterious to me now that when I lived in New Mexico I did not visit the Monastery of Christ in the Desert, north of Abiquiu, a crucial place for Merton in the last years of his life. I knew that he had considered leaving his monastery to live in the Benedictine community tucked in a red rock canyon along the Chama River, which he had visited twice in 1968 (the second time at the outset of his fateful journey to Asia), and I imagined that traces of his restless spirit lingered in that spare landscape, which he credited with helping to clear his mind. Merton's biographer reports that when he washed in the cold waters of the Chama he felt clean and awake; and when he met the artist Georgia O'Keeffe, who lived nearby, he deemed her one of those rare people "who quietly does everything right"—an insight that governed the composite biography that I was assembling about O'Keeffe, collecting scholarly essays and reminiscences by those who had known or worked for her.

What began as a geographical convenience (a local symposium on O'Keeffe's life and work had inspired an editor to commission the book) became for me an affair of the heart. Her paintings taught me to see flowers and canyons and bones in their essential strangeness; her letters opened new vistas on the nature of the artistic vocation; her physical beauty (preserved in photographs taken by her husband Alfred Stieglitz) left me spinning. She was for me the embodiment of art as well as desire, living as authentically as she painted, and when I visited her house in the course of my research I convinced myself that I could not afford an extra hour to drive to the monastery in which Merton might have produced yet more enduring works if his life had not been cut short. In fact I had more time on my hands in those days than in any other period of my adult life, and now I realized that what I lacked was the courage to explore the intimate connection between artistic and religious impulses—to make a true pilgrimage.

One summer day, not long after I had turned in the manuscript for my book about O'Keeffe, I was digging up a new garden, when to my consternation I found that I had to stop every few minutes to get a drink of water—which, curiously, did not slake my thirst. I wondered if I was getting sick—did this signal the onset of diabetes, which runs in my family?—or if living in the desert had somehow changed my metabolism. Through the afternoon and evening I worked, and drank water from the well, and only grew thirstier. The next day, though, I felt fine, and because I never experienced such a thirst again it came to stand in my imagination for the unquenchable thirst of the spiritual life.

This all came rushing back to me in Eh Chom's living room, when he rose to his feet, citing another obligation. During the proscription, he worked as a traditional healer, a *bomoh*, counseling couples with marital problems (his specialty, Eddin whispered with a grin). He was thus a busy man, and there was only time for him to take us on a quick tour of the temples by his house, a small dilapidated Thai structure and a larger, sturdier one, combining Thai and Chinese elements. He made a dismissive remark about the Chinese merchants whose donations were critical to the temples' upkeep, then led us along a path lined with garish statues of the Buddha and across the road to the largest sitting Buddha in Southeast Asia—a brown, golden-lipped figure ten stories tall surrounded by Chinese figures, pillars, and carvings. Eh Chom's second wife arrived on a motor scooter to take him to his appointment, and as they drove off Eddin said that while the Islamists despised this giant statue of the Buddha, which was ten years in the making, they had not forbidden its inauguration, in September 2001. The week-long celebration commenced with hundreds of Chinese Buddhists burning joss sticks and pinning pieces of gold foil to a teardrop-shaped heart displayed on a stage, and then they inserted into the heart a pair of gold and silver needles to signify their release from worldly attachments and rejection of hatred and greed—a symbolic act far removed from that of the al-Qaeda operatives who two days later crashed their planes into the Twin Towers. Like millions of people on 9/11, I had stared in disbelief at the carnage broadcast on television, wondering if, as the commentators kept saying, profound change was upon us. This Buddhist ceremony had continued, though, concluding with Thai monks installing the heart in the statue: a sign of the realm of pure light in which the enlightened dwell beyond change. And if I had thought that my travels in Malaysia would be undertaken in the light of a new dispensation now it occurred to me that from a Buddhist perspective perhaps nothing had changed at all. Back at my hotel, I sat down to make some notes on what I had seen since arriving in Kuala Lumpur the week before.

There was a crude swastika painted on the shrine to Ganesha, the elephant god, and as we started down the dirt path the sweet scent of a jasmine tree gave way to the smell of curry and then the stench of sewage. A dog barked, two chickens pecked at grain by a small house, and a baby crawled toward the door.

We entered the Kali temple in which Eddin performed his monthly ritual bath, a shed the size of a walk-in closet lined with shelves on which were laid offerings for the goddess: silver canisters filled with red or yellow dye, jars of honey and spirits, bowls of jasmine blossoms and dried flowers, a coconut, three bottles of milk, lemons stuck to the prongs of a trident. Eddin said that during one ceremony a king cobra had slithered into the temple and right back out again.

He had become a devotee of Kali during the troubles in 1997. The Asian financial crisis, Anwar Ibrahim's arrest, a clampdown on the media—these were connected in his mind to the mysterious rash he developed at that time. Repeated visits to the doctor over the course of seven months brought no relief, and just when he despaired of getting well something providential happened, or so it seemed to him. The newspaper he was working for sent him to the Brickfields neighborhood of Kuala Lumpur to do a feature on a Hindu temple saved from demolition by its priestess, an illiterate old woman who had returned from shopping one day to find a crew of men preparing to raze the shrine to make room for another apartment building to house the burgeoning Indian population. Eighty years before, an indentured Tamil railway worker, inspired by a dream to plant his trident here, had invited Kali, the mother goddess, the goddess of death and destruction, to enter this space, and now his spirited granddaughter told Eddin that in an age of incessant strife she had to preserve the temple; for Kali devours delusion, evil, and ignorance. Once she had answered his questions, she demanded to ask one of her own.

"You know why you really came here, don't you?" she said.

His suffering, she explained, was caused by Kali, Shiva's consort, who was inside him: Kali, the dark goddess of time and change, customarily adorned with a necklace of severed heads, earrings of children's corpses, and bracelets of serpents, her long hair in a wild tangle, blood smeared on her lips. The priestess advised Eddin to devote himself to the goddess, who danced on the battlefield after slaying the demon king—and within three months his rash was gone.

It was around this time that the paper put him in cold storage. Every day he would write a story, and then he would be summoned to the editor's office to watch him spike it. How the editor relished pushing the delete button, and reprimanding him for the tie he wore, his worsening attitude, anything at all. The final straw for Eddin was the order to attend the Basic English classes convened for Malay speakers.

"Fuck that," he said, and quit.

Providence entered the picture again, now through the British Council, which sent him to London to do his MA, and on his return he threw himself into his work at Pusaka, the origin of which he traced to a shadow puppet performance that he had attended in 1992, when he was studying politics at the University of Malaya. The spectacle of one man conducting an orchestra, improvising dialogue for scores of characters, and playing seven puppets at a time convinced him to apprentice himself to this master. So he took a bus to Kelantan, ignoring his mother's warnings that he might fall victim to black magic, and asked a taxi driver in Kota Bharu if he knew where the puppeteer lived. The taxi drove him straight to his house—which Eddin interpreted as a sign that this was the right thing for him to do. Then the puppeteer accepted him as a student, though for the first eighteen months of his apprenticeship he was not allowed to touch a puppet.

"It was all banter," he said, which is an essential part of instruction in traditional theater. But the puppet master was always observing him—how he held a cigarette, a cup of coffee—in order to discern his individual style.

"He told me from the beginning that I would never perform

like him," said Eddin, "but in my own way. After ten years of studying, I still haven't performed."

For acquiring the technical skills of puppetry was only part of his apprenticeship. More important was his immersion in Kelantan's culture, which led to the founding of Pusaka. Eddin's ambitions for his organization went beyond documenting and saving the traditional ceremonies: he wanted to expand their purview to engage urban communities and offer to the disaffected creative outlets rooted in the indigenous art forms of the land—admittedly a controversial idea.

"The government's strategy is to create a climate of fear," he said, "but Pusaka is here to ruffle the leaves, in the Malay phrase."

And ruffle them he did. His organization took its name from his childhood home (*putra pusaka*, "princely heritage"), and if he would not say whether he was the prince of the house he did recall with love the nurse who had taught him to speak Malay. (He had more complicated feelings about the gardener who had taught him to catch the king cobras nesting under the staircase and to smoke.) In the mixed heritage of the Malay Peninsula, with its varieties of religious experience and cultural practice, he looked for solutions to social problems, which neither the single-minded Islamists nor the inertia-bound ruling party knew how to address. *Amok* was a Malay word, he liked to tell me, insisting that in such a constricted society it was only natural for some to run amok, to go mad with rage, taking a dagger or a machete to anyone they met. The papers carried stories of men going on killing sprees for no apparent reason, but Eddin suspected that their suicidal frenzies were linked to a lack of creative means by which to express their disillusionment, their fundamental powerlessness. Take the bored young men of Kelantan, who had nothing better to do than visit prostitutes in Thailand and return infected with HIV or sign up with Jemaah

Islamiyah: the traditional ceremonies offered imaginative spaces in which to work out one's anxiety or despair. Eddin's devotion to Kali (who was, not coincidentally, the patron goddess of Kelantan) served a similar purpose.

In the temple, Pauline Fan, his helpmate and partner (another providential figure in his life, he said), took the flowers that he had bought from a street vendor and suggested he change into his ceremonial attire. She is a delicate Eurasian woman, a translator of Paul Celan and the manager of Pusaka, the calm eye in the storm that is Eddin Khoo. She laid the flowers on the altar, while he put on a white wrap, cinching it below the tattoo of a king cobra on his chest. The assistant to the priestess tolled the bell twice—the signal for Eddin to pour a canister of dye over the statues of Kali, Ganesha, and the snake goddess—and then the priestess held a candle made of camphor before him and Pauline. This ritual was repeated several times until the floor was covered with dye, and when Eddin went outside to wash off the priestess cleared the altar, wiped the tiles with a rag, mopped up the dye. Then she stopped to look at me, and after a moment she asked Pauline to translate for her. She said that although I was inclined to be a priest I need not worry about the external trappings of religion since I carried the spirit of faith in my heart; that I had two daughters; that there were tensions in my marriage; that I should resolve differences in my life quietly; that I should devote myself to my writing, having lost precious time in the last years because of other obligations; that my back and chest hurt; that I should not trust others too much; that whatever I put my mind to in the next five years would likely be successful, though for my own happiness I should spend my time writing; that I should drink more water. The priestess said that Kali was speaking through her, and that she had no choice but to tell me what Amma, the Mother, was reading in my soul.

She went into her house and returned with wedges of watermelon, which we ate at a table outside the temple, and then it was time for us to drive through heavy traffic to the weekly night market near Pauline's apartment, where hordes of shoppers looked over the goods on display in the stalls—fruits and vegetables and spices, clothes and utensils, balloons, toys. One man offered back scratchers for sale. A leper begged for money. A man in a white skullcap asked for donations for the construction of a mosque. We drifted along in the crowd, eating pancakes made of flour, sugar, and crushed peanuts, and washed them down with coconut milk. Eddin recalled his visit to an astrologer in India.

"You're three million years old," she told him, "and sometimes you feel it, don't you?"

"This will take fifty years for the United States to live down," said the Western official.

We were having drinks by the pool at the Hotel Intercontinental, in Kuala Lumpur, and as the sun sank through the haze of fires set by farmers clearing jungles in Sumatra the diplomat was considering the repercussions of the scandal at Abu Ghraib. Americans, he said, might forget the horrific crimes committed in their name, but the evidence—the images circulating on the Internet—might inflame passions in the Islamic world for generations. On the day that US senators examined photographs and videotapes of American soldiers abusing, humiliating, and torturing inmates at Abu Ghraib, Iraqi insurgents retaliated in a gruesome manner, Webcasting the beheading of an American businessman, Nicholas Berg. This was the backdrop to our conversation about cultural diplomacy, the exchange of information and ideas to enhance mutual understanding, a subject that I was researching for a report to the State Department—an all but impossible task, argued the official, without regime change in Washington.

"People like to talk about a neoconservative cabal in the White House," he said, referring to the chief architects of the Iraq War, Vice President Dick Cheney, Secretary of Defense Donald Rumsfeld, and his deputy, Paul Wolfowitz. "But what you really have is an ineptocracy: these people can't do anything right."

Talleyrand, France's prince of diplomats, observed that "The greatest danger in times of crisis comes from the zeal of those who are inexperienced." He was describing the need to curb the zeal of a young man in his employ at the embassy in London. But there is even greater danger in the zeal of the experienced: when youthful ardor goes unchecked, when idealism is not tempered by pragmatism but instead acquires political savvy and knowledge of the inner workings of government, then the chances of disaster increase. This is when people may run amok, as the wise elders surrounding a callow president in the Bush administration made plain; for now their dark vision was there for all the world to see.

Exhibit A was Abu Ghraib, which for the diplomat pointed to the White House's failure to prepare for the occupation of Iraq. The litany of decisions, which in the coming years would be recited to explain a foreign policy debacle unrivaled in American history (allowing Iraqis to loot their ministries—except oil—and museums, disbanding the Iraqi military, purging the government of Baath Party members, and so on), stemmed from the arrogant belief, said the diplomat, that we could remake the world with impunity. And if he thought that cultural diplomacy could mitigate some of the damage to our reputation he also feared that Bush's refusal to heed what Thomas Jefferson called "a decent respect to the opinions of mankind" or to consider the consequences of his actions might doom the republic.

From the vantage point of KL, as locals refer to Kuala Lumpur, which means "big muddy" in Malay, it looked as though the images from Abu Ghraib had forever muddied our good name. And we had no one to blame but ourselves.

"Torture's harvest," writes the journalist Mark Danner, "whatever it may truly be, is very unlikely to have outweighed [the] costs"—legal and moral. For the centerpiece of the Bush administration's prosecution of its war on terror—a system of military prisons at Bagram Airfield in Afghanistan, Guantánamo Bay Naval Base in Cuba, and Abu Ghraib, and secret prisons or "black sites" in Jordan, Thailand, and other countries, some with dubious human rights records, in which tens of thousands of men were interrogated, sometimes brutally—flouted the ideals of the American experiment in liberty. Details would eventually emerge about the depths to which the country had fallen. Indeed the CIA inspector general was about to issue a damning report on the agency's interrogation practices, concluding that it had repeatedly violated the Convention Against Torture. What "truths" were gleaned in confessions elicited by force, beyond US legal jurisdiction, were nothing compared to the consequences of the decision to ignore the Geneva Conventions on the treatment of prisoners of war. Indifference to criminality had corroded the soul, hollowed out the body politic, and diminished the country in the eyes of the world. I wondered how the president, a self-described born-again Christian, could sanction a policy that strayed so far from Christ's message.

"When you act alone," said the official, "you make mistakes."

What came to mind was the story of a friend who had lost his job not long before 9/11. On that September morning he was leaving his brownstone in the West Village—a short cab ride from the World Trade Center—to go to his lawyer's office and sign the paperwork for his severance package, when the first hijacked plane crashed into the Twin Towers. My friend, shaken by his professional setback, reacted to the national tragedy as if it was a personal affront: dust from the fallen buildings was hanging in the air thick with the stench of death when he fled with his family to their summer house on Long Island, convinced that more terrorist attacks were imminent. He resolved not to return; and as the days of his self-imposed exile turned into weeks he seized on rumors—of radiological bombs planted in Grand Central Station, of bridges and tunnels targeted by Islamic radicals, of smallpox released in Times Square—to justify his refusal to go back to the city that he had once loved with what I considered to be a humorous passion. That his wife and children missed their friends, their routines, seemed only to harden his attitude.

One night my friend's wife called to ask me to persuade him to return to the city, and so I told him that he could not allow terror to govern his life, invoking the example set by countless individuals I had met in Sarajevo—writers and professors, engineers and civil servants, ordinary men and women—who during the terrible years of the siege did not surrender to their fear but discovered instead new reserves of courage. This was crucial not only to their own survival, I said, but to the survival of their city. My friend angrily replied that no analogy could be drawn to his unique circumstances.

"September 11th is something new," he said. "Nothing can be compared to it."

Our conversation ended soon after.

Which in time prompted me to reflect more systematically on terror—and on the power of art, literature, and ceremony to counter it, to bolster the spirit in the presence of fear. The argument that I developed, which started with identifying the body's responses to fear (to flee, to lash out, to become paralyzed, to focus on the source of danger, to seek solutions, to rise

to the occasion—reactions that for better or worse define individuals as well as societies), went something like this: poetry
works by correspondence, linking one thing to another, past,
present, and future, in order to enlarge the reader's sensibility;
fiction cultivates empathy, inspiring us to imaginatively inhabit
other lives, other ways of being; and sacred ceremonies, which
in many traditions are exercises in analogy, serve to mitigate
various forms of terror, from individual existential anxieties
to societal threats, such as what Americans experienced on
9/11, when a new paradigm took shape—a cultural framework
whose parameters were still becoming clear the day that I
sipped scotch by the pool in KL, catching occasional whiffs of
smoke from the fires. The diplomat said that fear informed the
American body politic, making it easier for my countrymen
to think the worst of Muslims. For terror is the chief impedi-
ment of empathy and analogy, without which it is difficult to
make sense of what seems foreign or strange; when terror
blunts the mind's ability to find analogies, to put ourselves
in someone else's shoes, it becomes easier to fall for justifi-
cations of appalling deeds, like torture—"enhanced interrogation," in Bush administration parlance, a distortion of the
language integral to preparing Americans to accept hitherto
unimaginable excesses, like torture.

In the American response to 9/11 some Malaysians found
sanction for their darker impulses. Thus a cartoon on the front
page of the PAS party newspaper likened the scandal at Abu
Ghraib to the treatment of Islamic militants locked up in the
Kamunting Detention Center: *"Ini bukan Iraq tetapi ISA"*—
"This is not Iraq but the ISA" (Malaysia's internal security service). Inside the paper was another cartoon: from behind the
bars of a prison cell a shrouded figure cries, *Arrgh! Adoi!* Two
men walk by. *Prisoners of the USA?* one asks. *No,* says the other,
ISA! Indeed Human Rights Watch was about to issue a report

connecting Malaysian prison abuses to the war on terror. In August 2001, when Malaysia arrested several members of PAS, the White House condemned the government for its violations of human rights. After 9/11, though, Malaysia and other US allies were given a free hand to deal with Islamic militants as they wished. That some of the 9/11 hijackers had met in KL in January 2000 to discuss plans for the attack reinforced the argument that to secure information about terrorist plots quickly, the gloves had to come off. The ISA had videotaped the al-Qaeda summit, but without audio no one recognized the seriousness of the threat. More forceful action might have prevented 9/11, though the revelations of prisoner abuse at Abu Ghraib called into question the wisdom of the argument that there should be no limits in the war on terror.

The eighteenth-century writer Edmund Burke summed up the British failure to understand the American Revolution with words that still rang true for the diplomat: "No passion so effectually robs the mind of all its powers of acting and reasoning as fear." To which one might add this insight from the contemporary poet Geoffrey Hill: "Terror is opportune as is relief from terror." In my clearest moments I understood that it was but a step from terror to courage, but how difficult it is to take that step when terror grips the soul. Literature and faith, art and ceremony—they only go so far.

"Another round?" said the diplomat.

"Definitely," I said.

"Religious or cultural purity is a fundamentalist fantasy," V. S. Naipaul argues in *Beyond Belief: Islamic Excursions Among the Converted Peoples,* his follow-up account of travels in Indonesia, Iran, Pakistan, and Malaysia first detailed in *Among the Believers: An Islamic Journey.* The rise of Islamic fundamentalism alarmed the writer, and if I admired the precision of his descriptions of the people he met and the places he visited, his storytelling, and his elegant synthesis of information, I was also struck by his assertion that "the zeal of converts outside the Arab world is more fervent." It was the sort of sweeping generalization that inspires suspicion, even as I admired his attempt to explain the ferment in the region: "Islam is in its origins an Arab religion," he writes. "Everyone not an Arab who is a Muslim is a convert." That is the problem, according to Naipaul. He describes himself as "a manager of narrative," and the most problematic narrative for him is conversion, no doubt because his own biography, well known to his readers, is such a story: how a precocious schoolboy from Trinidad goes to Oxford on a scholarship and, by dint of hard work, transforms himself into a major English prose stylist, earning for his labors riches, a knighthood, the Nobel Prize in Literature. But religious transformation is another story—an act of erasure for which he has little sympathy:

> Islam is not simply a matter of conscience or private belief. It makes imperial demands. A convert's worldview alters. His holy places are in Arab lands; his sacred language is Arabic. His idea of history alters. He rejects his own; he becomes, whether he likes it or not, a part of the Arab story. The convert has to turn away from everything that is his. The disturbance for societies is immense, and even after a thousand years can remain unresolved; the turning away has to be done again and again. People develop fantasies about who and what they are; and in the Islam of converted countries there is an element of neurosis and nihilism. These countries can be easily set on the boil.

Of course the same holds for Christianity, which from its origin made conversion central to its theology, as Paul learned on the road to Damascus: "if anyone is in Christ, he is a new creation; old things have passed away; behold all things have become new." Conversion stories, like stories of healings and miracles, provide the foundations of Christian belief. Moreover, Christianity's holy places are located mainly in Arab and Jewish lands, only a handful of people read the languages in which the foundational texts were written, and in many societies that converted to Christianity the disturbances occasioned by the change of belief remain unresolved. Witness the schism between Eastern and Western Christendom, or the bloody aftermath of the Reformation and Counter-Reformation. What tribe cannot be brought to a boil? The Hundred Years' War, which some thought might be a model for the "long war" sparked by 9/11, proved that the converted peoples of Europe could be just as savage as anyone in the defense of faith. Naipaul's thesis, then, was as suspect as any essentialist argument which blurs individual differences. But what is more individual than matters of religion? The individual is the locus of literature, as the Nobel laureate brilliantly showed in his novels.

The problem for a writer with a thesis is that anecdotes, facts, and insights may be arranged to support a story line at odds with a nuanced rendering of the material: one mark of an enduring literary work. The history of Islam, like that of Christianity, another conquering state religion, is too complicated to support a simplistic narrative, at least not in literature, which functions by complexity, gradations of tone and hue. Islam spread to Southeast Asia via trade, not conquest, and though it has the same universal aspirations as Christianity it also has a tradition of tolerance for other faiths, other ways of negotiating one's time here below—a necessity for the preservation of Malaysia's cultural mosaic. Near my hotel in KL, for example, was an Anglican church, where I attended mass one Sunday morning. The congregation was Chinese, the language of the service English, the guitar-playing minister a familiar spirit from my childhood. The history of religion in Malaysia is a history of shared space—a fact that Naipaul glosses over in his bid to speak in grander terms about the failings of the converted and of the faith itself.

He is on firmer ground in his portraits of individuals. "For Anwar Ibrahim," he writes of the politician in *Among the Believers*, "Islam was the energizer and purifier that was needed in Malaysia; true Islam awakened people, especially Malays, and at the same time it saved them from the corruption of the racialist politics of Malaysia, the shabbiness of the money culture and easy Western imitation." Anwar was then at the start of his career, directing a Muslim youth movement which had become a potent political force. He was an attractive man, Naipaul decided; "and it added to his attractiveness that in spite of his great local authority he gave the impression of a man still learning, still thinking things out." The sketch of Anwar ends with Naipaul voicing regret that he did not have more time to talk with him. He wanted to travel with him, to see the country through his eyes, but there was no time.

I was also keen to speak with Anwar, who was still in prison during my first stay in Malaysia, and so it was Naipaul's image of a politician in his ascendency that I held in mind until I met him on a second visit to KL, in the summer of 2005. His fall from power had been dramatic, the overturning of his sodomy conviction a triumph, his release from prison a promise—of what, no one could say. He and his wife were packing up their house in an upscale neighborhood, preparing to move to a new residence, and the furnishings gave the impression of a work in progress. In the front hallway, on a table by a mirror, was a vase of peacock's feathers; the *kilim* in the next room was furled among cardboard boxes of books. Anwar served tea and chocolate cupcakes at the dining room table. Through a glass door I could see a guard on the patio performing his evening prayers, making prostrations in the shade.

"I went through the Riverside edition of Shakespeare four and a half times in prison," said Anwar, his eyes full of mirth. "If they had kept me for another six months I would have finished it five times!"

He cut a regal figure in his brown *jubah*, betraying no signs of the abuse that he had suffered in prison or of the back surgery that he had undergone in Germany upon his release ten months before. His 1998 arrest, on charges of corruption and sodomy, was widely seen as politics run amok, his true crime having been to challenge the authority of Prime Minister Tun Dr. Mahathir bin Mohamad, the country's guiding force for over two decades. Mahathir had been Anwar's patron, helping him rise through UNMO's ranks, grooming him to be his successor, until the Asian financial crisis forced their differences in governing philosophies out into the open. How to solve what looked like the beginning of a global financial meltdown? Anwar favored the free market recommendations put forth by the International Monetary Fund, Mahathir imposed currency and capitol controls, and when Anwar promised to investigate corruption in the ruling party, Mahathir responded in kind. A book was published in KL, titled *50 Reasons Why Anwar Cannot Become Prime Minister*, which accused him of engaging in sexual misconduct with his former speechwriter and his adopted brother—allegations that led to their arrest, imprisonment, and forty lashes of the rattan cane. Anwar was arrested on the strength of their confessions, later recanted, and tens of thousands of his supporters took to the streets in protest; his conviction was an occasion of national disillusionment and international outrage.

During his first six months in prison, when the guards abused him daily and he was not allowed to watch television or listen to the radio, Anwar established a routine to preserve his sanity, rising at five in the morning to perform his prayers, after which he would take breakfast, exercise, and read until dark. (Soon after his release from prison, at a conference of Muslim scholars in Istanbul, he rattled off the titles of several books, and then, fearing that he might sound pretentious, noted his special credentials: six years in solitary confinement. He advised the scholars to consider a stint in prison, if they wanted to get some reading done!) His favorite play, of course, was *Hamlet*, though he also loved *The Tempest*. Like the young prince, he had broken with a corrupt father figure, Mahathir; like Prospero, he had bid farewell to his audience, the Malaysian body politic, over which he had all but reigned for sixteen years. Now he was about to go to Australia to lecture on what he had learned from Shakespeare, notably the virtue of humility, and he was quick to acknowledge limits in his ability to understand others. If policy makers started from that premise, he said, they might have more sympathy for the Other.

"The problem," he said, "is that because the focus is on the Middle East we have no other lens through which to view our divisions."

Hence the need for a new vision of the Israeli-Palestinian conflict, which for Muslims was the primary issue—a fact that American policy makers ignored at their peril. He counseled the White House to play the role of honest broker in the region, engaging ally and enemy alike to resolve not only the Israeli-Palestinian conflict but to bring to an end the Iraq War, which enraged Muslims the world over; against the infamous "axis of evil" invoked by George W. Bush in his 2002 State of the Union address, which singled out Iraq, Iran, and North Korea for their defiance of the international community, Anwar called for an "axis of engagement" with Iraq's neighbors—Syria, Iran, Kuwait, Saudi Arabia, Turkey, and Jordan—in the common cause of peace.

But there was no sign of the White House removing its blinders about the failures of its policies in the region, said Anwar—which surprised him. He expected dictators to be in a state of denial, not American political leaders.

"Until you accept facts as they are," he said, "there will only be death, not just to Americans but to Iraqis. If you continue to reject facts, then the policy will be flawed."

Against this shortsightedness he set the wisdom of the Bard, who delighted and instructed him in his darkest moments, above all on the meaning of free will. For what prison taught Anwar to value most was freedom. The dehumanization of the individual, the systemic degradation of innocent men and women, the regimen of terror—these were the costs of Malaysia becoming a prison, he said, and vowed to liberate his countrymen. Unlike Hamlet, he seemed capable of acting on his beliefs, chief among them that Islamic governments had to carve out more space for freedom.

It was true that in drawing up UNMO's Islamic agenda he and Mahathir had been inspired by the Iranian Revolution (among other things, as minister of education, Anwar had banned the publication of Salman Rushdie's *The Satanic Verses*). But it was also true that Anwar hoped to create a Southeast Asian model for Islamic governance in keeping with the more tolerant interpretation of the faith introduced by the Sufi traders. We were speaking on the first anniversary of the Muslim terrorist bombings in London, which had killed more than fifty people—continuing proof of the crisis in modern Islam, according to Anwar. He insisted that radical Islam bore no relation to the teachings of the Prophet, to the traditions of tolerance and learning and love, to the interior journeys undertaken by the

Sufis who had brought from Arab lands the message to surrender to Allah. And he had taken a leading role in articulating a
moderate vision of his faith.

"Who Hijacked Islam?"—this was the title of a well-known
essay that he wrote in his prison cell just after 9/11 and published in *Time*. Islamic civilization, he argued, was forged in
part by wealthy men who supported universities and hospitals
and by princes who patronized scientists, philosophers, and
writers. And it was despair at the futility of political struggle
in autocratic Islamic countries that drove Osama bin Laden
to use his personal fortune "to wreak destruction rather than
promote creation." Anwar believed that the project of modernity had suffered in Muslim countries because of its complicity
with illegitimate power: "The great suspicion of modernity by
Muslims is often because it came without liberty," he said in a
lecture at Oxford; "it came with exploitation and brutal oppression first with colonialism, and later with indigenous military
or civilian authoritarianism." Where the state maintained total
control, blocking the development of a civic space in which to
work out a different destiny for the *ulama*, the community of
the faithful, there was bound to be resistance. And the alienation that marked Islamic society, the bitterness spawned by
the perception that modernity had left Muslims behind, led to
acts of desperation, like the 1998 *fatwa* issued by bin Laden:

> The ruling to kill all Americans and their
> allies—civilians and military—is an individual
> duty for every Muslim who can do it in any
> country where it is possible to do it, in order
> to liberate the al-Aqsa Mosque [in Jerusalem]
> and the holy mosque [in Mecca] from their
> grip, and in order for their armies to move out
> of all the lands of Islam, defeated and unable

to threaten any Muslims. This is in accordance
with the words of Almighty Allah, "and fight
the pagans all together as they fight you all together," and "fight them until there is no more
tumult or oppression, and there prevail justice
and faith in Allah."

For American allies read Israel; the despotic rulers of Saudi
Arabia (who had allowed the American military to build bases
on the holy land), Egypt, and other autocratic regimes in the
Middle East; and any Muslims who opposed al-Qaeda, which
sought to restore the caliphate that once stretched from Morocco
to Malaysia. Thus Muslims like Anwar who spoke out against
the dream of a theocracy rooted in the most extreme interpretation of *sharia* law (amputations, stonings) were judged to
be apostates—subject, that is, to the death penalty. If bin Laden
divided the world into *Dar al-Islam* (the Realm of Islam) and
Dar al-Harb (the Realm of War), Anwar had a more nuanced
approach, seeking to create *Dar al-Salaam* (the Realm of
Peace). And he would begin in Southeast Asia, since it had no
nostalgia for the caliphate, no myth of greatness. In Indonesia,
for example, Islamists, Hindus, nationalists, and secularists
had worked together to craft a constitution, debating ideas like
the framers of the American constitution.

"Yes, there were tensions between the different groups,"
Anwar said. "There were huge debates and disagreements. But
because they were all seated at a big table, like in Philadelphia,
the arguments were more substantive."

He looked to Indonesia for inspiration, believing that the
success or failure of the world's largest Muslim country to
create a workable democracy was crucial to the international
order. "This is the true and unprecedented drama of faith and
freedom of Islam in modern times," he said at Oxford. And it

held more promise than what was playing in the Middle East, where in the absence of a civic space Islamists exploited the sanctity of the mosque (where the authorities dared not intrude) to gain adherents, fueled by hatred of the West. The modern founder of radical Islam, the Egyptian writer Sayyid Qutb, executed in 1966, argued that all Westerners carried in their blood "the Crusader spirit"—a perception reinforced by George W. Bush's cavalier description of the war on terror as a crusade. Out of such infelicities of speech are clashes of civilization made, with writers on both sides furnishing arguments to harden attitudes—e.g. the British historian Anthony Pagden's assertion that in Islamic countries, "The present is linked to the past by a continuous and still unfulfilled narrative, the story of the struggle against the 'infidel' for the ultimate Muslim conquest of the entire world." But conquest is the dream of ideologues of every stripe. And if Anwar could not lift the scales off the eyes of the Islamists he would nonetheless work to ensure that their dogmatism did not blind the majority of Muslims, who wanted only to live in peace.

Presently we were joined by his wife, Dr. Wan Azizah Ismail. She is a beautiful woman, an ophthalmologist by training, who headed Keadilan, a coalition of parties that formed the main opposition to UNMO, and she would serve three terms in parliament before turning her seat over to him. (Anwar was not allowed to run for office until 2008, his corruption conviction having been upheld.) She teased him about serving chocolate cupcakes, and after fetching another pot of tea from the kitchen began to banter with him with what seemed to be unfeigned amusement. Whether there was any basis in fact for the sodomy charge leveled against him (he would be charged with the same crime some years hence, on the verge of his return to power, in what many saw as another politically motivated campaign), it struck at the heart of their marriage—and yet she betrayed no sign of bitterness. On the contrary. She finished his sentences with a light touch, which made him smile; their playfulness with each other suggested a deep bond. No one ever knows what goes on inside a marriage, but it is not easy to pretend to be playful, even for a politically savvy couple well versed in Shakespeare. She was witty, and the stories that he told to punctuate his points grew funnier in her presence.

For example, he once traveled to Pahang to give a speech for a cabinet minister who hoped to turn the province into a tourist destination. To prove that the area was free of crocodiles, the minister dove into the river, which prompted Anwar to quip that he was safe since crocodiles don't attack other crocodiles—a joke with a barb: the Malay word for crocodile also means "lecher." At lunch he was seated next to the minister's wife, who complained about her husband's wandering eye. Do you know how I survive? he said to her. My wife's an ophthalmologist, and every morning she puts a drop in each of my eyes so that only she is beautiful to me. The minister's wife said, Give me two drops!

When I asked Anwar what had become of the minister and his scheme to attract tourists to Pahang, he replied that in league with Mahathir the minister had managed to squander all the timber in his province, and now he was its governor.

"He sounds like all politicians," I said.

"Almost all," Anwar corrected me.

He was determined to rise above partisan politics. Unable to air his views in the local media ("We have freedom of speech," he explained with a grin. "We just don't have freedom after speech!"), he had started a blog to answer questions on any subject from his countrymen. Nor was he afraid to take them to task for criticizing atrocities committed by American soldiers at Abu Ghraib while ignoring or even condoning problems in their backyard—censorship, innocent people

detained without trial, rampant corruption. This was a forum
for him to work out his ideas about Islam and freedom, which
he had first tested in his political career, then reflected upon
in prison, and now hoped to put into practice. In dark circumstances he had discovered that clarity of vision is an effective
counter to terror, and in his new life he was trying to rally his
countrymen to see that it was in their interest to heed the call
of their better selves.

His theme was courage—which put me in mind of Georgia
O'Keeffe's confession that she was always afraid, and that her
fear had never stopped her. At the opening of her museum in
Santa Fe this had rattled around my mind. I was to appear on
a panel to discuss her work, and in the vestibule outside the
auditorium a man struck up a conversation with me. His father had worked for O'Keeffe as her gardener, and he was eager
to describe a ritual of hers: how every fall she would gather
hundreds of paintings that did not measure up to her exacting
standards and burn them in a bonfire. It was a ceremony of liberation, predicated on the realization that these works lacked
the clarity of line and color that she demanded. He remembered
how delighted she was to watch them go up in smoke—and it
occurred to me that this was how she freed herself to see anew,
to figure reality afresh, to strike out into unclaimed aesthetic
terrain. At every stage of her painting life she had transformed
herself, discovering new ways to render the world in images
of flowers, and bones from the desert, and ladders propped
against the adobe wall of her house, and clouds glimpsed from
above: step after step, always afraid, always alert to the next insight (*in* + *sight*). She aged gracefully in her paintings, fearless
in her explorations.

It was time to leave—Anwar had to pack for his trip—and I
suspected that when I went over my notes about our meeting it
would seem natural to invoke Shakespeare, not *Hamlet* or *The*

Tempest but *Julius Caesar,* the consummate drama of honor: "Cowards die many times before their deaths," Caesar tells his wife in the second act. "The valiant never taste of death but once." Anwar was still very much alive.

Palms lined the road to my hotel on the outskirts of KL. Laborers rested on the construction site of a new high-rise. The odor of rotting leaves and sewage wafted up from the metal grates on the sidewalk, along which I would walk in blazing heat to an Internet café, where for two ringgits (about fifty cents) I could check my e-mail. The café was filled at all hours of the day and night with young men playing video games, the most popular of which featured an American soldier walking down a street in Baghdad, shooting insurgents.

One day I joined an official from an opposition party for lunch at a Kelantan-style restaurant near a public housing project in KL. The official, who was preparing to run for parliament, brought along several volunteers—a toothless man who introduced himself as the president of the housing project's residential commission; a student from the University of Malaya; an insurance claims processor; a Chicago Bulls fan who worked as a clerk for a German company; a one-armed man who never spoke—all of whom welcomed the chance to tell me about the corruption of the ruling party, which was preventing them from organizing the residents of the project. What to do? said the official. We sat cross-legged at a low table, with a video of traditional musicians performing on the screen above, and feasted with our fingers on beef, chicken, fish, *petai* (a paste made from pungent seeds wrapped in curry leaves), sticky rice, various vegetable dishes, fried bananas. Over coffee the official criticized the government for its inability to tamp down the ethnic tensions, which had newly risen over the fate of a national hero, the first Malaysian to climb Mount Everest—a

Hindu, as it happened. Crippled later in life, the mountaineer was confined to a hospital bed until a Muslim shaman healed him—a miracle, the story went, that inspired him to convert to Islam. But there was evidence that he was delusional at the time of his conversion, and in any event his healing was short-lived, for he suffered a fatal stroke. When the religious police claimed his body, his widow filed an injunction in civil court asserting that he had been a practicing Hindu until his death. The matter was referred to a *sharia* court, which forbade her attendance, and so her husband was buried in a Muslim graveyard—which enraged the Indian and Chinese communities.

"What to do?" the official repeated.

What the volunteers next wanted to discuss, though, was a DVD being circulated of a documentary purporting to show that 9/11 was a plot devised by the CIA and Mossad (the Israeli intelligence service). How else to explain the fact that television cameras had been positioned to record the destruction if bombs had not been planted in the World Trade Center and the Pentagon? The clerk who idolized Michael Jordan led the anti-American charge, and nothing I said could convince him that al-Qaeda had hijacked the planes flown into the buildings, not even when I reminded him that Osama bin Laden had taken credit for the attack. We parted on a sour note.

When we were out of earshot the official took my arm. "Do you see how their thinking has been corrupted?" he said. "And they're more enlightened than most people in this country." He did not expect to win his election.

Later that night, I hailed a taxi to take me to my hotel. The Tamil driver stopped at the light to pick up a young woman in a brown T-shirt and jeans, and at once began to lecture her, as if resuming a conversation, which seemed to verge on argument. From time to time she nodded, which led the driver, a wiry man with long hair and a thin mustache, to talk even faster, waving his hands, his two-inch-long fingernails gleaming in the headlights of the passing cars. The air conditioner was broken, gasoline fumes filled the taxi. Suddenly the driver turned to ask me where I was from and if I was a Christian. He gave my answers some thought, and then, pointing at the woman, said in a thick accent, We are anti-Muslim. I asked if he was Christian or Hindu. TOG, he replied, an acronym he had to repeat several times until I figured out that he was saying *Tool of God*—though something may have been lost in translation.

He fell silent, and then, inexplicably, turned onto an unlit road, which wound through a park or a rubber plantation. There were no cars or houses in sight, and when I asked him where we were going he pulled over to the side of the road and got out. The woman waited until she saw him light a cigarette before she reached for my hand. Do you want a massage? she said. Not tonight, I said. No problem, she replied, and called to the driver. He grimaced, stubbing out his cigarette, and drove me to my hotel without another word. The fare was sixty ringgits. He said he had no change for a hundred.

Khalil Ibrahim's self-portrait, in a retrospective exhibition at a gallery in the Petronas Twin Towers, was an essay in double vision: the artist stood before a table, an unfinished floral painting at his back, the left side of his face in such thick shadow that only the arm of his eyeglasses could be seen. But it was impossible to tell where the light came from, since the blank part of the canvas behind him, which was as bright and harsh as sunlight, had a shadow of its own—as if another figure were lurking somewhere in the studo—or what the source of the different shadows might be. The artist's lips were turned downward, few of the paintbrushes wedged into a dark can were illuminated, and it was difficult to decide which was more disturbing, the penetrating gaze of his lit eye or the speck of light in his dark one. The painting spoke to something essential about my experience of KL: it felt as if every conversation, gesture, and silence contained a shadow.

Yet the self-portrait seemed to bear little relationship to the droll, round man who warmly greeted me and his old friend Eddin, or to the other sketches and paintings drawn from fifty years of work for *A Continued Dialogue,* a whirl of flowing lines and vibrant colors, in images of dancing women and fishermen, of palm groves and boats on the sea, spread over all the flat and curving walls of the gallery. I took the title to mean that the artist's dialogue was not only with his materials but with the complicated issue of identity that shaped so much of the national discourse, and I was intrigued by the stylistic variety of his land- and seascapes, which ranged from the abstract to the figurative. He painted in oil, acrylic, and watercolor; he made batiks and gouaches; he celebrated the human body, notably in a series of ink drawings titled *The Spirit of the East,* which featured groups of women on the beach, spinning and swirling and stretching toward the sky.

"Malays are a very sensual people," said Eddin.

Ibrahim was born in a *kampong* near Kota Bharu, the son of a Sumatran sent to Kelantan to be educated in an Islamic school, and from an early age he yearned to be an artist, despite the traditional Islamic suspicion of figurative representation. (It is written in the Hadith, the stories and sayings attributed to the Prophet, that "He who creates pictures in this world will be ordered to breathe life into them on the Day of Judgment, but he will be unable to do so.") Ibrahim drew, made shadow puppets out of cardboard, and took classes with a Singapore-trained art teacher. Ignoring his father's wish for him to become a teacher, he devoted himself to painting, selling his works to British colonial and army officers; when his family moved to a *kampong* in Pahang his work brought him to the attention of a district officer, who convinced him to seek formal training abroad. And so it was that in 1959, two years after independence, Ibrahim won a scholarship to Central Saint Martins College of Art in London, and there he learned the elements of composition, color, and anatomy, tutored by artists steeped in the European academic tradition. He drew still lifes, worked with models, visited galleries and museums in London and on the Continent. A decisive encounter with Rubens: the Flemish artist's portraiture fed his developing interest in the human form, and by the time he returned to Malaysia in 1965 (with a Swiss-born wife) he had not only internalized the history of Western art but discovered the rudiments of his artistic vision—in the body.

His subject, broadly speaking, was life in the coastal villages of Kelantan—fishermen and their boats, women walking by the sea, swirling figures in bright greens, yellows, reds, and blues: the lives of ordinary people, set against the lush backdrop of the tropics, and the communities that they form.

"I am deeply involved in the activities of people in groups," he once said.

While Eddin asked him about friends they had in common, I took another look around the exhibit. From a painting of six women strolling into a splash of sunlight I turned to gaze through the window at the women passing by, laden with bags of designer clothes, and then it hit me: the planners of 9/11 had probably been here, had perhaps even wandered down this gleaming hall—a realization that made me shudder. I remembered how the ash was still falling when I visited Ground Zero late one afternoon in November 2001. The wooden walkway I climbed to peer into the twisted wreckage was slippery with soot; the stench of death filled the cold air. Men and women wept. Sidewalk vendors hawked American flags, T-shirts, hats emblazoned with NYFD and NYPD insignia. A young woman embraced a policeman. I circled the site, conscious of what was missing—and of how absence can be described through what is there: the skeletal remains of a building; a makeshift shrine of plastic flowers and teddy bears; a chamber orchestra rehearsing in a church with plastic sheets covering the pews. The mind reels before such destruction—which is why so many turned to poetry in the days following 9/11. For poetry, Robert Frost reminds us, offers a temporary stay against confusion.

By way of contrast, the Petronas Twin Towers, the tallest twin buildings on earth, completed in 1998 (just after the Asian financial crisis) to house the state oil and gas company and its subsidiaries, were beacons of prosperity, with the rest of the office space leased to Boeing, IBM, Microsoft, and other Fortune 500 companies, and all six levels of the shopping mall crowded on a weekday afternoon. The Petronas Group, one of the so-called "New Seven Sisters" of the petroleum industry (along with companies in Russia, Iran, China, Venezuela, Saudi Arabia, and Brazil), played a huge role in the national economy—exploring, refining, and distributing oil and natural gas; operating pipelines; manufacturing petrochemicals; trading and shipping and developing real estate—and was helping to integrate it into the international economy. It was fueling globalization, that is, as relentlessly as the financial service firms located in the World Trade Center in New York City had once moved capital around the globe.

Two pairs of towers celebrating economic might, two visions of modernity: a double-sided mirror of the international order.

What could not be seen in this mirror before 9/11, what remained in shadow, was the backlash against the forces of dislocation unleashed by globalization—the uncertainty that, for example, contributed to the rise of Islamic fundamentalism. Nor were those who walked the corridors of power and money (not to mention the majority of intellectuals and writers) always alert to the potentially violent link between dispossession and fervency: acts of terror in the service of the divine have shaped civilization sometimes as decisively as the ethical codes

and ideals of justice vouchsafed to prophets. For faith and terror are inextricably linked, inspiring some to create works of
genius and some to take up arms. It was no accident that al-
Qaeda operatives finalized plans for their attack on the World
Trade Center in the shadow of the Petronas Twin Towers. If
only the import of their summit had not eluded the intelligence
community—and yet how often we fail to comprehend the
meaning of something until it is too late.

Ibrahim lifted the plastic cover off a table displaying a
selection of his sketchbooks, every page of which seemed
to burst with ideas—figures in every conceivable pose, with
notes scrawled in the margins: a microcosm of a world in flux,
I decided, caught in the act of disappearing. Ibrahim said that
he was always drawing, and from a side pocket of his combat-
style trousers he pulled out a sketchbook filled with pictures
of the visitors to his exhibition, all of them, men and women,
rendered in the nude.

"I naked them," he said with a smile, "because I love the
body."

This seemed to me to be a good definition of any work of
the spirit.

On the road to Kota Bharu, at the sight of a policeman flagging
down a pickup truck, Eddin took pleasure in describing the ritual
about to unfold: the policeman would sidle up to the truck, de-
mand to see the driver's license, and say, *How to solve this?*—the
signal for a bribe. The amount was negotiable, like everything
in this crazy country, my friend said, including the proscription
on traditional ceremonies in Kelantan. It turned out that performances could be arranged for educational and research purposes,
a tourist version of shadow puppetry was put on every week in
Kota Bharu, and the authorities knew that ritual healings like
main puteri took place in some of the remotest villages. What

was not negotiable, said Eddin, nodding at the driver and the policeman across the road, was the fact that until a certain sum traded hands the journey would not continue.

How to solve this? This is a question constantly posed to individuals and nations; our answers, personal and collective, determine how posterity judges us. After 9/11, the American body politic answered the question in dramatic fashion, with the vice president declaring that the government would now work "on the dark side," Congress granting the White House license to devise its war on terror with minimal oversight, the media and the public largely acquiescing to the administration's violations of international treaties, infringements on civil liberties, and so on. Utilitarian arguments acquired the patina of grandeur, at least in the eyes of their defenders, and as ad hoc arrangements hardened into permanent structures the worst excesses of human behavior emerged.

How to solve this? Abu Ghraib was one answer.

Eddin sped up, but soon had to pull over to the side of the road—not to pay off a policeman but to change a flat tire. We worked in the withering heat to jack up the car, the melting tar sticking to the soles of our shoes, the lug nuts almost instantly becoming too hot to touch, and my shirt was soaked with sweat by the time we resumed our journey. My heart sank when I learned that we were some distance from the next town, where we could stop for tea, and the watery quality of the light on the long stretch of road that took us through paddy fields and rubber plantations made me thirstier yet.

"Water, water everywhere," Eddin said. "Nor any drop to drink."

It was not unusual for him to invoke *The Rime of the Ancient Mariner* to describe a situation. Coleridge's tale of an ill-fated sea voyage was a touchstone for Eddin, and there was something in his manner that reminded me of how the Mariner buttonholes the Wedding-Guest to tell his story of sailing on a ship toward the South Pole, through mist and snow and ice, until the Albatross appears, bearing good luck, it seems. For the ice entrapping the ship splits apart, the helmsmen finds a passage through, and a south wind pushes them onward, with the Albatross following—to the delight of the crew—until the day that the Mariner inexplicably shoots it with his crossbow, setting in motion a tragedy he is condemned to "teach" to strangers like the Wedding-Guest.

His shipmates all agree that killing the bird was "a hellish thing," since it brought a fair breeze. Yet when the breeze keeps blowing they convince themselves that the Albatross actually brought the fog and mist, and so they justify its sacrifice until the ship enters the Pacific, where at once it is becalmed, the sun parching every tongue, the water burning "like a witch's oils," death-fires dancing in the rigging at night. The sailors hang the Albatross around the Mariner's neck to ward off its avenging spirit. Then a ghost ship arrives bearing a Spectre-Woman and her Death-mate to slay the crew, two hundred men in all. Only the Mariner is spared, and for a full week he lies on deck surrounded by the dead: a ghastly scene capped by the appearance of weirdly beautiful water-snakes coiling and swimming, leaving tracks like flashes of golden fire. "A spring of love gushed from my heart," he tells the Wedding-Guest, "and I blessed them unaware"—the prayer that frees him of the yoke of the Albatross, which sinks "Like lead into the sea."

Into a deep sleep he sinks, and when he is roused from a dream of buckets filling with dew his thirst is slaked by rain, the wind rises, and his dead shipmates return to their positions, a ghostly crew to sail him home. Now he falls into a trance, in which he hears two voices discussing the penance that he has done—and his obligation to do more. He prays to wake, the ship enters the harbor, and at the sight of crimson shadows rising from the depths he turns to see the deck littered once more with corpses, atop each of which is a man in white: a band of seraphs signaling to the land. A boat approaches with three figures onboard, splitting the bay, and when the ship, like the Albatross, "went down like lead," they fetch the Mariner from the water. His first words cause the Pilot to faint, and when he takes up the oars the Pilot's boy concludes that he is the Devil. Only the praying Hermit possesses the wits to ask: "What manner of man art thou?"

The Mariner recounts the story of his crime and punishment, the telling of which frees him momentarily from the agony that in the future will periodically overcome him, forcing him to travel from land to land until he chances upon someone like the Wedding-Guest, who "cannot choose but hear." It is true that the Wedding-Guest's reactions to his story are like unto what many feel before the sublime: indifference gives way to impatience and anger, then to fear and fascination and finally, perhaps, to gratitude. Who can bear to hear such an awful tale? Yet we yearn for its truth with the desire of the parched sailors who dream of slaking their thirst, which is why *The Rime of the Ancient Mariner* endures in the imagination, like Coleridge's other dream work, *Kubla Khan*.

The poem defies rational analysis, demanding that readers surrender to its musical and mysterious logic, which carries them into a supernatural world, where a different set of rules applies—no less stringent than what we imagine governs daily life. Told in the popular form of a ballad, which is rooted in oral tradition, the narrative unfolds at a brisk pace, luring the ear from rhyme to rhyme, dramatizing the strangest events in what seems to be an inevitable sequence. *The willing suspension of disbelief*: this phrase, coined by Coleridge to justify in the name of a larger truth the fantastic elements in his poem, is a useful formula for explaining the structure of belief, which depends upon giving oneself over to a story that can both enchant and explain the meaning of one's walk in the sun. The more implausible the tale, the more rigorous the writer must be to make it believable: *In the beginning was the Word. . . .* And the formula applies not just to poetry and religion but to every aspect of experience. We want to believe, hoping against hope that what we believe is true: that our beloved feels as we do; that our calling is the right one; that our time here below matters. Most of our decisions—to attend a particular school, a house of worship, a film; to marry, take a job, raise children; to travel to one place instead of another; to vote for someone; to launch a war; to negotiate for peace; to make a record of our deeds—are predicated on hope, however misguided, for ourselves and our families, for our tribe and country, for posterity and the planet, for God.

The willing suspension of disbelief leads some to clarity, others to blind faith. In Coleridge's waking dream lie truths of a philosophical and religious order—that we are judged and punished for our actions; that prayer and love are intertwined; that expiation requires confession, a story—that a fanatic can translate into a nightmare. But clarity and faith need not be at odds, as writers in every religious tradition make plain, and an idea shared by most faiths—that vision is always partial—can instill the humility required for the marriage of clarity and faith: one theme of Coleridge's poem. He strikes a balance between what he knows and what he does not know, leaving unexplained certain crucial matters, beginning with the Mariner's decision to kill the Albatross. Why did he commit the crime? The poet lets the reader imagine that the Mariner is afflicted by some anxiety, the only relief for which is to kill the bird that in sea lore carries the souls of lost sailors. Nor does he explain how the Mariner's silent blessing of the water-snakes restores him to human society, what compels him to stop certain strangers to tell his tale of guilt and redemption, or why the Wedding-Guest stays to listen. We cannot presume to understand everything, he seems to say, and therein lies hope for our salvation.

The marriage of clarity and faith was doomed for a poet condemned to become addicted to laudanum, which he took to relieve his pain and anxiety, and yet in some of his opium-tinctured dreams he sounded the depths of human under-standing, articulating questions of last things—questions that the Wedding-Guest, who will rise the next morning "A sadder and a wiser man," will ponder as he reflects on his encounter with the Mariner, the spirit of Death-in-Life.

This spectral sense was what Eddin treasured in Coleridge, since it was very close to the Malay spirit; the altered states of consciousness that the Romantic poet sought in dream were what my friend found in Kelantan; the Voices of the Spirits in *The Rime of the Ancient Mariner* reminded him of conversations between the shaman and the *minduk* in *main puteri*. I could not help but wonder how much of *main puteri* was believable to the people of Kelantan, and Eddin replied with a story about a Malay who hired three shamans to make him chief minister of the region. The shamans, two men and a woman, demanded three million ringgits, for which they led him through a series of initiations, in the last of which they used machetes to hack him into thirty-six pieces, the Malay presumably believing that he was invincible. More proof, said Eddin, of the corruption of power and belief. The shamans were hanged.

"This is a country comfortable with schizophrenia," he said.

In *The Long Day Wanes*, Burgess's comic trilogy about the last days of colonial rule in Malaya, a British schoolteacher's gin-soaked marriage falls apart against the backdrop of Chinese Communist guerrillas plotting in the jungle. If the path to Malayan independence in 1957 involved considerably less bloodshed than the end of the Palestine Mandate, fifty years later, American strategists confronting a growing insurgency in Iraq would debate the merits of the British model for containing violence in Malaya—the so-called "oil-spot strategy" by which an occupying force establishes security in a small area to win the hearts and minds of the local population, creating a political space in which to foster a spirit of compromise, and then expands that area, like oil spreading. But the British had occupied Malaya for nearly two centuries before they had to confront the Communist insurgency, and their knowledge of their subjects was what enabled them to devise, in a timely fashion (and time was of the essence), the strategy of quickly resettling Chinese communities to prevent them from offering support to the guerrillas. Resettlement had its costs, though: Malays still regard the Chinese with suspicion.

When one order succeeds another, as in the Malayan Emergency, there is usually hell to pay, as Burgess intimates in a conversation between the British schoolteacher, Victor Crabbe, and Lin Cheng Po, an Oxford-educated Chinese solicitor who would prefer to live in England. Their ostensible subject is terrorism on the island of Penang, but what they are really discussing is the anger that lies just beneath the surface of daily life—an unintended consequence of the traditional colonial strategy of dividing and conquering the peoples of an occupied land, of pitting one ethnic, tribal, or religious group against another in order to maintain control:

> "Who starts it all?" asked Crabbe.
> "My dear chap, that's rather a naïve question, isn't it? It just starts. Some blame the Malays, others the Chinese. Perhaps a Malay shakes his fist at a Chettiar money-lender, and for some obscure reason, that sets off a brawl in a Chinese cabaret. Or a British tommy gets tight in KL and the Tamils start spitting at a Sikh policeman. The fact is that the component

races of this exquisite and impossible country
just don't get on. There was, it's true, a sort of
illusion of getting on when the British were in
full control. But self-determination's a ridiculous idea in a mixed-up place like this. There's
no nation. There's no common culture, language, literature, religion. I know the Malays
want to impose all these things on the others,
but that obviously won't work. Damn it all,
their language isn't civilized, they've got about
two or three books—dull and ill-written, their
version of Islam is unrealistic and hypocriti-
cal." He drank his tea and, like any Englishman
in the tropics, began to sweat after it. "When
we British finally leave there's going to be hell.
And we're leaving pretty fast."

The bill for this came due in the deadly race riots of 1969,
long after the sun had set on the British Empire. Malaysia was
still wobbling under the debt. Americans may be uncomfortable with the notion that a global military presence and the
occupation of Afghanistan and Iraq constitute an empire, but
after 9/11 it was common to hear scholars, strategists, and
policy makers extolling the virtues of such an enterprise, glossing over the fact that imperial undertakings require vast ex-
penditures of blood and treasure: reordering the world cannot
be done on the cheap, as American soldiers, diplomats, and
policy makers were discovering in Baghdad's Green Zone, with
bloody consequences.

This was the substance of my conversation with Eddin in
Kota Bharu's central market. It was sweltering, and as we walked
among bins of spices and rice, basins of fish, and tables lined
with plucked, headless chickens, my friend drew my attention

to the mix of people—a Chinese woman offering bananas, an Indian woman displaying batiks, a Malay woman arranging turtle eggs in a pyramid: hundreds and hundreds of sellers and buyers and people strolling by. We climbed to the second floor to get a panoramic view of the market—long tables covered with fruits and vegetables, men in white skullcaps examining goods, women in bright sarongs fanning themselves—and there Eddin quoted a British historian, "Take a knife to a Malay and you'll find a Hindu." His gaze settled on a pious young man hectoring a group of teenagers.

"It's the Chinese Restaurant Syndrome," he said dismissively. "The louder the storefront, the worse the food. The more you proclaim Islam, the less it works"—which was why Kelantan had the highest rates of HIV/AIDS infection and drug addiction. The Islamists had nothing more to offer to the young.

In the stalls outside the market, among the piles of fruits and vegetables, I smelled the fabled *durian* before I saw it—a large melon with a thorny husk and a thoroughly disagreeable odor. At Eddin's suggestion I tried a bite and promptly gagged. It was, in Burgess's memorable words, "like eating sweet raspberry blancmange in the lavatory." Eddin admitted that *durian* had the flavor of an open sewer line, but he loved it.

The proscription on traditional ceremonies had forced the shadow puppeteer to tap rubber for a living, for a quarter of what he had earned in the theater, and rising in the middle of the night to work had taken its toll on the elderly *dalang*, who spoke in a halting manner. He had served his apprenticeship during the independence movement, when hundreds of shadow puppet troupes worked in Kelantan, and he remarked that only three remained by the time that Eddin Khoo began his research; now there were more, thanks to Pusaka's efforts to promote the Thai drama, *wayang kulit*, and to the interest generated by the ban, without which it might have vanished. Nevertheless it seemed that the *dalang*, a wiry toothless man in blue jeans and an olive shirt, with large spectacles and even larger ears, embodied a dying tradition. He was recovering from a stroke suffered in 2000, and when Eddin and I visited him at his smallholding in Kok Lanas he greeted us with the sad news that he had lost his false teeth and thus could no longer sing.

Abdullah bin Ibrahim, the famous red shirt *dalang* (a moniker won in a puppeteer duel, the prize for which was a dozen red shirts), was also known as the hooligan *dalang* for his irreverent style, his naughtiness, which he attributed to his *angin*. Those who wish to practice *wayang kulit*, he said, have different *angin*. Everyone has *angin*, of course, but those in the healing and creative arts have more of it than others; the ban thus cost them not only their livelihood but in some cases also their health. Blockage of the *angin* was general among Kelantanese performers, and Eddin blamed the Islamists for crippling this *dalang*: he had no outlet for his creative energy.

Nor had his three sons inherited the *angin* for shadow play—or for much else, said Eddin in a voice laced with contempt. They were lying on hammocks strung between rubber trees, sullenly looking us over, and did not stir when their three sisters rode up on a motorbike groaning under their weight. Near a pile of burning debris grazed a cow named Limousine, a baby monkey chained to a tree licked its toes (the *dalang* was training it to pick coconuts), turkeys and chickens rooted around cages of wild birds.

We followed the *dalang* into his workshop—an unlit barn with wood shavings on the floor, a carpet embroidered with a design of the Great Mosque in Mecca nailed to one wall, an ironing board set up by the only window, under a cage in which a zebra dove softly cooed; in a bowl hanging from the rafters were the *dalang*'s favorite puppets, wrapped in a yellow cloth (the royal color); his apprentice, an older man in a green-and-white sarong with a grimy towel draped over his bare chest, was scraping and pounding leather to fashion into a new puppet. Low on cash, the *dalang* had sold some of his puppets to the national gallery, along with one of the two drums bequeathed to him by his teacher, his beloved *dalang*. Pusaka had commissioned him to create another set of puppets, which he removed now from a wooden case for us to examine.

In the dim light I could not at first appreciate the intricate designs worked into the water buffalo hides, which were pressed together like the folded wings of an owl. But on closer inspection I could see how carefully each figure had been cut, stretched, stitched, painted, and gilded, then attached to a series of rods whittled from buffalo horns to bring to life a range of characters—fantastic and wicked and wise—from the Ramayana, the Hindu epic performed throughout the Subcontinent. Each *dalang* adapts for his healing rituals and performances of the epic different aspects of Rama, the seventh incarnation of Vishnu, supreme god of the Vaishnavism branch of Hinduism, creating characters to represent different human inclinations—empathy and evil, loyalty and darkness, gentleness and sensuality. This *dalang* preferred the naughty one, though Eddin added that he loved them all; otherwise they would not perform for him.

What extravagant demands he made on them. The red shirt *dalang*'s version of the epic took a month to perform—five shows a week, each lasting four hours—and in his prime he could play seventy different puppets a night, seven at once, propped on a banana stalk, their movements elaborately choreographed and cast on a cotton screen lit by an oil lamp. Healings were just as demanding: he would examine the patient, diagnose the

problem, and return to his workshop to discuss with his puppets what to do; a *wayang kulit* would be organized to celebrate
the patient's recovery.

All gone. I felt my anger rising at PAS's decision to ban such
a source of delight, such healing energy. It defied reason for an
Islamic party to cut off in the name of Islamic purity one of the
traditions crucial to the reception of Islam in Southeast Asia,
but no one ever accused those who traffic in fear of accurately
remembering history. The *dalang* had begun selling tickets
to his performances in 1957, at the height of the resistance to
British rule, and if it seemed that he had always been at war—
with the colonial order, with the cinema, with his body, with
time itself—clearly his defeat at the hands of PAS was the most
painful of all; for it struck at the core of his identity.

"After Independence," he said in a garbled voice, his hands
in constant motion, as if working his puppets, "I wanted to
be like the cinema. But the people preferred *wayang*. Once
I performed in a *kampong* while they were showing a film in
an open theater. I told my musicians to play louder—and the
people came over to hear us!"

Now he chose two puppets and set them against each
other, conducting a duel that seemed closer in spirit to dance
than a violent confrontation. One leapt at the other, arms
flying, and then scurried backward, staging a dramatic retreat, pursued by his nemesis through the wood shavings
on the floor, forward and back they went, heads bobbing,
raising their arms to threaten or defend themselves, ducking
and weaving and twirling, their wizened master clucking and
shaking with joy.

"You can tell who the real *dalang* is in a fight scene," said
Eddin. "The real ones are playful."

Art *is* play, even when the subject matter is dark, for creativity depends upon the freedom of the spirit to range wherever

it likes in search of materials, pattern, meaning; and in the *dalang's* workshop I found myself drifting back to childhood, to the pleasures of watching cartoons on Saturday mornings, captivated by the escapades of Quick Draw McGraw and Ricochet Rabbit, Wile E. Coyote and Roadrunner—characters inspired by shadow play, a precursor to animated films. The stories, terrifying as they were, made me howl with laughter, even when I was sick in bed, with pillows heaped around my fevered body; and now by a strange logic I recalled the cartoon figures in the small cardboard box that at the age of seven I would hold up to my eyes, reluctantly performing the exercises prescribed by an ophthalmologist to align my crossed eyes. But the figures would not fuse, not even after I had undergone a pair of surgeries to correct my vision, and so began my preoccupation with the limitations of sight. For what is the creative process if not an attempt to see what lies at the edge of understanding?

As it happens, my first published article, which appeared in our local newspaper when I was twelve, profiled a blind neighbor, Morris Frank, the founder of the Seeing Eye. From Switzerland he had brought the revolutionary idea of training dogs to guide the blind, and it was a badge of honor among my friends to raise puppies for the Seeing Eye, which was headquartered near our village in northern New Jersey. My mother said that Mr. Frank's guide dog, Buddy, a German shepherd, was smarter than most people, and I inherited her view that dogs possess uncanny knowledge about human behavior—though I do not remember whether I raised this in my interview with Mr. Frank, who was by then an old man. What I do remember is a story that my mother told about him: how one day he was burning leaves in his backyard, unaware of the fact that there was poison ivy in the pile; the smoke he inhaled triggered an allergic reaction, which almost killed him. The story haunted me, and indeed the image of a blind man breathing what I called "itching smoke" in the title poem of my first collection, *Workbook,* had become in my mind an emblem of the pain that may be involved in discovering the truth.

The *dalang*'s pain, physical and spiritual, rooted in the banning of *wayang kulit,* differed in kind from what Morris Frank had suffered after burning leaves one autumn day, but it revealed an enduring truth: that the powerful often fear the ways in which art, in the form of entertainment or healing, of articulating difficult questions, of interrogating the order of things, may speak truth to power. Debilitated as he was, the combative *dalang* retained his playfulness, and the stylized dueling of his puppets reminds us that *wayang kulit,* like all art, all forms of serious play, can clarify our walk in the sun, framing experience as a form of vision predicated on what might be glimpsed in and through the shadows. This terrified PAS.

By way of contrast, the Indonesian government had recently succeeded in having *wayang kulit* designated as a UNESCO Masterpiece of Oral and Intangible Heritage of Humanity—a tribute to the traditional ceremonies of the entire region, which put pressure on the authorities in Kelantan to engage local performers. But this *dalang* ignored PAS's overtures, preferring to spend his final years passing on the rudiments of his craft than talking to politicians; what he offered to his apprentice and Eddin was an intangible good, the value of which, like that of most spiritual things, could not be measured: access to a tradition of pleasure and instruction and solace integral to society.

Three times a *dalang* formally enters this tradition—at his initiation, midway through his career, and when he hands on his teachings—in a ritual requiring every ounce of his energy. First he feeds the puppets, the spirits, laying out a feast for them that goes on for three days and nights; then, dressed in a yellow robe, he inhabits the puppets, imitating all their movements; ten people could not hold this *dalang* back when he entered the tradition at midcareer. The date of his final entrance into the tradition depended upon his apprentice, who told us that as long as his teacher was alive he would keep learning from him. Eddin teased him about the length of his preparation (which had begun over twenty-five years before), though he admitted that after a decade of study he himself was not ready for initiation—an elaborate ceremony in which the puppets are sealed in a wooden case and then dropped into the river for the initiate to retrieve. It aggrieved Eddin that the *dalang*'s sons showed no interest in carrying on his work. And he feared that the *dalang* would die before he could enter the tradition for the last time. Nor did his apprentice look like he could easily manage a dive to the bottom of the river. But for *wayang kulit* to survive the apprentice, quite literally, had to make the plunge.

Thunder rumbled in the west as the last light of day streamed in the window through which I could see a grove of banana trees on a small hill. Dust motes hung in the air. The zebra dove ruffled its wings, cooed in its cage.

Figurines of animals fashioned out of rice flour and water—these were the first offerings that the *pesakit* placed around the doll-sized spirit house propped on a stand at the back of the stage. Candles burned by the four corners of the spirit house and in the coconut husk atop an adjacent post; from house and post hung palm fronds, *pelapsas,* tied together with double slip knots, the untying of which would release the *pesakit* from the bonds of illness before the night was over. In Malay cosmology, the spirits manifest themselves as animals—tigers, wolves, sea creatures— and a *main puteri* concludes with the feeding and appeasing of these spirits before the *minduk* runs through the forest to throw the figurines into the river.

An even larger crowd had assembled than on the first night of the ceremony, and as the *pesakit* set out her offerings

to the spirits—a blue bucket of jasmine and platters of bananas, sweets, hard-boiled eggs, and yellow flower blossoms,
all blessed with incense pulled from the nearby fire pit—a
pigeon-toed man swept the sand around the stage. The *pesakit*
wore a beige sarong and a yellow veil, the royal color, befitting
the diagnosis that she wished to be the center of attention, to
live the life of royal leisure. Her attendants sat in a row next
to the *minduk*, who held a pipe between his toes, bantering
with the shaman. The crowd grew silent when the candles were
extinguished, the *minduk* and the musicians took up their instruments, and then the shaman scattered jasmine blossoms
on the stage, summoning the spirits and their ancestors—
consecrating the space, Eddin explained, to secure a relationship between the audience and the performers.

"We still have our ancestors," he said, translating the *minduk's* invocation, a chant that was *haraam*, although it praised
Allah. "We still have their bones, we still have their wings, and
now they will meet here. Peace be upon you. Come."

The mnemonic opening recalled the people to their pre-
Islamic origins, preserving the memory of their lineage in the
Malay Archipelago, in the same manner that in the Old and
New Testaments, in the book of Numbers and the Gospel of
Matthew, respectively, genealogies are rehearsed to establish
the history and authority of the chosen people, the prophets,
God, the Son of Man. For rituals remind the faithful not only
of the tenets of their religion but of their place in the world,
schooling their memory in the signal events and figures of
their history in order to instruct them in the conduct of their
lives and inspire their devotion to the divine. It is easier to
maintain the record of a religion in written form (also to develop a theology), which is why the proscription against traditional ceremonies had the effect of erasing the memory of the
Kelantanese: what is not written down, what floats on the air

of its own creation, may be carried off by the wind, despite the efforts of someone like Eddin to record as many performances of it as possible. In the chants, and the music and dance, and the conversation of the spirits inhabiting the stage tonight, was a history about to vanish, leaving only traces in the words and gestures of the people who might carry on with little knowledge of what came before.

Kelantan means "land of lightning," and lightning was flashing in the distance, as it had during the first performance. The atmosphere around the stage was also electric: evidently the *pesakit's* revelation the night before had riled some young men milling in the trees. They shouted slurs at her until an elderly man said something to them in a sharp tone of voice. The commotion stopped almost as soon as it had begun.

"Inhibition is an elemental part of Malay society," Eddin was saying, ignoring the ruckus, and that was why the shaman had urged the *pesakit* to cast off her inhibitions on the first night and act out the repressed feelings of her ancestors. Her leaping around the stage was a sign that her soul had left her body, her dancing a token of the marriage of the earthly and celestial, all held together by the shaman's tears—emblems of the altered state of consciousness that drew my friend to Kelantan. The *pesakit* had a spectral bearing, and it seemed to me that the sadness etched into her sepulchral face was of ancient origin. Would she find relief from her pain tonight? How would she fare in the *kampong* now that her secret was out? And the audience—what would they take from this? The shaman and the *minduk* were the authors of a play, the ending of which remained a mystery even to them—unlike, say, the prayers performed five times daily by most of the crowd, the words of which they could recite in their sleep.

Character, complications, climax: these are the ingredients of drama, which in the Aristotelian scheme of things leads to a cleansing of the emotions—catharsis, from the Greek word to purify. No one knew how the complications faced by the princess would be resolved, and that suspense held our attention. What could be more complicated, or grievous, than to grow up as a transvestite in a *kampong*? Yet in this ceremony it seemed that the *pesakit* had discovered a space in which to become her true self: a princess. And her neighbors and kin had found a way to make room for her. Perhaps the future of Islam depended upon preserving such indigenous ways to include within the fabric of the community the marginalized, the Other?

The shaman cast jasmine on the pillow in front of the *minduk*, and together they interrogated the blossoms to determine which of the four winds would be drawn out of the *pesakit* seated on a mat at center stage. Then the *minduk* drew his bow over the strings of his *rebab*, an instrument believed to have been carved from the spine and scattered bones of Adam, the original man, to guide his descendents, and now it set the tempo for a ceremony that was closer in spirit to a jazz concert, part provocation, part arousal, composed in the changing key of the *pesakit*'s needs. Eddin was struck by the fact that the tempo of this performance was much slower than on the first night.

"It's strange," he said. "There's a lot of sadness tonight, a lot of wailing."

At some invisible signal the *pesakit* jumped to her feet, whirled toward the *minduk* and the shaman, and fell before them, laying her head on the pillow, as if to sleep. The *minduk* proceeded to question her through the shaman, who knelt behind her, summoning spirits to convince her that she had entered a palace. A royal destiny awaits the dead in the afterlife, Kelantanese believe, and to play the princess is to die a ritual death, leaving the tormented self to find relief from afflictions in this life. The shaman retrieved from the spirit house the figurine of a cow and, along with the first shaman from the night

before, the *minduk,* and the *serunai* player, interrogated it for
some time before placing it between the *pesakit's* legs. The
minduk gazed at her, as if to discern something, then touched
her shoulder, softly, and glided across the stage to place the
figurine in the coconut husk atop the post. He untied a slip-
knotted palm frond, releasing the spirit, and brought another
figurine to interrogate the *pesakit,* a process that he repeated
several times, his demeanor changing with each spirit that inhabited him. Now he caressed the *pesakit* like a lover, now he
jostled her, as if to wake her from her trance. The mournful
song of the *rebab* and the *serunai*—the call of the devil, according to some Islamists—sounded in the night.

"The spirit is released not through a process of possession
but of expression," said Eddin, carefully distinguishing between
the different states of consciousness that we were witnessing. The shaman had to maintain control, refusing to fall into
a trance so as to become a vessel through which poured the
voices of the spirits, one of whom prompted the *pesakit* to ask
the other shaman to take over: she needed a gentler, sadder
poetry.

"Basically this is psychotherapy," said Eddin.

This was the point made by the anthropologist Carol
Laderman, who notes that Kelantan's healing rituals can produce in the patient the distance necessary to confront emo-
tional wounds, a keystone of psychotherapy, and certainly
the *pesakit's* revelation about her sexuality would furnish an
analyst with plenty of material. There is, of course, a ceremonial aspect to psychotherapy, as pioneering spirits of the discipline like Freud and Jung suggested, and indeed to any form
of interrogation, for good or ill, as leaked scripts of the interrogation sessions conducted by the CIA and the US military
made plain—elaborately staged dramas, performed in black
sites and prisons like Abu Ghraib, to elicit confessions that

bore no relationship to the truth, just as priests in the Spanish Inquisition perverted the sacrament of confession to purify the faith. But at its best a ceremony enacts the full range of human emotions in the service of interrogating the soul, articulating ways of knowing, pleading to the gods, defining one's right relationship to family and community, tribe and country, the earth and the divine. It is how we call to mind our best selves, cleanse our worst impulses, undergo catharsis.

How to purge the body politic of its terror? Begin with the individual.

To know. To be known. To see. To be seen. To seek the truth. To seek thy face. To sort it out. To assemble the facts. To tell the story straight. To come clean. This was what the *pesakit* had done, and I wondered if she felt bolstered, or terrified.

"This is a pretty negotiable case," said Eddin, meaning that the *pesakit*'s family would not have to organize another ceremony for her, at least not in the near term.

The shaman set a small leather sailboat between the *pesakit*'s legs, and after a little while he picked it up to store it under the spirit house, returning to cast jasmine blossoms over the *pesakit*, who was holding a blue pillow in her lap. One of her attendants came to sit by her, accompanied by an autistic child, who lay down behind her. From time to time the music stopped, the shaman and the *minduk* bantered, the crowd chimed in. Near midnight, a cell phone rang, and then another. The shaman moved the spirit house in front of the post, lit the candles, and when the singing resumed the *pesakit* danced across the stage to the spirit house. There she dropped to her knees to raise overhead a platter of food for the spirits released tonight. The second shaman pulled her up to dance with him, the first shaman snuffed out the candles and started to dance with the *minduk*, and when an old man joined them onstage the crowd went wild.

This went on for some time before the *pesakit* fell down,

seemingly unconscious, and long minutes passed before she came to her senses, stood up, and took a ceremonial turn around the spirit house. The shamans ate sweets, threw baby powder over everyone on stage, cinched white cords around their waists. The first shaman carried off the coconut husk, while a man with a white skullcap and the *minduk* took the spirit house to the river. The stage emptied except for the *pesakit* sitting in the corner. The second shaman, tossing jasmine blossoms on the ground, went over to her.

"You are healed," he told her, "for now."

Her attendants brought out trays of coffee, and as the crowd dispersed Eddin explained how animistic knowledge, Hindu-Buddhist symbolism, and Islamic mysticism flowed together in this folk tradition, which was sustained by the local communities. I thought how this ritualized search for the truth stood in counterpoint to the barbaric rituals unveiled at Abu Ghraib—the one designed to discover a healing truth, the other to provoke false confessions about terrorist plots.

"Of all the forms that have been banned," said my friend, "this one has the best chance of surviving, because it's the one that is most needed."

Everything is negotiable, was Eddin's explanation for the incongruities of daily life in a country stitched together in the usual ways (geography, religion, politics, art, desire, conflict, ceremony), which ultimately defied comprehension. Thus the shaman's last words to the *pesakit* were instructive: *you are healed, for now.* There was no question that she seemed to be in better spirits, her aches and pains and despair having been alleviated, perhaps because she believed in the ceremony, or wanted to believe.

Belief is a curious thing. We want to believe that we will recover from an illness, that our plans will work out, that we made the right decision. The beloved is beautiful as long as the lover believes in what they are creating together. What else is desire but the cherry-picking of intelligence? The narratives that we construct for our lives are not easily shaken—until they are. And then? And then we begin again, in a new dispensation, where we have the chance to listen either to our good angels or our bad. Like poetry, the shaman's benediction was a momentary stay against confusion. For healings are always provisional, sometimes lasting only as long as the ceremony itself.

PART II

EXPEDITION

EXPEDITION

I

In May 1920, a Frenchman set off from Beijing, traveling with friends for three weeks by car and train, by horse- and camelback, through the Gobi Desert and the Mongolian steppe to Urga, soon to be renamed Ulaanbaatar—a voyage inspired in part by his book-length poem, *Anabasis,* which he had written not long after his diplomatic posting to China, in 1917. This was the first of several masterpieces by the twentieth century's preeminent poet-diplomat, Aléxis Saint-Léger Léger, also known as Saint-John Perse, a public figure and prophetic poet who wished to have his work read as "a single and long sentence without caesura"—a sentence for which he was awarded the Nobel Prize in 1960. Léger published *Anabasis* in 1924, under his *nom de plume* (a name supposedly chosen for musical reasons, though Perse is French for Persian), and if his meditation on what the Swedish Academy called "a mysterious warlike expedition into the Asian deserts" does not refer directly to the *Anabasis* of Xenophon, the ancient historian who recounted the disastrous journey of Greek mercenaries to seize the Persian throne only to be routed in Mesopotamia, still it reminds us of the intimate connection between literary expeditions and those undertaken by soldiers, missionaries, and explorers.

Aléxis Saint-Léger Léger was born in 1887, on the island of Guadalupe, in the French Antilles, two hundred years after his

family had settled in the Caribbean. His was a happy childhood—
his family belonged to the class of plantation owners who ruled
the Isles des Vents—and his poems teem with images of the tropics: royal palms and sugar cane and coco plums; coffee, spices,
waterfalls. Above his family's coffee plantation was a rumbling
volcano, typhoons swept in from the sea, and in the port of
Pointe-à-Pitre, among the freighters, whalers, and ocean liners,
Léger met travelers from Africa and India, China and Europe,
and heard many languages. He was a child of the trade winds,
with his own boat to sail beyond the shelter of the cove and out
onto the open sea, a horse to ride on the beach, a telescope with
which to explore the heavens.

And there was a Hindu servant who took a special interest
in him when he was seven. His mother and sisters had gone
to France for the summer, his younger sister having died (the
fragrance of her mahogany coffin would enter his poem, "To
Celebrate a Childhood"), and in their absence the servant told
him stories about Shiva, Lord of the Three Faces, who created
and destroyed the world. One night she crept into his room,
painted his palms and the soles of his feet with ochre, and took
him to a temple at the edge of the woods, where he joined the
Indian worshippers in chanting to a statue of Shiva, a seated
figure on an altar surrounded by stone idols. Then she carried
him to the houses of the plantation laborers to touch the fore-
heads of the sick—Indian and Malay, Chinese and Japanese:
"men of every blood," he remembered.

The schoolboy's favorite haunt was the port, among the
prophets and sorcerers, carcasses of cattle and catches of fish,
"the kegs of sugar drip[ping] on the Quays of marcasite painted
in great festoons with fuel oil." He was avid for the mariners' stories, which along with the impressions of their ships he recorded
in a notebook—a habit that he retained in the diplomatic service;
their every gesture—tying knots, folding sails—captivated him;

the list of their ports of call shaped his imagination as decisively as the natural splendor of the island and the stories of his Hindu servant.

His idyll came to an end in 1897, when a large earthquake struck the island. Walls fell, the sea surged into Pointe-à-Pitre, corpses piled up in the market. The Légers' property and fortunes were devastated; henceforth dispossession marked the poet's life; when at the age of twelve he set sail with his family for France, scion of a vanished colonial order, he must have mourned what he left behind—his horse and toys, his friends and servants—and wondered what lay in store for him. The journey passed without incident, but upon arrival the Légers discovered that during the initial loading process the crates containing their library had been dropped into the sea—and no effort had been made to dry them out; the books had turned into a black mass; the only surviving sheet was the title page of a first edition of Baudelaire's *Les Fleurs du Mal.* Perse never forgot the smell of the putrefying books, which may help to explain why his work is free of the stench of the library: "his word is fresher to us than new water," he wrote of a mythical poet, an archetypal figure in his imagination. "Freshness and promise of freshness."

Not that he was averse to studying. His *baccalaureates* were distinguished—he excelled in Latin and Greek, philosophy and rhetoric—and he was writing mature poems before he enrolled as a law student at the University of Bordeaux. He translated Pindar's odes, schooling his ear on their music, and rounded off his literary apprenticeship with the publication of his first book, *Praises and Other Poems,* in 1911—the same year that he wrote for advice about his future to Paul Claudel, the poet-diplomat with whom he is often compared. Indeed their friendship, their shared vocation and service in China, and the fact that in their major works they employed the same long line, the verset of the Psalms and Proverbs—all suggest that they were kindred spirits.

And yet their differences were profound. Claudel, a devout Catholic who once considered joining a monastery, tried in vain to lure the agnostic Perse back into the fold of the church. And though Claudel was as self-centered as Perse was discrete he set the young man on his path, noting in a letter to him that he seemed bent on finding "the limits of a 'work.'" Perse, who had decided that his own work was lifeless, replied in a prophetic fashion: "I would simply like, some day, to have the privilege of leading an 'undertaking' the way an *Anabasis* is conducted by its leaders. (The very word seems to me so beautiful that I should like to come across the work worthy of such a title. It haunts me.)" In fact he created such a work, and then he led an expedition across the Asian vast—twin undertakings integral to understanding that sliver of modern experience in which poetry and politics occasionally rub up against each other.

The first secretary in the French legation wrote *Anabasis* in a Taoist temple rented from its monks, in the mountains west of the capital, and one overcast summer morning I drove there with the poet Xi Chuan and two of his acquaintances, a filmmaker working on a documentary about Perse's life in China and the architectural preservationist who had discovered the ruins of the Dragon Fountain Temple. What was for the diplomat a one-day journey on horseback would take us less than an hour, even in traffic, and once underway Xi Chuan translated the preservationist's account of finding the temple: how the posthumous publication of a Chinese student's Parisian research convinced him that Tao Yu must be what the locals referred to as *Frenchland*, the French Embassy having purchased it at some point. From the outer ring of the city we sped through the countryside on a highway, with a handsomely landscaped meridian of boxwood hedges and red poppies, and in a town

at the base of the mountains we left a tree-lined street to follow a dirt road past a walled compound incongruously named
The Center of Literary Exercises—Xi Chuan had no idea what it
could be. Up a narrow lane, beyond cornfields and sunflowers,
brick huts and produce stands selling honey, peaches, and ap-
ples, we entered the woods, where the road turned to mud, and
parked under a steep hillside. It had rained overnight, and in stifling heat and humidity we climbed an overgrown trail. By the
time we reached the ridge I was drenched in sweat.

The preservationist had mapped thirty temples in the immediate area (Buddhist, Confucian, and Taoist)—an amaz-
ing feat, given the difficulty of the terrain and the fact that
Japanese forces had burned most of them down in the 1930s,
these mountains being a Communist stronghold; only a
trained eye would have noticed the foundation under a thick
cover of ferns and shrubs or the stone inscription indicating
that the temple had been built in the 1890s, during the reign of
the last emperor. Beyond some dragonflies and a patch of daylilies was a pair of silver apricots or ginkgos planted by monks
during the Ming dynasty (1368–1644)—symbols of ancient
China, like the panda bear. A rainbow-colored banner was
draped over the gate to a peach orchard; the pine tree twisting above the remnants of the north wall had taken root after
Perse's time. The monks had let him stay in the most sacred
part of the sanctuary, which was also the coolest, and in a letter to his mother he reported that his camp bed was "set up at
the foot of the platform of the gods, with all the big windows
open to the pure night." From the river far below he heard
stone drums calling the ferryman; in the distance—all haze
this morning—he saw "the pale yellow line of the first camel-
routes that lead off into the northwest and into Central Asia."
Someday he would set out in that direction, along "the vanishing traces of the old nomadic empire and its marches where
the roads have no markers."

There is a photograph of the poet lounging with two friends on a hay pile under the pagoda of Tao Yuan, in a summer suit and bowler, with a bow tie and mustache—an image that stands in sharp contrast to the turmoil that he witnessed during his first year in China. He had been posted to Beijing in an emergency (a case of what he called "Chinese hysteria" had led to riots in the French concession in Tianjin), where he took exception to the high-handed European way of dealing with the Chinese. Better to let tempers cool than to act in the heat of the moment, was his instinct. And his efforts to get to know his neighbors taught him that they had an altogether different conception of time, which had to be factored into every encounter. Against the advice of colleagues unwilling or afraid to venture out of the diplomatic quarter, he explored as much of "the real China" as his busy schedule allowed; in the evenings he played chess with local politicians who unwittingly let him glimpse "something of the old, underlying human substratum that, no matter what we say, is infinitely variable. Their logic is not ours." Silence was the rule in China, Perse decided, despite all the noise and hankering after money and social status; in the intellectual and political ferment from which a modern state was rising, it seemed to him that keeping silent was an individual's only right. Fortunately he did not maintain his own vow of poetic silence, which he had taken upon entering the diplomatic service. And so it was that when he took up his pen again silence was the secret theme of his poetry—the silence of the vast; of the elements; of the desert, sea, and sky. In *Anabasis* he heard "the swarms of silence in the hives of light," a rich metaphor for the relationship between gestation and activity, a dynamic that sometimes leads to revelation.

The fall of the Qing dynasty in 1912 had brought to a close two thousand years of imperial history, and with world war raging in Europe in the summer of 1917 little notice was taken in foreign capitals of the revolutions breaking out in China's provinces and the coup d'état staged in Beijing—which emptied in terror, the Chinese disappearing, Perse wrote, "like so many insects burrowing out of sight into the sea-sand." The imperial restoration lasted for just twelve days, a firestorm that reduced the city to smoking ruins, and after surveying the damage Perse rode to his mountain retreat to reflect on China's first experience of democracy. He composed for the ambassador a private, and hilarious, account of his role in securing the release of the presidential family and concubines from the imperial forces, parodying the language of diplomacy: "The First Lady herself, hiding her face from the crowd behind a fan, and in the measure that two green patches pressed against her temples because of a splitting headache permitted, fixed her gaze steadfastly on the non-existent threat of death." But this "report" was mistakenly added to the diplomatic mail pouch sent to the Ministry of Foreign Affairs in the Quai d'Orsay, which frowned upon such antics. Perse's sense of humor might have cost him his career, if not for his close friendship with Philippe Berthelot, who was then in charge of political affairs.

It was to Berthelot that Perse had written an extraordinary letter within weeks of his arrival in China, which revealed his ability to size up people and situations, his clarity of vision, his uncommonly good sense—essential diplomatic traits also on display in his poetry. Part travelogue, part political analysis, the letter teems with mordant observations, witty asides, and prophetic statements. It is remarkable how much he grasped so early in his tenure, how clearly he foresaw what would come to pass. "A whole future is here at stake," he wrote, "completely committed to a new form of civilization, in search of social institutions more suitable to China than to imitations of institutions and regimes suitable to the great Western democracies." Then the crucial insight:

> The ideas of Karl Marx and of Engels already exert their subtle attraction on all the young Chinese intellectuals; and in the long run, after any number of subversions and transitional experiments, but perhaps even before the unification of China is achieved, nothing will stop the march of the Chinese community towards a collectivism very close to the most orthodox Leninist communism. . . . They are a people open to every influence, thanks to their capacity for assimilation and to the very existence of reactions jaded by long usage.

In short, Perse glimpsed the collectivist future of the Middle Kingdom thirty years before Mao Tse-tung and his comrades established the People's Republic of China (PRC). Which raises the question: how did a young diplomat at the start of his first tour, in an unimaginably complex country whose language he did not speak, predict one of the key political developments of the twentieth century? Prophesy is linked to what Christian mystics call discernment—seeing clearly, without the blinkers of received ideas or opinions. And this gift, always in short supply among the clerics, poets, and politicians most likely to claim it, is essential to good judgment. Perse had no patience for those who relied on outdated theories to guide their thinking—for example, the "cliché of the age-old rural structure of China" dear to the diplomatic corps. Indeed he employed literary reasoning (the poet lives in fear of clichés) to make a political point: those who imagine that rural traditions are a stay against change delude themselves. For Perse the sight of a peasant gazing for the first time at an airplane in the sky, "with what placid unconcern and lack of surprise," was proof that despite their old ways the Chinese would readily adapt to modernity. What separated him from other observers was the quality of his attention: he not only viewed his surroundings with the eye of a poet storing up images for future work but analyzed details with the rigor of a diplomat entrusted with a delicate mission. He knew that poor decisions follow from a lack of proper knowledge of the facts on the ground. Now was no time for ignorance, willful or otherwise.

This was in Perse's judgment "an equinoctial moment in history," when great care had to be exercised to avert disaster. He was by no means sanguine that France's political leadership understood the gravity of the situation—a common sentiment in every foreign service—and with ever more violent storms approaching (the Bolshevik Revolution, the rise of Nazism, World War II) his belief in the special vigilance demanded of policy makers would be strengthened. He knew that in a crisis even a slight miscalculation can have grave repercussions. "It sometimes takes only the smallest object to determine which slope a river will run down," he concluded. Where the water goes determines history, and in the coming years he would help to shape its course.

He took to heart his mentor's suggestion that "no professional or human education is complete without a sojourn in the Far East," his slow sea voyage from the Continent having left its mark on him: "Every day of the trip I felt that by degrees I was becoming a different man, and every day I had an ever-stronger feeling of how relative are all things in this world." And the fruits of his learning, his sense of connection between one thing and another, are everywhere on display in *Anabasis,* which he began after dispatching his mock "report" on the coup d'état. It may have been in the same antic spirit that in the space of a few weeks Perse drafted one of the strangest poems of the twentieth century—a work, as he said, intended to be "the poem of the loneliness of action. Action among men quite as much as the action of the human spirit upon itself."

Anabasis is the quintessential travel narrative, the journey of journeys, which seems to proceed in an elliptical fashion. T. S. Eliot, who published a translation of the poem in 1930, described it as "a series of images of migration, of conquest of vast spaces in Asiatic wastes, of destruction and foundation of cities and civilizations of any races or epochs of the ancient East." Not that this is immediately clear, as Eliot himself admitted. Better to read it six times through and let its images sink into your memory than to puzzle out its meaning, which might become apparent only later. Eliot believed that "the reader of a poem should take at least as much trouble as a barrister reading an important decision on a complicated case," and certainly *Anabasis* makes such demands on readers. Nor was the equation of law and poetry accidental. For as some have noted the logic of poetry is analogous to the logic of law: each has a language, structure, and method designed to serve the truth. And if the logic of law is ultimately concerned with justice, poetry obeys an imaginative logic, which may seem elusive but which can work its way mysteriously into the reader's heart. Eliot includes in the afterward to his translation a French scholar's description of the poem, which is divided into ten cantos:

I. Arrival of the Conqueror at the site of the city which he is about to build.
II. Tracing the plan of the city.
III. Consultation of augurs.
IV. Foundation of the city.
V. Restlessness towards further explorations and conquests.

VI. Schemes for foundation and conquest.
VII. Decision to fare forth.
VIII. March through the desert.
IX. Arrival at the threshold of a great new country.
X. Acclimation, festivities, repose. Yet the urge toward another departure, this time with the mariner.

This is not the outline of your average modernist poem, even of those which feature discontinuous narratives. And the ceremonial diction is also unfamiliar. "Under the bronze leaves a colt was foaled. Came such an one who laid bitter bay in our hands. Stranger. Who passed." Thus begins *Anabasis* in Eliot's translation. The reader may be forgiven for recoiling at the antique phrasing. A more faithful translation of the second sentence might read: "Someone laid bay leaves in our hands." But Perse seems to have approved of Eliot's tone, and not just because the dean of English poetry could ease his entry into another literary milieu. Perse was a masterful rhetorician—which sets him against the current of our time, when arguments in the high style are customarily met with suspicion. But rhetoric was more than an ornamental flourish for him—it was a means of rendering with utmost precision the complexities of experience: "So I haunted the City of your dreams, and I established in the desolate markets the pure commerce of my soul, among you // invisible and insistent as a fire of thorns in the gale."

What holds the poem together? A pair of songs framing a series of monologues delivered by a shape-shifting speaker; the musicality of the language (alas, largely lost in translation); and a set of recurring images. Thus the colt foaled in the first song, when the Stranger meets a tribe of nomads, returns in the final song, when the speaker halts his horse by "the tree of the doves" to hear that his brother, the poet, has written something

new—perhaps a hymn of desire and departures titled *Anabasis.*
Indeed the speaker seems also to be the Stranger, the Poet, and
the Prince—emblematic figures who delight in the cataclysmic
ways of nature, in the winds and waves and changing contours
of the earth. They are all in love with a young nomad woman
who inspires prophesies of blessing and bounty. And they do
not cower before the challenges of history, constantly setting
forth, as if to suggest that renewal lies in ceaseless movement.
The pleasures of creation, the privileges of rank, the pain of
exile—nothing is alien to those who embody the spirit of the
steppe. The cities they found, the ceremonies they perform,
the decisions they take to move on—all belong to the human
drive to pass beyond the boundaries of the known world, the
unquenchable desire that spurred Perse's explorations.

"From now on my life will be that of the wanderer, the
absent one," he wrote to his uncle. Perse was a solitary figure
who transformed a deep well of loneliness into signs of rebirth:
"Solitude! the blue egg laid by a great sea-bird, and the bays
at morning all littered with gold lemons!" In the temple ruins,
gazing at what were once the caravan routes to Mongolia, I
heard the silence from which works of the spirit emerge. And
I imagined the glee with which Perse emptied himself into his
poem: after months of diplomatic activity he had embarked
upon a daring literary journey, and what he would chart in this
interior landscape was a new map of the mind.

The preservationist uncovered a charred rock on which
were carved the characters 桃園—the garden of peach trees, in
Xi Chuan's translation. He added that if you pronounced them
in another way they would mean the source of a stream. I wondered how Perse had interpreted them. He addressed his letters
from Tao-Yu, perhaps misunderstanding what the monks called
their home, and on at least one occasion he referred to Dragon
Fountain Temple as being Buddhist. The preservationist said

that it was probably Taoist, but he did not know much more than that. Nevertheless the local authorities had asked him to rebuild the temple, but where to begin? Lacking drawings or blueprints, he would have to resort to guesswork.

The orchard had gone wild, the spring was covered over, and my mind was racing with an idea about Perse's decision to write an epic poem of exploration, conquest, and settlement. Inspiration is notoriously difficult to describe—what poet really knows how a poem comes into being?—and yet I liked to try to imagine the source of *Anabasis*, which presents its images, its poetic case, in an elliptical fashion, without visible connections, obeying the logic of a river whose headwaters lie in a hidden spring. I spun out my idea for Xi Chuan: the name given to the Chinese dynasty founded by the Mongol conqueror Kublai Khan was Yuan, meaning origin, and perhaps in sight of the route to Xanadu, the fabled capital of what was once the world's largest empire, Perse heard in the name of this sanctuary something that triggered his imagination: a dream of origins.

Xi Chuan smiled at my conjecture. "Maybe," he said.

Then again *yuan* is also the word for the Chinese currency.

On we drove to the Tomb of the Seventh Prince, the last emperor's grandfather, and in the mountains that for centuries before the Communist era had attracted pilgrims to their tea houses and shrines the filmmaker lamented his inability to raise enough funds to finish his film. There was just no market for documentaries in China.

Under a stand of pines, near the long stairway leading up to the tomb, was a stone wall on which Xi Chuan laid out canned porridge, yogurt, bread, cheese, smoked meats, and small fish in chili sauce, and over lunch I had another thought, which I kept to myself: that the preservationist's effort to reconstruct the temple, the details of which could only be imagined, was not so different from the filmmaker's desire to recreate Perse's tour of the Middle Kingdom. To do their work, in the absence of information on the one hand and money on the other, they would have to be as inventive as Perse was in casting himself into the characters of nomads on the march, transforming his memories and observations, from the Caribbean to Europe to China, into an unsettling vision of society: "A great principle of violence dictated our customs."

This principle governs *The Last Emperor*, the Academy Award-winning film that offered the West its first feature-length view of China after the Cultural Revolution. The Italian director Bernardo Bertolucci, who lacked neither information nor money when he made his film, some of which is set in the Forbidden City in Beijing, lavished attention on the ceremonies marking the final days of the Manchurian dynasty—Buddhist monks at prayer, soldiers on parade: rituals devised to keep disorder at bay. The film is a study of the imperial life and then the playboy and proletarian afterlives of the last emperor to lose the Mandate of Heaven, Puyi, an otherwise ordinary man who fell from the heights of power to end up working as a gardener. I recalled some of the commentary sparked by its premiere in 1987: everyone seemed to have an opinion about China's future—though no one managed to predict the looming massacre in Tiananmen Square.

The film opens in 1950, with Puyi's forced repatriation after five years in a Soviet prison. His brief restoration during the 1917 coup was the prelude to his nominal return to power in 1932, in the Japanese puppet state of Manchuria, the Qing's historic homeland, which ended with the defeat of imperial Japan and his arrest by the Soviet Army. In the first sequence of the film, shot in black-and-white, Chinese Communist guards herd him and other collaborators into the train station on the Russian-Manchurian border, and there the last emperor locks himself in the washroom to slit his wrists. The redness of the blood spreading through the water in the sink becomes a visual motif: the color linking ancient China to the modern inheritor of the Mandate of Heaven, the poet, calligrapher, and charismatic revolutionary Mao Tse-tung, whose portrait dipped in red is still ubiquitous in China. Thus the redness of the doors and walls of the Forbidden City from which the boy crowned emperor in 1908, when he was three years old, was not permitted to leave until his abdication in 1924 of what was by then a purely ceremonial post. And the redness of the monks' robes and concubines' dresses; of the bridal chamber on his wedding night and his wife's lipstick smeared on his face; of the urns in which the eunuchs kept their organs so that they could be buried whole. And the redness of the banners and flags of the new order; of the seal on the letter granting his release after a decade in a reeducation camp; of the armbands worn by the Red Guard who carried out the edicts of the Cultural Revolution in which millions upon millions of Chinese lost their lives.

The brilliant sea of red offsets the grey prison in which Puyi is "reeducated" to fit into the new society. Stripped of everything—title, belongings, dignity—and subjected to extensive interrogations, the Son of Heaven turns this exercise in humiliation into a journey through his past, a search for the meaning of his life. His written confession does not satisfy the governor, who draws out the real truth in a series of flashbacks tracing the decline of the empire from the inside. For example, Puyi recalls the day that he cut off his queue, his long braid of hair: a symbol of a political order that must rise to the challenges of modernity, or else it will be swept into the dustbins of history. "The emperor before me was murdered because he wanted to reform the empire, is that not so, Mr. Johnson?" he asks his Scottish tutor. "Yes, your Majesty, probably," his tutor replies.

Lacking the power to modernize his country, the emperor vows instead to reform the Forbidden City—"a theater without an audience," he calls it, in which the actors have stayed behind to steal the scenery. But even these reforms come to nothing. He expels the eunuchs for robbing his storerooms, which are promptly burned to the ground, and it is not long before an army regiment marches into the Forbidden City, interrupting his tennis match to put him and his wives and concubines to flight. What transformations he undergoes: now he is singing for friends in a nightclub in Shanghai, now he serves in Manchuria at the pleasure of the Japanese, now he labors in a botanical garden in Beijing. It seems miraculous that he survived until 1967, dying of natural causes in the first wave of the Cultural Revolution. Likewise miraculous is the fact that his father's tomb, plundered by the revolutionaries to fund their fight against the Japanese (who spared it because the emperor was their puppet), and then restored by the Communists, escaped the frenzy of destruction unleashed by Mao during the Cultural Revolution, in his war on the Four Olds—Old Customs, Old Culture, Old Habits, Old Ideas.

A waist-high patch of corn was growing in a small stone enclosure at the base of the stairway so far below the tomb that only the yellow-tiled roof of the temple was visible. Smooth pieces of slate flanked the stone steps, between which grew clumps of grass and moss, and at each of several landings there was something to behold—a statue of a sacred turtle in a pagoda, a bridge over a stream, cypresses and junipers and white-skinned pines. It felt as though we were climbing to heaven, and we were out of breath when we reached a rusted gate beyond which lay another bridge, another flight of stairs, and then a courtyard recognizable to millions of moviegoers not from *The Last Emperor* but as the setting for a fight sequence in Quentin Tarantino's *Kill Bill*.

Xi Chuan stood behind a U-shaped brick wall, patterned after the Echo Wall in the Imperial Vault of Heaven in Beijing, and instructed me to stand at the other end.

"We call this the Turn-Around Wall," he said softly, and it sounded as if he was whispering a secret into my ear.

Daylilies encircled the white-skinned pines around the tombs of the prince's three wives, near one of which was a *stele* commemorating a gingko felled at the behest of the empress Dowager Cixi. A gingko growing on the prince's tomb—this was for her a sign that one of the prince's descendants would be the next emperor: an infuriating prospect. But fortune did not look kindly on her attempt to circumvent fate—the consequences, that is, of her despotic reign, which lasted for close to half a century: the monk who cut down the tree died soon after, and upon her death in 1908 the prince's grandson was installed as the twelfth, and last, emperor of the Qing dynasty.

Historians have long detected echoes of imperial customs in the Communist order, and just as Xi Chuan's voice carried information from the other side of the Turn-Around Wall (that the tombs were raised from the ruins of a temple dating from the Tang dynasty twelve centuries before), so I imagined that I heard something from the distant past in the chirping of a cricket: a familiar sound to Perse, who as he prepared to write *Anabasis* told his mother that in his hermitage, in the silence of the night, he could hear time passing—"that special time that seems to pass so much more slowly here in China than elsewhere." Beyond the graveyard was the prince's house, which now belonged to the Ministry of Business, and past roses, potted palms, and bamboo was a shrine to the Buddha; inscribed on a rock were verses, which Xi Chuan translated for me: "A stream that sounds like jade, which day and night sings through the clouds and stone. Now I know the clarity of the stream, and use this water to wash my heart and ear, to enjoy my fame."

But change was the dominant theme of the day. Perse raised concern in his letter to Berthelot about "safeguard[ing] the future of the special entente that exists between France and China," which did not survive the Communist takeover, and at our final stop, the estate of the French doctor, attached to the embassy, who accompanied the poet on his journey to Mongolia, I felt as if I had entered a lost world—*Frenchland*, in local parlance. The family chapel stripped of everything but the altar stone, the grass growing through the leaves matted on the bottom of the swimming pool, the rotten staircase in the stone tower once used as a clinic for revolutionaries: the government's seizure of foreign property in 1953 ended a way of life, the fruits of which included works of literary genius— enduring testimony to France's engagement, poetic and diplomatic, with China. In a clearing in the woods was a rickety play structure with a set of rusted gymnastic rings which did not look as if they could hold a child. I gave them a tug, and when they did not break I pulled myself up to hang there for a while.

The Great Wall rose above us, a brown, dusty sentinel staggering off in slopes of green—our first point of reference on the journey to Ulaanbaatar. The train had left Beijing early in the morning, and while my colleague poured tea for us from a thermos I pried open the window to get a better look at the fortifications, which for more than a millennium had protected China's northern border. The Great Wall defined the Middle Kingdom from the founding of the Qin dynasty in 214 BC to the rise of the Qing in 1644, stretching for thousands of kilometers from east to west, along the southern edge of Inner Mongolia: a monument to the eternal human quest for security.

This quest is the key to unlocking Chinese history, which reads like an essay in unification—by the Han Chinese (the dominant ethnic group), Mongols, Manchurians, Communists:

dynasties and kingdoms and military governments. The configuration of the Great Wall reflects the persistent fear of attack from the north, and indeed the borders of modern China were drawn by the Mongols. Genghis Khan unified the tribes of the steppe in 1206, and when he set out to conquer the world he first invaded the Middle Kingdom, routing the dynasties in western and northern China. Then he laid siege to Beijing in 1215 (the city burned for a month); and although his dream of seizing all of China was deferred until his grandson, Kublai Khan, could take the southern heartland in 1279, extending the largest land empire in history to the South China Sea, he established governing structures, lines of communication, and trading routes that in the words of the cultural anthropologist Jack Weatherford "created the nucleus of a universal culture and world system. This new global culture continued to grow," Weatherford writes,

> long after the demise of the Mongol Empire,
> and through continued development over the
> coming centuries, it became the foundation
> for the modern world system with the original
> Mongol emphases on free commerce, open
> communication, shared knowledge, secular
> politics, religious coexistence, international
> law, and diplomatic immunity.

On a hot Saturday morning in July 2006, on the eight hundredth anniversary of the founding of the Mongol Empire, my friend Stephen Vlastos and I sipped tea on a train passing the Great Wall—which is really a series of stone and earthen walls built at different times. (The true length of the Great Wall has yet to be calculated.) It had long been my dream to retrace Perse's expedition through the desert and steppe to Ulaanbaatar. Alas,

I had neither the time nor the resources—camel, car, horse—to match his travels, but I could book passage on the train that took him part of the way. For this thirty-hour trip through a landscape central to Perse's (and my) imagination I tucked into my satchel his *Collected Poems* and a volume of his correspondence; also a notebook filled with impressions from my previous travels to China. This was to be a journey to the origins—of the modern world, of my favorite poet's later work, of my own fascination with the vast.

Stephen, a tall, bearded man with a deliberate way of speaking, was making his first trip to China—a fact owing more to geopolitics than to the changing circumstances of an academic life. He had planned to study Chinese history in graduate school, but in the 1960s, when American scholars had little hope of doing research in Communist China, he turned his attention to Japan, writing about peasant uprisings. He joined the history department at the University of Iowa, and now, after a stint in administration directing the Center for Asian and Pacific Studies, he had treated himself to a month of intensive Chinese studies at Nanking University. Native speakers were impressed with his linguistic ability.

Perse's lack of Chinese (a history could be written on the relationship between a diplomatic corps' facility in the local language and its ability to advance its interests) may explain his casual dismissal of modern Chinese poetry. To Paul Valéry he wrote that it was not worth discussing: "Chinese concepts of poetry, which are always subordinated to the requirements of the most academic kind of conformity, never touch upon the true source of the mystery of poetry." What he did not know was that a literary revolution was underway: Chinese writers, schooled in European literature, particularly Nietzsche, were breaking free of the classical literary tradition, addressing the burning issues of the day—modernization, democracy, nationhood—in colloquial language.

Their writings created a sense of possibility, articulating a vision of a society liberated from its Confucian past; their readers called them heroes. Indeed the May Fourth Movement—named after the student demonstrations during the Paris Peace Conference in 1919 against the decision taken by the Allied Powers to cede German-held territories in China to Japan—begat not only modern Chinese literature but the modern Chinese state. For the protests ended in violence, the students' idealism turned to despair, and from the ashes of the May Fourth Movement arose the Chinese Communist Party.

Perse may not have read the avant-garde journals in which the idea of China was being redefined, but he did grasp the consequences of China's shameful treatment at the Peace Conference. On the eve of his departure for Mongolia he wrote to his mother to lament the West's betrayal of his adopted homeland, which had sided with the Allies in the Great War—for naught. This was what Chinese writers called *bainian guochi*—"one hundred years of national humiliation." An upsurge in nationalism was inevitable, Perse thought; also a clash of civilizations. "A splendid opportunity has here been lost to assure China's future orientation toward the concert of Western Powers," he concluded. "Only Soviet Russia will gain any immediate advantage from all this." He too had lost a chance: to become the diplomatic counselor to the presidency of the Chinese Republic, a position that he had eagerly sought so that he could stay in China. But what use was he now? The Chinese would view him as a parasite. Better to return to Paris.

The train took us past a temple painted red and yellow, a billboard advertising the upcoming Beijing Summer Olympics, peasants working in the fields, and then switched tracks in a station where men pushed carts along the platform, offering juice and water, smoked sausage and chicken. The journey resumed, and beyond some grave mounds and poplars and cornfields was a valley divided by a river, on the northern side of which were horses, vineyards, a deserted village surrounded by stone walls. In the next compartment were two Mongolian women, one of whom served as the conductor, and the aroma of garlic from the stew they were cooking on a hot plate filled the corridor.

What a relief it was to get out of Beijing, which was frantically making itself over for the Olympics, razing neighborhoods to erect a dazzling array of stadiums and training centers and skyscrapers, all connected by scores of new roads and tunnels, bridges and canals: building, building, building. The government was investing billions of dollars in the city's infrastructure, and it was not hard to be swept up in the excitement generated by the construction: there was so much scaffolding and hammering and dust. And what my Chinese colleagues radiated at every turn, in meetings and at banquets, was pride: the Beijing Olympics would announce the beginning of the Chinese Century, they seemed to say—an increasingly common fear in American foreign policy circles.

But for now it was pleasant to gaze at the jagged mountains in the distance, or leaf through my notebook, or talk with my friend. Our conversation drifted from politics to film to family. Stephen, a philosopher's son, described his childhood in a college town. I recalled the trans-Canadian train trip that my wife and I had taken during our courtship—the elegant dining service, the moose by the tracks. And so the hours passed.

The sweep of the land outside the window put me in mind of my first journey to China, in the spring of 2002, when among other things I began to appreciate the scope of Perse's achievement. One morning in Beijing, just before sunrise, I went for a run along a boulevard leading to Tiananmen Square, a greensward in which elderly men and women were doing calisthenics or performing tai chi, and there was something in their stylized gestures, in their ceremonial aspect, that cast Perse in a new light for me. I seemed to be watching a meditation that reached back to the beginning of time, which made me think that the sense of space integral to his poetics was a function less of his travels over the expanses of the earth, his reflections on law and history, and his readings of Claudel, than of his service in China. The mystery of poetry is as elusive as the mystery of love or faith—one reason why we reread poems—and I suspected that the mystery of his work was connected to the crowd gathering in Tiananmen Square for the changing of the flags. He saw into the heart of a magnificent civilization, which in his words enlarged his "earthly vision on this narrow planet," and was changed, utterly, just as I was changed by reading his poems, which had somehow brought me to this train berth.

I was not, strictly speaking, following in his footsteps—my experience of China was glancing, my stay in Mongolia would be brief—and yet I hoped that this abbreviated journey, at another decisive historical moment, might offer perspective on our changing world. I was traveling under the sign of the war in Iraq, a British colonial invention which furnished American policy makers with the dream of empire—and which, as in many imperial adventures, had become a nightmare. Few expeditions turn out the way they are planned, and few understood this better than the author of *Anabasis*.

Or, come to think of it, the authors of the Mongol Empire. Perse's itinerary might have followed the long-forgotten route of Kublai Khan's funeral cortege from China to a mountain in Mongolia, where he was laid to rest in an unmarked grave beside Genghis Khan. Kublai Khan fulfilled his grandfather's dream of conquering China, and although their empire disappeared within a century of his death in 1294, its influence still shapes "this narrow planet," thanks to the writings of the Venetian merchant and explorer, Marco Polo. His account of his travels along the Silk Road, of his colorful experiences at the court of Kublai Khan, of the riches available in the land that he called Cathay—these gripped the European imagination. Indeed Christopher Columbus set sail for the New World to open a new trading route to Cathay—and to learn more about the Great Khan, dead for nearly two centuries; his copy of *The Travels of Marco Polo* (a "practical guide," according to Jack Weatherford) included notes in preparation for his arrival at Xanadu; the aboriginal peoples that he encountered in the Caribbean he named Indians, imagining that he had made landfall just south of the Mongol Empire. America, then, was discovered by a sailor under the spell of a vision vouchsafed to a man half a world away—a vision inherited by merchants, soldiers, and missionaries, not to mention Perse, at least while he was writing *Anabasis.*

China's only Nobel laureate in literature, the exiled playwright and novelist Gao Xinching, said in his lecture to the Swedish Academy that "literature fills in the gaps of history." What *Anabasis* fills in are the textures of empire, the secret history of which is always animated by desire: "Restlessness towards further explorations and conquests"—the scholar's description of Perse's fifth canto holds for the Mongol conquerors. They did not know how to stop themselves.

Dust on the wind. The lush hills had given way to arid hills, shepherds and sheep to yurts and new roads under construction, and before long our window was covered with dust. When the train stopped in a desert town to take on passengers, I went outside to stretch my legs, and tasted the dust, which blows all the way to California.

Perse considered writing a book about dust when he was in China, and in his last poem, "Drought," which dates from 1972, he argues that "the spirit's great campaigns" will begin only after drought has covered the earth and language has been stripped of its false conceits, its "scarlet muck." Out of emptiness, then, renewal, as he himself learned throughout his life. Perhaps that was the key to his success, as a poet and a diplomat: his sense of the vast and the experience of repeatedly starting over inculcated in him the humility integral to the creation of poetry and the practice of diplomacy—the art of the possible. He took the long view, which has distinguished the wise since Adam's time ("you are dust," God said, "and to dust you shall return"), and he had the advantage of knowing his own mind. "My greatest strength," he told his mother, "though no one suspects it, lies, as a matter of fact, in my personal detachment and total lack of ambition—contrary to what people think, and will always think, about me."

Thus after his journey to Mongolia he returned to Paris; and in the interregnum between world wars he played a leading role in the creation of the new order sketched out at the Paris Peace Conference, rising through the ranks of the foreign ministry to become known as Europe's greatest living diplomat. It was said that foreign ministers come and go, but Léger remains. And he was entrusted with increasingly important tasks, including drafting the Briand-Kellogg Pact—a visionary treaty that renounced war as an instrument of politics, reversing von Clausewitz's dictum, and proposed establishing an organization of European nations, setting in motion an idea that after the war led to the creation of the European Economic Community, the precursor to the European Union. In 1933, the year that Hitler seized power in Germany, he was appointed secretary general of foreign affairs.

The relationship between literature and politics is by definition fraught. This is especially true for writers engaged in matters of state, whether as politicians or diplomats. If writers articulate questions central to the human condition, politicians and diplomats must provide answers; combining these activities is difficult, if not impossible, since the writer's commitment to truth must inevitably test the politician's desire to shape public opinion to suit his or her agenda or the diplomat's instructions. Perse's idealism often put him at odds with his superiors, a succession of foreign ministers paralyzed by the threat that Hitler posed, and if he had to carry out assignments that went against his grain he also had the opportunity to observe at close hand Mussolini, Hitler, and Stalin—only the last of whom, he noted, had a sense of humor; their coldly calculating designs on Europe left him with no illusions about the human propensity for evil; the resolution that he displayed before the approaching catastrophe cost him dearly.

He confronted Hitler at the Munich Conference, demanding to know whether he thought Czechoslovakia should survive or not. The dictator, startled, fixed on him what the poet recalled as the eyes of a dead fish, and then began to shriek like a madman. Perse pleaded with his delegation not to appease him, which earned him Hitler's wrath. Nor as the crisis gathered steam could he evade the machinations of some in his government. For his independence, eloquence, and hauteur had earned him enemies on both the Right and Left; his downfall was engineered soon after the war broke out.

Perse, a marked man, fled just before the Germans invaded Paris, going first to his family home to visit his ailing mother, then to London, and then to America. The Gestapo agents dispatched to his apartment found a copy of the Treaty of Versailles and a bound volume containing the only manuscripts of five long poems, a play, and a political testament. On the treaty they scrawled, in bad French, "Grand Bien vous fasse a vous défenseur de la derniere victoire française!" ("A lot of good it did you, you defender of the last French victory!") The manuscripts disappeared. And searches after the war, in

Germany and the Soviet Union, yielded nothing: an incalculable loss. It is said that Perse chose *Anabasis* almost at random from several works completed in China to give to André Gide at the publishing firm of Gallimard, and in Paris he continued writing despite his duties at the foreign ministry. What insights, impressions, and turns of phrase he must have recorded in his notebook during meetings called to determine Europe's fate, then refined at night in his study. But whatever hope there was that after the Berlin Wall came down his manuscripts might be found in a Soviet vault has vanished.

Stripped of his citizenship and possessions by the Vichy government, Perse took refuge in Washington, arriving with little more than his pride. It was only with misgivings that he accepted an offer from the poet Archibald MacLeish, then serving as Librarian of Congress, to become a consultant in French literature. Nor did he view his position at the library as a sinecure, assembling, for example, a bibliography titled *A Selection of Works for an Understanding of World Affairs Since 1914.* At the same time he vowed never to write again, even turning down offers to publish his political memoirs. And yet in the summer of 1941, as he wandered around the dunes on Long Beach Island in New Jersey, poetry returned to him in the form of a meditation on his changed status. "Exile," which he described as "a poem born of nothing, a poem composed from nothing," begins with a memorable line, "Doors open on the sands, doors open on exile"; what he discovered passing through those doors were marvelous rooms containing the poems that he is remembered for: hymns of praise to the elements—rain and snow, wind and sea. For his recognition of the universal nature of exile—from childhood, from one's homeland, from life itself—freed him to create a language in which to address his deepest concerns: "Syntax of lightning!" he writes. "O pure speech of exile!"

This is the diction that he employs in "Rains," a long prayer to be baptized in all the waters of the earth: "wash, O Rains! the sorrowful faces of the violent, the gentle faces of the violent . . . for their paths are narrow and their dwellings uncertain." He wrote it in a hotel in Savannah, in 1943, when the outcome of the war remained in doubt. He was dining with his friends, Attorney General Francis Biddle and his wife Katherine, and when a rainstorm began he rose from the table without a word, returned to his room, and sat all night by his open window until, at daybreak, he wrote his poem.

Francis Biddle may have recognized in his friend the onset of poetic inspiration—he himself was the author of a novel, a biography of Oliver Wendell Holmes, and a pair of memoirs—and it is tempting to try to imagine his impression of the bleary-eyed poet at breakfast the next morning. Biddle, who would serve as a judge on the International Military Tribunal at Nuremberg, is remembered chiefly for signing off on Franklin Delano Roosevelt's wartime decision to intern Japanese-Americans in relocation camps. Thus it may be said that he understood better than most the contradiction between poetry and politics, and perhaps he envied his friend's newfound freedom to focus his attention on writing. For the despair that Perse felt in exile seemed to dissolve in his petition to the rains to wash "the people's history from the tall tables of memory."

This act of purification was the prerequisite to his next work, a book-length poem, *Winds*, which is a meditation on the forces, natural and manmade, that shape landscapes and lives. "Wherever there is movement," he said, "there my interest is aroused." Once he was captivated by the movement of human history. Now in exile he contemplated the motions of the earth—which in the desert took tangible expression for me in the taste of the dust on my tongue. The conductor spat on the ground, signaling to the passengers to board the train, and there was something in the slow wave of her hand against the blue sky that brought to mind my first journey to China, when the shaping power of the winds had made a deep impression on me. I returned to our compartment, where Stephen was reading, and soon we were joined by an outgoing German woman who worked for an international development agency. She specialized in erosion control.

"The world is becoming one big desert," she told us.

Outside the dusty window were spindly tree seedlings planted along the tracks, and from time to time a solitary mud house appeared. The sky turned overcast—probably a dust storm, the German woman explained—which prompted me to search through my notebook for an entry that I had made four years earlier, in another desert. And so it was that I began to reconstruct my own journey into the Middle Kingdom.

II

On the Silk Road in Gansu Province, at the Jade Gate, the soldier taking tolls warned us about sandstorms, which in northwest China are common in the spring, and as we continued along a single rutted lane Mr. Niu recalled the sandstorm that he and his wife had survived on their honeymoon: how the wind picked up, day turned into night, a black cloud blew out the front window of the bus carrying them; how the injured driver steered into a hillside to keep the bus from being blown over; how the sand stripped all the paint off of the bus, which after the storm shone in the sun.

"You're a lucky man," I said, not for the first time.

Mr. Niu, my guide from the Chinese Writers' Association, was a retired military officer with an eye for the absurd. He was quick to extol his country's progress—the number of highways built, of skyscrapers raised, of trees planted to ward off global warming—and quicker yet to note its incongruities, with which he had long experience. He grew up in a family of peasants, and one day his father, who had only a rudimentary education, was forced to move from his village to take charge of a hospital in Beijing.

"You see," said Mr. Niu—this was how he prefaced his statements—"my father didn't know anything about medicine!" Then he let out a belly laugh.

He had inherited his father's luck—he had not owned a television set twenty years ago, and now he traveled the world—as well as his faith in the wisdom of the Party, which had just sent him to Iran for a conference on translating fiction into film. When it was his turn to read his paper, which he had neglected to write, he sang instead a bawdy drinking song, explaining to his hosts that it was a harvest song.

"You see," he said, "they loved it."

Through flat grey desert pocked with thorn bushes and creeping junipers we drove for hours, bouncing up and down in cement draws, shielding our eyes from the sunlight, until we came to Yumen Pass—which the spring wind never crosses, according to the Tang dynasty poet Wang Wei. We got out of the van to stretch our legs. The desolation of the place unnerved me. Wisps of clouds in a barren sky. Swallows circling the ruins of an adobe house and paddock, their high squeaking cries carried off in a cold wind. On the horizon was a line of white buildings at the missile testing site.

There was a story about a nearby *stele*—a stone monument bearing an inscription to mark the death of a donkey, whose foal had stood over her for six days without eating until it died. A peasant buried the donkey, and was about to eat the foal when a motorcyclist stopped to rest. He was following the Silk Road across the Gobi Desert, and the peasant's story about the grieving foal intrigued him. He interpreted it as a sign not to eat the donkey flesh, offering to erect a *stele* in honor of its filial piety; as a promissory note, he gave the peasant a prayer wheel that he had bought in Tibet.

"If I don't return," he said, "if I should die in the desert, you may sell this amulet to buy yourself meat. Just don't eat the donkey."

But he did return to build a black *stele*, which draws pilgrims from around the country—though on this day we were the only ones driving through the sand past a small oasis to find the *stele* halfway up a dune, in thick scrub. From there Mr. Niu and I scrambled to the top of the dune to take a look at the missile site. His thoughts turned to his military career. He prized the discipline instilled by military service, though he would not say why he wanted his son to forego it. But he did describe in detail the interminable trip that he had made as a recruit to western China during the Cultural Revolution: ten days in a bus on even worse roads than what we were driving on had left its mark on him.

"You see," he said—and then nothing more.

On we drove to China's newest national park, Yadan, the Uyghur word for "steep mounds"—the stone formations, crusted with salt, carved by the wind into the shapes of silver cities and islands, animals and boats, afloat on a sea of sand hundreds of kilometers square. When we entered from the north, in blinding afternoon sunlight, the soldiers lounging in the shade of a freestanding map of Yadan were in no hurry to escort us to the bus, which would take us eight kilometers inside the park—whereupon Mr. Niu and I set off down a long corridor of stone, trudging through the hot sand in silence.

The wind whistled by the mounds, which rose twenty or more meters above us. Ghost City is what locals call the park, because at night the wind in the *yadan* creates the sound of birdsong, dogs barking, bells ringing, honking car horns, the shrieks of children. It is said that dead souls reside in the castles and towers, pavilions and squares, gleaming in the sunlight. Long ago, they served as a bulwark against invaders, protecting a thriving crossroads called Loulan, which disappeared in the seventh century. No one knows what caused the downfall of a city blessed with forests and a lake—though deforestation seems a likely culprit. Sandstorms filled the lake and covered the city, a small part of which has been excavated. Some say that the haunting night cries belong to the former inhabitants of Loulan. What remains is an arid land at the edge of which atomic weapons are tested.

A young Asian man had been following us at a distance, and now as he closed in on us it turned out that both Mr. Niu and I had imagined that he was sent to spy on us.

"I thought the Cultural Revolution was over," Mr. Niu joked.

Like many of his contemporaries Mr. Niu had denounced his own father, who was then forced to confess his failings in public; by way of defense Mr. Niu said that everyone had gone crazy then. We had a good laugh when we learned that our "spy" was a Japanese tourist eager for our company.

I wandered off to collect white stones and pieces of obsidian. The sands stretched to the horizon, and in the presence of the vast, Perse's true subject, it occurred to me that his experience of the Asian desert, with its harsh light and fierce winds, turned him into the most original poet of his age. For in his chronicle of modern life he links the earth and its movements to the governing forces, the passions, of mankind.

"Divinity ebbed from the great works of the spirit," he declares in *Winds*, which he wrote as a houseguest on an island near Dark Harbor, Maine. The war was winding down, and from his isolated perch, where he could indulge his passions for botany, entomology, and geology, he watched "the land in its long lines, on its longest strophes, running, from sea to sea, to loftier scriptures, in the distant unrolling of this world's most beautiful texts." *Winds*, his longest poem to date, unfurls in ribbons of versets, which carry the full force of the winds "Over all the faces of this world." The winds offer "council of force and violence," but "the poet is still with us. And in the councils of the Western sky recurrent signs are in the ascendant."

The bus parked on a plateau, from which we could see a large formation resembling a fleet of ships under sail—a sight certain to give invaders pause. I could not imagine a worse fate than to be cast adrift on the high sea of this desert. Perse must have felt the same here, for upon his return he wrote to the novelist Joseph Conrad that "China is surely the country least suited to a seaman." He considered Conrad to be "the only real poet of the sea," someone who would understand how in the western regions of China he had experienced "the same alienation that is produced in us by the strange anonymity of certain seas." To his fellow mariner Perse wrote that in this arid reach he felt something "extraplanetary":

> Here boundless earth is the most perfect imag-
> inable simulacrum of the sea—a mirror image,
> like the very ghost of the sea. The obsessive
> memory of the sea makes itself strangely felt
> here. A mystery that I myself can attest to is
> that, in the Asiatic highlands and in the very
> heart of the desert, horse and rider still in-
> stinctively turn toward the east, where lies the
> invisible table of the sea and the source of salt.
> The silent countryside seems, at that moment,
> to awaken a distant sea-murmur in one's ears.

That murmur, awakened again in the New World, provided the music for Perse's masterpiece, *Seamarks*, which appeared in 1957. This celebration of the sea sums up a lifetime of reflection on what he called the fifth element, which conditioned his early island life and his exile in America, where he spent his free time sailing and exploring coastlines from the Gulf of Mexico to Maine. He liked to visit maritime museums and shipwrecks; to loll in the dunes of Cape Cod and swim in the icy waters off Monhegan Island; to combine, as one critic writes, "a life of action with that of dream." The march to the sea was for him an emblem of our thirst for the divine; in the timeless encounter between land and sea he discovered "higher celebrations of the spirit and graver spiritual adventures," which culminated in a forty-page-long hymn to love in its earthly and celestial forms, a paean to creation in the tradition of *The Song of Songs*. "I have seen the first night open out and all its blue of true pearl," he declares, and in this glimpse of eternity he sketches a vision of the world in its original promise:

> The land and its black does descend to
> the low-tide marks of the sea. And the sea,
> with bare feet, withdraws over the sands. The
> continents edged with gold voyage in their
> haloes. The enlarged islands yield to the medal
> collection of the shores their great planed
> coins of polished wood, or of leather; and half-
> opened pods, in the shape of hulls, which have
> emptied their cells, their basins, expose their
> partitions, white and dry, like rowers' benches.
> Floating seeds bury themselves where they
> come to rest. And from them grow trees for
> the cabinetmaker's art.

The publication of *Seamarks* coincided with his return to France, where some of his admirers bought him a house on the

Mediterranean, and henceforth he divided his time between the New and Old Worlds. Honors came his way, culminating in the Nobel Prize; his lecture to the Swedish Academy, devoted to praising poetry, implicitly drew a line between the work of Aléxis Léger (who after the war had refused to rejoin the diplomatic service, retiring at the rank of ambassador) and the author of *Seamarks*. Can the poet's earthenware lamp suffice in the face of the nuclear threat? he asked. "Yes," he said, "if its clay remind us of our own." The last line of his lecture might serve as a credo for those despairing of poetry's marginal place in contemporary society: "And it is enough for the poet to be the guilty conscience of his time."

Bins of fruits, nuts, and vegetables; jade bracelets and drinking cups; toy camels and used books: the night market in Dunhuang, an oasis city at the edge of the Gobi Desert, in Gansu Province. School had just let out, and children in blue-and-white sweat suits strolled by the stalls, enjoying a few moments of idleness before starting their homework. I needed a geography lesson, and for a few yuan I bought an old map of China on which I saw that we were close to the juncture of the Silk Road's northern and southern routes, along which goods were traded for over a thousand years, from the Han dynasty to the Ming. Merchants and monks, soldiers and explorers—they followed the Silk Road from Asia to Europe and North Africa and back, through the harsh deserts and over steep mountain passes, traveling thousands of kilometers on horse- and camel-back, in caravans and on foot, carrying silk, porcelain, precious stones, grains, spices, artistic styles, ideas and beliefs and innovations, the plague: blueprints for the modern world.

The ruins of the Great Wall's western end curl around what was once a military outpost. Dunhuang means "blazing beacon"—a reference to the signal fires lit in its watchtowers to warn of approaching armies—and with rising trade it drew all sorts of nomadic spirits, becoming a thriving crossroads where different cultures and confessions met, mixed, and shaped one another until the late Middle Ages, when the opening of sea routes and an increasingly hazardous Silk Road reduced traffic to Dunhuang to a trickle. The city was now a backwater in the largely empty stretch of land between Mongolia and Tibet, but its rich past was inscribed in the Mogao Caves just south of town—a complex of grottoes carved into a sandstone cliff, two kilometers long, at the foot of the Dunes of the Singing Sands: a thousand caves, half of them decorated with murals and sculptures, which trace the development of Buddhism and Buddhist art through the centuries and incidentally offer a detailed portrait of life on the Silk Road.

The story goes that in 366 AD a wandering monk named Yuezun had a vision of golden lights in the cliff, which looked to him like a thousand Buddhas, whereupon he dug a cave for himself and built a shrine to the Awakened One. Others followed suit, hollowing out meditation caves, temples, and assembly halls, on the walls and ceilings of which they painted frescoes of the Buddha (past, present, and future) and legends from his life (his wandering and enlightenment, his deeds and sermons under the bodhi tree, his death and the mourning of his followers); illustrations of his teachings; portraits of bodhisattvas; patterns of miniature Buddhas—and much more: animals, mythical figures, saints, patrons, emperors. And scenes from daily life—weddings and funerals, planting and harvesting, jewelry- and winemaking—and history: caravans on the Silk Road, armies on the march. And dancers and musicians. And athletes—wrestlers, weight lifters, horseback riders. The story of a prince sacrificing himself to a tigress so that she could save her cubs from starvation. The story of five hundred blind thieves regaining their sight. Not to mention all the

sculptures, carved porticoes, and texts detailing nearly everything known at the time—prayer books, dictionaries, government documents, speeches and silk paintings and star maps,
works on Confucianism, Zoroastrianism, and Nestorianism: a
secret library dubbed "the ocean of ancient knowledge." Here
was visible expression of what the Tao Te Ching calls "the ten
thousand things"—the universe, that is, or at least what monks
and nuns could observe and imagine of it.

What surprised me as I stood one morning in searing heat
before the Caves of the Thousand Buddhas, a buff-colored wall
of openings, stairways, and porticoes which gives no hint of the
artistic treasures hidden within, and then as I toured the dozen
or so caves open to the public, gazing at haloed bodhisattvas and
the Buddha in attitudes that brought to mind Byzantine iconog-
raphy, was the yearning that I felt to live as close to the divine as
the men and women who had made this place. Generations of
anchorites had testified to their experience of faith, recording
some portion of their time here below, and their work inspired
in me a dream of beginnings—which came as a shock.

I had just finished writing a spiritual autobiography, tracing my pilgrimages to the Holy Mountain of Athos in northern
Greece, my efforts to make sense of my walk in the sun, and my
deepening love for the Orthodox Church, its beautiful ceremonies and rites, its rich theology and traditions, its complicated
history and politics. And now it seemed that I was mistaken
in imagining that I had answered once and for all the questions at the heart of my book—how to seek the divine? how
to live authentically? how to discover the proper relationship
between art and the sacred? For in these caves, where it was
much cooler than outside, the signs of devotion inscribed on
the walls stirred in me some of the same thoughts and feelings as the sayings of the Desert Fathers, the Egyptian ascetics
who had inaugurated the Christian monastic tradition not long

before Yuezun was vouchsafed a vision here. What in my mind connected the Buddhist monk to the early Christians was the desire to retreat to a cave in the desert, far from the seat of power, to draw closer to the divine. For a moment I could not distinguish between one faith and the other, which was as it should be in a sanctuary at the juncture of four civilizations—Indian, Chinese, Persian, and Greek. And when we entered a cave whose wall portraits of the Buddha had been defaced I saw how the faiths also shared a history of desecration.

Our guide, a young woman with a British accent (she had a degree in tourism), told us that White Russian soldiers had peeled gold leaf from the frescoes of the Buddha, etched their names in the statuary, and cooked meals in the caves, blackening the walls with smoke. But during the Cultural Revolution Premier Zhou Enlei had ordered the cementing over of the walls to protect them from the Red Guard.

"You see," said Mr. Niu, "you have to admire Zhou Enlai."

I saved my admiration for the monk behind the tradition of cultural exchange, spanning ten dynasties, on display in these caves. He put me in mind of certain figures in Perse's work: the Prince, the Stranger, the Poet—visionaries who undertake expeditions, inhabit other ways of being, make us see. Agents of change, that is. The Mexican poet Octavio Paz wrote in an appreciation of Perse that "history separates, poetry unites." And no one had a clearer understanding of that distinction than the French diplomat, who brought to his poetry, his union of image and idea, of sound and rhythm, a historical consciousness. He attended to what is here and now—for what is inspiration if not a matter of opening oneself up to the world?—with the largest imaginable view of human actions.

I must have had an abstracted look on my face, for Mr. Niu made me stop in front of a sculpture of the Buddha and then proceeded to explain how his travels had convinced him that respect for human rights was ingrained in the Western imagination.

"In ancient Greek sculpture the figure is an individual," he said, "even when it's a god. In China gods are transcendent, like emperors. Which is why we always follow them, even when they go crazy, like Mao in the Cultural Revolution."

Not everyone followed Mao. In the museum there was an exhibition of Tibetan statuary, dating from the thirteenth to seventeenth centuries, which had arrived during the Cultural Revolution. The Red Guard in Tibet sent a convoy of artifacts north to be melted down, and some scholars internally exiled to Dunhuang risked their lives convincing the drivers to leave the best pieces here. Before a handless statue titled *The God Facing in Three Directions*, which had a hole in its chest (left by Red Guards avid for gold), stood an elderly American woman, who said that in twenty years of visiting China, her son having married a woman from Beijing, she had watched expressions of apathy on the faces of nearly everyone she met give way to something new.

"There's so much energy now," she said, in a tone of wonder.

Outside, the sunlight was blinding and the dust was general—on the ground, in the wind. What better setting for seekers of freedom from the dust of human attachments, the endless cycle of sorrow and suffering, than a place where you could never escape the dust that was for Perse a symbol of the mutability of existence, the ceaselessness of movement, the possibility of rebirth? The Buddha was enlightened in a forest in northern India, and in northern China his thought flowered in the desert, the aridity of which helped to preserve the art and texts integral to his vision of the spiritual life. In the eleventh century, fearing an Islamic invasion, monks sealed in a cave an extraordinary collection of writings, paintings, prints, embroidery, and other objects: fifty thousand artifacts in what came to be known as the Library Cave, the so-called Encyclopedia of the Middle Ages, which remained hidden for the better part of eight centuries.

It was not until 1900, in the twilight of the Qing dynasty, that a wandering monk who had settled here to clean and restore the artwork damaged by the elements stumbled upon the Library Cave; his petitions to the emperor to preserve his find went unanswered; hence foreign scholars collected thousands of valuable items for the British Museum, the Bibliothèque Nationale, and the National Museum of India. Interest in the materials gave rise to an academic discipline, Dunhuang Studies, and what scholars pieced together from texts composed in various languages (Chinese, Sanskrit, Tibetan, and Mongolian, as well as lesser-known tongues like Hui, Yutien, and Turfan), including a ninth-century woodblock scroll (the world's oldest printed document), was a history of Chinese Buddhism: a complex story of mixing and matching.

This was also, of course, a story of conquest. In the eighth century Tibetan armies occupied Dunhuang, which turned out to be a blessing in disguise when a Taoist emperor came to power in China and outlawed Buddhism; while his minions were closing monasteries and melting down Buddhist statues for coins, Tibetan Buddhist monks introduced to the Mogao Caves a new symbolic system, which survived the expulsion of the occupiers in 848. Local Buddhist clans established a semi-autonomous city-state, between Chinese warlords and the approaching Islamic forces of the Arab caliphate, and governed until Genghis Khan destroyed Dunhuang in 1227. He spared Mogao, though, and under the influence of Tibetan monks in his court new caves were dug until the early part of the Yuan dynasty. Indeed Mogao thrived until about the time that Kublai Khan completed his unification of China. For Arab armies were on the march in Central Asia, where Islam would replace

Buddhism, and when the Silk Road was abandoned in the Ming dynasty Dunhuang, reestablished as a military outpost only to be retaken by Tibet, all but vanished from history. The caves fell out of use except for local celebrations. The Buddhist center was forgotten for five centuries.

Then a wandering monk stopped to see what was here, and so began the work of saving the caves from the ravages of time. Now it is a UNESCO World Heritage site, with conservators from the Getty Museum helping to preserve its art, and as I entered the Nine-Story Temple, in which rises a statue of the Buddha chiseled from a rock wall more than seven stories high, I marveled at what had survived. By the statue's giant feet I craned my neck upward, trying to imagine the view from the opening in the wall by the Buddha's eyes. Mr. Niu joked that with the Taliban's destruction of the Buddhas of Bamiyan, a pair of monumental statues carved fifteen hundred years ago in a cliff on the Silk Road in Afghanistan, this statue had moved up on the list of the world's tallest standing Buddhas. Bamiyan resembled Mogao in its spiritual vitality, its monasteries and frescoed caves and shrines; its statues had survived earlier Islamic invasions only to be condemned by the Taliban government as idols, which violated the Islamic prohibition against representations of the divine; the dynamiting of what the Taliban called the gods of the infidels drew worldwide protests in the months before 9/11, as a crime against Afghanistan's cultural heritage, like unto those committed by purifiers through the ages: Byzantine iconoclasts, Ottoman clerics, Protestant reformers, Nazi book-burners, Soviet commissars, the Red Guard, the Khmer Rouge, Islamists in the Middle East and South Asia.

But this statue was still whole. What did the Buddha see? Sand and dust. For the deserts around Dunhuang are growing, thanks to overgrazing, and the history of Silk Road towns disappearing under swelling dunes may not be over. Soon there may be more areas like the Dunes of the Singing Sands, which rise hundreds of meters from the riverbed—a popular attraction for tourists and locals who coast down the shifting slopes on aluminum saucers. I myself would climb its Staircase to Heaven before the end of the day, step by step up a series of wooden ladders laid on the hot sand, then slide back down with the wind in my face and the sun burning through my shirt. What a thrill it was to sail on a dune, skipping from wave to wave, spinning around and around. Perhaps a day was coming when the drought conjured in Perse's final poem would cover the earth.

Ghosts under the land—this is what people in Xi'an call the terra-cotta warriors created for China's first emperor. Qin Shi Huang, who ascended to the throne in 246 BC at the age of thirteen and ruled for thirty-six years, was terrified of death, so he commissioned the construction of a clay army to maintain his rule in the afterlife—life-sized guardians of a hidden universe, thousands strong, accompanied by hundreds of horses and chariots. He had conquered the Warring States, unifying China (the name of which comes from the word Qin, the western state in which he was born), and begun to build the Great Wall; now he hoped to expand his empire into the next world, creating an underground city, with palaces and towers and gates, connected to his mausoleum a kilometer away. It was said that he buried Confucian scholars alive (he had already burned their books), and all his wives and concubines were sealed in the tomb with him, along with his courtiers and craftsmen (to keep the splendor of the necropolis secret). And there were terra-cotta officials and scribes to help him administer his empire, acrobats and wrestlers to entertain him, cranes and geese and swans to take wing: a world unto itself.

The emperor, desperate to find the elixir of life, appears to have been accidentally poisoned by his alchemists. But it is unfair to blame his mad bid for immortality on their decision to dose him with mercury, for construction on his necropolis began soon after he ascended to the throne and was unfinished at the time of his death. Nor did his dynasty long survive him. He made no provisions for a successor, and in the ensuing disorder, from which the Han dynasty would arise in 206 BC, his tomb was looted, its wooden structures burned, and the scale of his ambition to rule from the beyond was forgotten until 1974, when peasants digging a well discovered a figurine. How did his terra-cotta army survive the Cultural Revolution, when every vestige of history was under assault? A popular revisionist view of Shi Huang as a visionary ruler, published in 1972 (the year that Richard Nixon went to China), made comparisons with Mao inevitable. Indeed the Communist leader, who boasted of burying alive a hundred times as many intellectuals as the first emperor, was no less determined to stamp out Confucianism—an Old Idea which was repressed in the Cultural Revolution. But even as the Red Guard destroyed temples and monasteries and palaces this necropolis was protected. Outside the excavation, Mr. Niu said that a farmer caught stealing a terra-cotta figure was beheaded.

"You see," he added, "the government doesn't fool around."

In a shed the size of an aircraft hangar were pits containing hundreds of warriors in body armor and headdresses, lined up in battle formation. It takes archaeologists a year to reconstruct some figures, each of which possesses its own individual character. Their skillfully carved lips and noses, their goatees, their expressive eyes—they look as if they were modeled after real people. Shi Huang united warring tribes, a feat of military genius later duplicated by Genghis Khan, and the various ethnic groups under his command were represented in his army for the afterlife. But this exhibit was no essay in diversity uncovered from history's substratum. Shi Huang was a tyrant of the first order: the Great Wall and his necropolis were enormous public works projects designed in part to control the diverse peoples that he governed; countless lives were lost in the construction of his edifices against terror—a necessary cost of maintaining security, within and without, he must have thought, and his own hold on power. Which he wielded ruthlessly, for better or worse. On the one hand, he terrorized his subjects, the majority of whom were condemned to lead short, miserable lives, and destroyed a significant part of their cultural heritage; on the other, he commissioned the writing of a uniform legal code, standardized the currency and script, developed a system of weights and measures—created, in short, what is now the world's oldest intact political entity.

For which he demanded that a new history be written, free of the taint of the past. For if his immortal dynasty was to spring full-blown into the world, then everything that described what had come before must be erased—poetry, and history, and the writings of the Hundred Schools of Thought: Taoism, Confucianism, and scores of philosophies that flourished in the centuries prior to the Qin dynasty. All went up in smoke in a war on memory that rivaled the burning of the library in Alexandria. It was the Argentine writer Jorge Luis Borges who grasped the true connection between the building of the Great Wall and the burning of the books: "the wall in space and the bonfire in time were magic barriers intended to stop death." In vain, of course: the emperor died, some texts survived the conflagration, and the Great Wall could not deter the nomadic hordes forever.

Some political leaders build on their predecessors' achievements, some destroy them. It is a question of character: the courageous are not threatened by their inheritance, but use it wisely to advance the interests of their people. Not so the cowardly, who may think that the world revolves around them. Borges knew better: "Perhaps the burning of the libraries and the building of the wall," he wrote, "are acts that in some secret way erase each other." The first emperor's legacy may be everywhere on display in modern China—in the ruins of the Great Wall, in the terra-cotta army marching in place, in the general configuration of the state—but it is Confucius who continues to instruct: "A person can spread the Way, but the Way is not to aggrandize a person."

Why was Shu Huang threatened by an itinerant scholar who lived centuries before him? Perhaps because he lacked the virtues that Confucius cultivated—humanity, justice, and courtesy. The just leader is wise, and if wisdom is born of education— "How can one be humane without knowledge?" Confucius asks—then just leaders may be distinguished by their desire to learn more than what it takes to maintain power. History, geography, culture: knowledge of the world is crucial to the judicious exercise of power. And the complicated inheritance bequeathed by China's first emperor, a mixture of delusion and achievement that perhaps only Mao could fully appreciate, makes plain the wisdom of the Confucian ideal of rooting government in morality: a recurring theme in Chinese history. Confucianism became the state religion of the Han dynasty, played a more or less official role until the end of the Qing dynasty, and after its suppression in the Cultural Revolution was gradually revived. Writers reinterpreted its tenets for a society opening itself to the world, and now the Party had adopted it to promote social cohesion. Orders went out to create a harmonious society, Confucian texts were restored to the curriculum, Confucius institutes offering programs in Chinese language and culture were established around the world, including one at my university. In short, an old ethical system was summoned to fill the moral vacuum left by a discredited ideology.

This political development was presaged long before by poets alert to the invisible presences underfoot and in the air, in the music and movement of language, in the gaps of history. Thus while May Fourth Movement literati debated China's Confucian legacy, the American poet Ezra Pound looked to China for inspiration. He took his artistic credo—*Make it new*—from an inscription on the bathtub of the Shang dynasty founder, in the second millennium BC; what he made new, through the prism of his invented China, was a way of interpreting experience in poetic imagery designed to endure for as long as an artifact unearthed from the past. Gertrude Stein called Pound the village explainer ("Very useful if you happen to be a village; if not, not"), and he was at his best when he confined his remarks to the village of poets; when, for example, he said that an image is a vortex, "a radiant node or cluster . . . from which, and through which, and into which, ideas are constantly rushing," people listened, myself included. His instructions to treat things directly, to write economically, and to "compose in the sequence of the musical phrase, not the sequence of the metronome"—these encouraged generations of poets, including a Chinese student at Cornell, who in 1917 issued a manifesto known as "Eight Don't-isms" (don't imitate the ancients, don't use allusions, and so on), a call for a new way of writing that fed the May Fourth Movement. Literary advances may be made by adventurous spirits who find in the past something to turn to good effect—a form, a style of thought; what Pound discovered in writings from a land that he never visited oriented generations of readers to the East, even as his ideas inspired anti-imperial protesters in China. He was, in Eliot's words, "the inventor of Chinese poetry for our time." And I was one of the beneficiaries of his invention.

My first serious encounter with this imaginary China was at Berkeley. I had left a small college in Vermont to follow my girlfriend to the Bay Area, and when I moved into a walkup apartment near the university I had two goals: to keep my girlfriend's wayward heart from straying and to become a poet. My girlfriend's father, a prominent stock investor, did not approve of either idea. He encouraged her to see other men, and on the rare occasions that he did speak to me it was to suggest that I study for a joint degree in business and law and write in my spare time. I enrolled instead in a modern American poetry seminar, which began with *Cathay,* Pound's collection of translations of Chinese poems, and concluded with selections from his *Cantos*—"a poem including history," he called it, significant parts of which were inspired by Confucius. *Cathay,* another name for China, was my introduction to the Orient, and I was taken with the Chinese aspects of *The Cantos*. It hardly mattered to me that even Pound considered his poem incoherent—that his effort to weave together disparate strands of knowledge and experience had failed. Some of his lines bore straight into my soul. "What thou lov'st remains," I recited to myself on long runs in the Berkeley hills, hoping that he was right.

The woman leading our seminar, a young assistant professor who took an interest in my fledgling literary efforts, turned to Pound's prosody (the ancient Greek and Anglo-Saxon rhythms heard anew, the patterns of images borrowed from the Chinese), and in an attempt to find a language for the despair that I felt over my love life I wrote imitations of *Cathay*—which, fortunately, disappeared long ago. One day on a run, zigzagging downhill through a grove of eucalyptus trees, I stepped into a hole, wrenching my back. It felt as if I had been shot, and by the time I staggered to the road to flag down a passing driver it seemed that every muscle from my neck to my hips was in spasm. A week in traction in the hospital brought some relief, and upon my release I stayed in bed for another week, heavily medicated. My girlfriend ministered to me; and at first it seemed as if things between us were on the mend. But as time wore on something about my injury upset her, maybe the plain fact of my frailty, which I tried to dispel one night, rising unsteadily to my feet in a haze of Valium and Percocet, swaying like a drunken sailor at the edge of my bed. "What are you *doing*?" she cried. I did not know what to say—and then I was diving into the wall, from which a jutting nail sank into my forearm. I felt nothing, not then and not in the morning, when my girlfriend said that she was leaving. Nor did I return to class when my back spasms let up, partly because I had fallen behind, partly because I was so depressed. Unprepared for the final exam, I fidgeted in my seat for a few minutes, glancing from the questions to the clock on the wall, until I closed my blue book without writing a word and left.

The look of pained surprise on my professor's face haunted me at the bar to which I repaired for the rest of the afternoon. It was dark by the time I got back to the apartment that I shared with a Chinese student. I knew little about him—he had little English—except that he cooked with a wok, filling the air with the aroma of garlic and ginger and peanut oil, and practiced the martial art of nunchaku at all hours of the day and night. The sound of whirling sticks ceased as I walked by his room, and then he was at my door, sweating heavily, with a message from my professor. She was not angry, she said when I called, only mystified by my behavior, which mystified me as well. She asked me to come to her office the next day to retake the exam, and when I arrived she gave me back my blue book, with instructions to explicate a poem from *Cathay*. I wrote as if possessed, making new connections between the old text and my life. Many years passed before I recognized her gesture for what it was: a lesson in compassion.

Which might have served me in my later reflections on Pound's wartime activities in Italy. His propaganda on behalf of Benito Mussolini's regime—over one hundred radio broadcasts, some so incoherent that Italian officials wondered if he was passing secrets to the Allies—led me to reject not only the poet but his poems, the best of which transcend, perhaps, his treachery. His was a fool's errand: convinced that central bankers were to blame for the world's ills ("That stupid, suburban anti-semitic prejudice," as he came to view it), and despairing of the American war on his adopted homeland, he imagined that he could bring an end to the hostilities. In May 1945, he was arrested at his home in the village of Rapallo, above the Ligurian Sea, and during an interrogation in Genoa he offered to negotiate a just peace with Japan, appealing as a translator of Confucius not to its militarists but to its traditional culture. In a cable to President Truman (which the FBI did not send) he predicted: "CAN WHAT VIOLENCE CANNOT. CHINA ALSO WILL OBEY THE VOICE OF CONFUCIUS." He said to an American journalist that if he was not shot for treason his chances of seeing Truman were good.

He was transported instead to a prison camp north of Pisa and confined in a steel cage; exposed to the elements, in the heat and dust, with the sun beating down on him by day and floodlights trained on him at night, forbidden contact with anybody, he suffered a nervous breakdown, later reporting that he had "burst a mainspring." He was moved to an officer's tent; and in the coming months, between shadowboxing and ranting against "the dunghill usurers," he wrote on one side of a sheaf of papers *The Pisan Cantos*, a book-length poem for which he would receive the prestigious Bollingen Prize, and on the other translated two Confucian texts—*The Great Digest* and *The Doctrine of the Mean*, which he titled *The Unwobbling Pivot*. How to account for the beauty of certain passages in *The Pisan Cantos*, an extravaganza of poetry and history, which is also a requiem for Italian fascism? Or the discrepancy between Pound's Confucian ideals—that good governance, for example, is rooted in governance of the self—and his raving? Impossible to reconcile the work and presence of such a complicated man.

There is no more riveting figure of a poet undone by politics than Pound. And as the rebellious son of a banker, in a failing relationship with an investor's daughter, I took comfort in his denunciations of usury, which seemed to justify my decision to pursue a vocation separate from commerce. But I did not realize how his idée fixe about finance unhinged him. And it was only later that I began to wonder how a poet blessed with such a sophisticated ear for rhythms old and new could not hear the false notes in his simplistic ideas. Pound had no business experience or grasp of economic theory, which did not dissuade him from thinking that he could cure all the world's ills. Facts were inconvenient for him, as they are for anyone blinded by an idea; in this he reminded me of some writers who rose to prominence in the Yugoslav wars of succession, ardent nationalists whose fixation on the perfidy of other religious confessions or ethnic groups led them to support violent measures against their neighbors. Like Pound, they lost sight of the writer's obligation to test the general truth of an idea against the reality of individual experience; like Pound, they betrayed their countrymen, their literary gifts, and what Perse in his Nobel lecture referred to as the "honor" of poetry.

It is thus instructive to compare Pound to Perse. For the American was a casualty of the conflict between poetry and politics, which the Frenchman skillfully navigated, perhaps because he tempered his lofty ideals with solid observation—interrogating his beliefs, that is. Perse's preparation for the foreign service, for example, included traveling to Hamburg, Germany, to study the port—the complicated web of relationships governing its operation, the intricacies of commerce, the logic of maritime law, all of which informed his diplomatic efforts and his writing of *Seamarks*. (It is worth noting that the city built in the fourth canto of *Anabasis* is a harbor city.) Perse was in love with the sea, but he also understood how differently mariners, ship owners, and longshoremen, not to mention marine biologists and historians, regard the tides, the weather, and the markets. He professed to disdain books, but the bibliography on world affairs that he prepared for the Library of Congress reveals the breadth of his reading—nearly nine hundred titles in history, economics, and politics, ranging from the writings of Winston Churchill to John Maynard Keynes to Woodrow Wilson, with excursions into the issues shaping the major countries on every continent. And he wore his learning lightly, unlike Pound, who scattered across his pages references from his reading, like rock salt. Perse had a larger view of the world than Pound—and yet Pound looms larger in the literary imagination than Perse, whose poems have fallen out of fashion, at least in America.

Coincidentally Perse's friends played leading roles in determining Pound's fate. Francis Biddle charged him with treason, and upon his return to Washington to stand trial, Archibald MacLeish campaigned to have him spared on the grounds of mental unfitness. Whether or not Pound was insane (there is some debate on this point), he was committed to Saint Elizabeth's Hospital, where for twelve years he wrote, translated, and received guests, with a likely death sentence facing him if he should ever be deemed competent to stand trial. Perse disliked Pound's poems and probably the man himself, but he followed his case closely, as well as the fallout from his Bollingen Prize. (The headline in the *New York Times* read, "Pound, in Mental Clinic, Wins Prize for Poetry Penned in Treason Cell.") In a letter to Allen Tate, one of Pound's supporters for the prize, Perse wrote: "I've also thought about you throughout all the activities you have initiated here during the past year to stimulate and defend the life of the mind, with all due respect for its limits." And he must have thought it ironic to be the beneficiary of the same source of largesse as Pound:

the Bollingen Foundation provided Perse with annual grants from 1946 to 1966—his principal means of support after he resigned from the Library of Congress. His friends continued to lobby on Pound's behalf, winning his release from Saint Elizabeth's in 1958. The disgraced poet returned to Italy (one year after Perse made his first trip back to France) to live out his life in seclusion. "I cannot make it cohere," Pound confesses toward the end of *The Cantos*, acknowledging the failure of his grand poetic project (and maybe the politics informing it), while Perse's collected poems read, as he hoped, like "a single and long sentence without caesura."

I am haunted by Pound, because his work was central to my education, poetic and sentimental, and because I know how easily aesthetic and political imperatives can be confused. He was not alone among artists in offering his talents to a totalitarian regime. Éluard, Neruda, Sartre—the twentieth century was awash in writers who sold their souls for political systems promising to answer every human need. But his fall from grace was the most spectacular. He bet that he was on the right side of history, and lost. How could he be so blind? I wonder. But as soon as the question rises in my mind I recall the biblical injunction not to look at the speck in your brother's eye without considering the plank in your own. And who can quarrel with his decision to raise the issue of good governance, which was in the air after World War I, as it is in every period of crisis, including our own Age of Terror: it is the writer's prerogative to take on any subject. That Pound could not see what was right before his eyes is a common failing. The heart has its own reasons, and in the grip of passion, personal, political, or religious, it can be difficult to see the truth.

How did Perse avoid this trap? We do not know what he wrote between the wars, the Gestapo having confiscated his manuscripts, so we cannot be certain that he always distinguished between his literary art and the art of the possible. It is also true that most of his major poems postdate his diplomatic service; his literary career can thus be divided into a before and an after, even as his nom de plume separated his political and poetic selves. But there is more to this story than the bifurcation of a life. I suspect that Perse's refusal to apprehend reality in purely aesthetic terms enabled him to see things in their true context. His interest in natural sciences deepened his sense of his place in the great chain of being—contact with the earth can be a defense against aestheticism—while his studies, travels, and statesmanship broadened his outlook on human affairs.

Ghosts under the land: the terra-cotta warriors are the most visible representatives of what lies all around us—the history of human thought and action, noble and demonic, engaged and indifferent, shaping our every word and gesture. Confucius, the Buddha, Pound, Perse: these were some of the ghosts informing my travels through the Celestial Empire, along with countless others of whom I might discover nothing in a lifetime of writing and reflecting, of excavating my experience. But perhaps those writers, thinkers, and spiritual guides whom we recognize as our travel companions speak for the silent others always at our side? In their words we plot our itineraries through our interior landscapes.

This was the drift of my thinking when I stumbled on a monograph titled *Forged Genealogies: Saint-John Perse's Conversations with Culture,* which includes the delightful fact that Perse's principal reading in China consisted of pamphlets from travel agencies and cruise ship lines—a not insignificant source of knowledge, in his view. The scholar Carol Rigelot traces the literary influences on his work, the ghostly presences lurking in his lines, and in this mapping of his poems I grasped what it was that drew me to him: his determination to create a new paradigm of poetic activity, like unto the book of Genesis, in which the discourse between poet and statesman might yield other ways of imagining our time here below. In *Anabasis*, Rigelot explains, Perse inscribes images and ideas borrowed from the Bible, Plato, Marco Polo, Jules Verne, Paul Claudel, Pierre Loti, and Victor Segalen—a process of citation, homage, dialogue, and rejoinder, which is hidden in the text and may become clear only after several readings. The cities founded in *Anabasis* thus rise from the ruins of Plato's *res publica*, although in Perse's conception of the ideal city, of justice writ large, poetic intuition is something to value, not fear. His City of Poetry, in which the diversity of daily life is celebrated, transcends the ideal cities laid out in religious and philosophical tracts from time immemorial. And his vision of the human condition, at once just and brimming with life, was precisely the opposite of that on display in the necropolis conceived by China's first emperor.

It was Victor Segalen, man of many hats (poet, novelist, librettist, literary theorist, sinologist, archaeologist, naval doctor attached to the French embassy in Beijing), who on an expedition in 1914 located the tomb of Shi Huang, a discovery forgotten until peasants unearthed a terra-cotta warrior sixty years later. The Great War cut short Segalen's tour of China—he went back to France to serve briefly at the front—and it is unclear if he met Perse when he returned in 1917 to work as a medical officer. Certainly they had much to share—a love of poetry, China, and travel, they had even gone to the same university—and indeed Segalen's magnetic book of prose poems, *Stèles*, inspired by the monuments ubiquitous in China, was dedicated to Perse's mentor, Claudel. Published in 1912, in an edition of eighty-one copies (to match the number of paving stones on the upper tier of the Altar of Heaven, in the Forbidden City), *Stèles* might seem suited to Perse's taste.

For it presents a timeless vision of China, translating a static form—funerary art—into poems extolling the virtues of jade, yellow earth, and the wisdom of ten thousand years, which abides not in stone walls but in the uninterrupted generations of the Han.

But he also praises a mistress who quickens his desire, like "water on red coals"; urges a sleeping dragon to rise up and dazzle us; honors a prince doomed by his love of forbidden delights. "The Chinese stone Steles," he explains,

> contain the most tiresome of literature: the
> praise of official virtues, a Buddhist ex-voto,
> the pronouncement of a decree, a call to good
> mores. It is therefore neither the spirit nor
> the letter, but simply the form 'Steles' that I
> have borrowed.—I deliberately seek in China
> not ideas, not subjects; but forms which are
> uncommon, varied and in an elevated style.

Segalen possessed the same ceremonial sensibility as Perse, along with his interest in what lay north of Beijing. "Look," he writes in "The Pass": "through the gate in the Long Wall, all grassy Mongolia spreads its winnowing fan to the sky's sill,

> Promising everything: the trek, the gallop in the
>   plains, the lumbering
> journey with its endless stages, the boundless
>   release, the soaring flight, the dispersion.

But Perse dismissed *Stèles* as "arty-arty," perhaps because he resented his elder's success in adapting an ancient form to his own devices, or perhaps because he understood that Segalen's love of the Chinese dynastic order had blinded him to the fact that it was dying. Segalen's faith was in beauty, which may or may not contain the truth; the prospect of change in the Middle Kingdom was more than he could bear. He died just after the student demonstrations that gave rise to the May Fourth Movement.

In a study of Segalen's literary encounters with China, the scholar Yvonne Hsieh takes the author of *Stèles* to task for his failure to recognize political realities—that the Han Chinese were desperate to rid themselves of the Manchurian regime and develop a modern economy free of foreign influence—Japanese, European, and American. By way of contrast, Hsieh invokes Perse's farsightedness:

> Ironically, it is precisely because Alexis Leger
> knew little about China's 'glorious' past that
> he had few regrets over its disappearance and
> could thus direct his attention solely to the
> future development of the nation. Segalen's
> very erudition and emotional attachment
> to imperial China prevented any impartial
> judgment of the historical events he had the
> privilege to witness.

How to see? A vexing question. For all their poetic gifts Pound and Segalen were blind to the political realities of their day, which makes Perse's combination of political acumen and poetic genius all the more remarkable.

Alas, there was no time to see the emperor's tomb, and on the drive to dinner in Xi'an, as Mr. Niu described in great detail the local specialty awaiting us—dumplings shaped like roosters, ducks, and fish—I remembered a sign in an exhibit at the Confucius Temple in Beijing, which informed viewers that the sage's highest political aspiration "was to establish a society of 'great harmony,' where public good is prevailed." In this ungrammatical translation was a history of missed opportunities: fertile ground for poets. For poetry connects this to that, the visible to the invisible. Thus in a mountain temple Perse summons ghosts from his past, his reading, and his imagination, inventing an expedition which he himself will undertake. *Anabasis* is a kingdom of connection, like all good poems, and it is also a microcosm of the world figured as a journey, whose readers are invited to accompany the poet into the vast. What an itinerary Perse offers. Missed connections abound in poetry and politics alike; nevertheless we may imagine Segalen and Pound and Perse meeting on a page of the Book of Books—describing wonders etched in funerary stone, instructing us to love well, sifting through a notebook to find an exact image for the Orient. This is what the traveler endlessly seeks.

"Chinese people are always looking at their food and saying, 'What is this?'" Wang Meng laughed. "It's the same with our country, our politics. We have five thousand years of history, and no technique—except in cooking. That's where we put all our energy."

We were in an elegant restaurant in Beijing, and from the lazy Susan rotating on the table the elderly novelist passed me a dish called Eight Things, only three of which I could identify (beef, peppers, tofu), then told a story about the Cultural Revolution: how he had been sentenced to sixteen years of hard labor in Xinjiang, an autonomous province in western China, working long hours with the peasants in the fields; how he learned Uyghur from his Muslim neighbors, who befriended him although they did not share his taste for liquor; how it was too dangerous to write fiction or even to keep a journal. One year after his "rehabilitation" he went to the University of Iowa's International Writing Program, a residency for distinguished writers from around the world (which I now directed), and there he worked on a novel and took English lessons; four years later he was named minister of culture—a post that he eventually lost for his support of the democracy movement, which was quashed in the Tiananmen Square massacre in June 1989. But the political winds had changed again, and it was in his position as vice president of the Chinese Writers' Association that he had arranged this banquet, each course of which started with a toast. I was half drunk by the time I foolishly asked him about the future of Tibet.

He put down his chopsticks and glared at me. "Tibetans," he said angrily, "were slaves until the Communists arrived."

Every conversation around the table stopped.

The history of Tibet is particularly contested. What the Chinese call *Shitsang*, the Western Treasury, was actually a Mongolian gift: the mountain kingdom was conquered first by Genghis Khan's son, Obedei, then incorporated into the Chinese dynasty founded by Kublai Khan; the Manchurians granted it nominal autonomy, allowing Tibet's spiritual leader, Dalai Lama (*dalai* is the Mongolian word for "ocean"), to rule his people, and with the fall of the Qing dynasty in 1911, Tibet regained its independence for the first time in seven centuries. This was short-lived. The Red Army invaded Tibet in 1949, claiming it as "an inalienable part of China," and thus began an occupation, in which a million Tibetans lost their lives, monasteries were leveled, and the indigenous culture was systematically destroyed. In 1959 the fourteenth Dalai Lama fled with thousands of his followers to India to establish a government in exile, from which issued a steady stream of appeals to the conscience of the world to remember the Tibetans' plight.

One autumn afternoon in Beijing, I had visited the Tibetan Lamasery of Harmony and Peace to see the Buddhist art preserved there. The temple complex was built at the end of the seventeenth century and housed by turns court eunuchs, the emperor's son, and monks from Mongolia and Tibet. Down the tree-lined Imperial Path, through the Gate of Luminous

Peace, I passed a drum tower, a bell tower, pavilions of *steles* inscribed in Manchu, Mandarin, Mongolian, and Tibetan, and walked through a series of courtyards, which diminished in size even as the halls surrounding them grew. Signs forbidding the lighting of incense due to high winds did not deter the pilgrims; smoke swirled from devotional bins outside the temples; before three bronze sculptures, of the Buddhas of the past, present, and future, pilgrims knelt, watched over by a Mongolian monk who was sweeping the floor.

In the Pavilion of Infinite Happiness stood a Buddha carved from a single piece of white sandalwood eighteen meters high, with bright ribbons hanging from his hands—yellow and green and blue and violet. It was getting late, and I was cold. But my curiosity got the better of me when I saw a sign for an exhibit of Tibetan Buddhist statuary. Once inside the hall I could not take my eyes off the art, which many Tibetans would regard as stolen property. In a display case of golden figures of the Buddha was this inscription: "The Buddha usually is in a cassock and seating cross-legged on a lotus throne. The hands of Buddha show the Mudras which symbolize wisdom, virtue, etc." The *et cetera* spoke volumes.

I needed such wisdom now, having inadvertently crossed a line with my host. The silence in the restaurant was unbearable.

"Slaves!" Wang Meng repeated, his voice rising.

I wished that I had not drunk so much wine—and that he would stop staring at me while I tried to think of a graceful way to change the subject.

Finally I said, "How many countries have you visited?"

The novelist smiled.

"Forty-three," he replied. "Have you tried the duck eggs yet?"

"Tell me, Mr. Niu," I said, "do they still teach Marxism to the Communist Party cadres?"

Mr. Niu sighed.

"It's a long story," he said.

"We have a long drive," I replied.

"Very well," he said, for he could not resist telling a story.

Mr. Niu was a gifted raconteur. But a series of mishaps on our trip from Shanghai to the pagodas and gardens of Suzhou—the driver hired to take us to the so-called Venice of the Orient (the industrial city is built around polluted canals flowing from the Yangtze River) kept getting lost, then the van broke down in front of a military barracks, and then, after assuring the wary soldiers at the gate that a tow truck was en route to take the van to a garage, Mr. Niu hailed a taxi to drive us back to Shanghai—had unsettled my ordinarily unflappable guide. It took him a minute to collect his thoughts.

"You see, the three main tenets of Marxism remain valid," he began. "First, one should take a scientific view of the situation."

I nodded.

"Second"—and here he paused, a look of consternation sweeping over his face—"oh, well, never mind."

But if he no longer remembered that Marxist triad he could tell a story about the Communist Party restyling itself along capitalist lines to stay in power. How to repudiate the revolution upon which its authority rested without undermining its foundations? This was the story of a carefully constructed illusion. It began with Deng Xiaoping's decision, in 1979, to create a special economic zone in Shenzhen, a fishing village near Hong Kong, in which to encourage private enterprise, foreign investment, and the development of a market economy. Deng, who was Chairman Mao's successor in all but name, was convinced that in the wreckage of the Cultural Revolution the Party must create a form of socialism with Chinese characteristics—a socialist market economy, which was of course a contradiction in terms. But he persisted, replacing the Cultural Revolution's campaign against the Four Olds with Four Modernizations, in agriculture, industry, science and technology, and the military. Deng's determination to open China up to the rest of the world had led to tremendous economic growth (the joke was that the national bird was the construction crane), fueled by what the economic historian Niall Fergusson called "Chimerica"—a system whereby American consumers bought Chinese-made goods, the Chinese government bought American debt, and everyone was happy, save for American workers who lost their manufacturing jobs to cheaper labor in China, antiglobalization and environmental activists who warned of impending catastrophe, and economists wary of the growing American current account deficit with China.

The riots in the French concession, which brought Perse to the Middle Kingdom, signaled the beginning of the end of the Sino-Franco relationship, while my journey took place in what might be the last days of "Chimerica"—the latest incarnation of globalization, the empire of connection first envisioned by Genghis Khan. I would not repeat Pound's mistake of imagining that I understood how the system worked. And indeed the economic crash of 2008 was still in the offing. But like many American parents I had been asked by my children to explain why their toys and clothes were made in China, and if I sometimes wondered if this was a sustainable system I pushed away my doubts. Nor did Mr. Niu care to dwell on any problems generated by the new dispensation. He was proud of the skill and efficiency displayed by the authorities in reorienting his country toward the future—which, he admitted, needed spiritual mooring. Perhaps that was why he could not remember his lessons in Marxism? I joked. He did not laugh.

He had an easier time remembering the three main tenets of Chinese Buddhism, refracted in his telling through the lens of Confucianism: that you must purify yourself; that you must maintain order and harmony in your family; and that you must do something for your country. He had nothing but contempt for Indian Buddhism and for India in general—a dirty country, he sneered. And as we drove by factories belching foul-smelling smoke, farmers spraying insecticide in rice paddies, and ponds dotted with small boats from which peasants were throwing food for the fish, he grew quiet for a while before recalling how for his own safety his father had sent him to his relatives in the village during the Cultural Revolution; how he had returned to Beijing after a month, sick of the mosquitoes; how on a visit to that village not long ago he had seen how well his relatives were doing for themselves—much better, in fact, than the millions of poor people of India, which had never undergone land reform.

"Anything else you want to know?" he said.

III

Coal cars passed, their black dust flying over the barren ground, carrying fuel perhaps to one of the new power plants opening weekly in China. The government had just released figures showing an annual economic growth rate of ten percent—which was why in the last five years China had been responsible for more than half of the increase in the world's emissions of carbon dioxide. Americans consumed about three times as much oil per day as the Chinese, but this was changing. Likewise the notion that the threat posed by climate change could be ignored: the central question for policy makers in a country with hundreds of millions of people hoping to join the middle class was how to manage its growth. I recalled the day that Mr. Niu had praised China's reforestation project. We were driving in Beijing, toward the Forbidden City, and he was explaining how the trees planted to slow the march of deserts across his country would soak up greenhouse gases, when our van clipped the side mirror of another van. The drivers settled their claims against each other in less than five minutes, with our driver handing over the equivalent of fifteen dollars to have the mirror repaired.

"You see," Mr. Niu explained. "It's better than waiting for the police."

How to regulate a society racing into the future, hell-bent on prosperity? And who could comprehend its changes? "So vast is our land that no fable could do justice to its vastness," Kafka wrote in "The Great Wall of China," a story begun in the same year that Perse composed his Chinese fable, *Anabasis*. Observers aplenty were offering new fables for China, the most pressing of which concerned its use of natural resources. All the talk in environmental circles was about the need to develop forms of renewable energy—solar and wind power, wave farms, geothermal heat—and all I could see from the train was coal. But I knew that with ingenuity, investment, and a little luck the future might include wind farms on the Mongolian steppe. Imagine the power that could be harnessed from the winds whipping over the desert ("very great winds over all the faces of this world," as Perse wrote in *Winds*), scattering black dust across the sea. I had seen enough of China to imagine that anything was possible. But I had also covered a war caused in part by economic dislocation. If "Chimerica" failed, all hell could break loose.

We did not know that we had just five minutes to get off the train at the border before the doors were locked. Experienced travelers made for the shopping mall, a neon-lit expanse beyond the last station in China, while Stephen and I suffered through the changing of the bogies. Chinese rail lines are standard gauge, Mongolian and Russian are broad, and at the border the carriages must be lifted from one set of bogies—the wheeled wagon on which they ride—and set down on another, a squealing, wrenching affair that went on for hours. It sounded as if someone was scratching a nail across a blackboard, and my back stiffened with each jolt, my head pounded, I felt seasick. Yet after a while I began to drift in and out of sleep, dreaming or reflecting (everything seemed to blur) about the worlds through which we were passing—from metropolis to desert to steppe, from the remnants of the Communist order to the promise of capitalism, from tyranny to liberty.

In an article published in *Foreign Affairs*, "The Rise of China and the Future of the West," G. John Ikenberry argues that if the liberal international order built largely by the United States after World War II—an open system defined and regulated by the United Nations, the World Trade Organization, the International Monetary Fund, and other institutions—was reformed to suit the changed economic, political, and security conditions of the twenty-first century, then China would find reasons to work within this liberal order instead of marshalling forces to oppose it, as rising powers have traditionally done. Unfortunately the Bush administration's reflexive unilateralism on a range of issues—from climate change to NATO's role in Afghanistan to the invasion of Iraq—ruined any hope of forging a consensus among our allies to reform the international institutions, devised in the main by our forefathers, which continue to serve American interests.

Timing is everything in diplomacy: the White House had missed its chance to shape the system to its liking, acting as if it was no longer bound by rules drawn up by its predecessors, Republicans and Democrats alike—rules established, for our own good and that of our competitors, to promote human rights, free trade, transparency. A tragic error. For the American moment of unrivaled power will pass. One day China's economy may overtake ours, and a new international order will emerge, which may not be to our liking. "If the defining struggle of the twenty-first century is between China and the United States, China will have the advantage," Ikenberry warns. "If the defining struggle is between China and a revived Western system, the West will triumph."

Once, in a night market in Hong Kong, astonished by the amount of goods for sale (an entire block was taken up with buckets of sea turtles), it came to me with a sudden force that the future belonged to China. There was such energy in the air—crowds of men and women haggling with one another, their voices rising in the warm evening air. They won, I thought. They won. Then I experienced a feeling of relief, as if I were a student excused from exams. I felt just as relieved at the sight of the passengers returning laden with packages and plastic bags. Then I had another thought: how would this country fare if the entire economic system had a break-of-gauge?

The train lurched forward. My back was in full spasm.

Mongolia: a mythical place in my imagination. In my study was a print by an artist from Inner Mongolia of a long-haired faceless figure in a red robe, riding one of five black horses over the snow-bound steppe, under a blue sky—an image that put me in mind of Perse. For horseback riding was his chief pleasure in China. "And right here in Peking," he wrote to his mother on the eve of his expedition to Mongolia,

> during my hours of solitude, these desert
> expanses that extend through the west and
> northwest of China have exerted a hold on my
> thoughts, a fascination that approaches hal-
> lucination. The bits of the African desert that
> I glimpsed on the edges of the Red Sea never
> stirred my imagination nearly as much as
> these high Central Asiatic expanses. And quite

apart from the mysterious physical attraction that this sort of thing always has for me, I am boundlessly curious about the repercussions on my inner self that may be set off by such a complete involvement of my whole being and by all the unknown ultra-human elements that may be revealed to me.

It is impossible to gauge all the repercussions of Perse's discoveries on the Asian expanses. But his subsequent diplomatic activities and poems suggest that his expedition did involve his whole being in a search for the meaning of what in *Anabasis* he called "the firesmoke of mankind everywhere"—a line that I recalled before dawn, standing at the window in the corridor of the train to watch the landscape roll by. The May Fourth protests, the Great Depression, the rise of Stalin and Hitler, World War II, the nuclear arms race, concern over climate change— these lay in the future when Perse wrote his line, which seems to grow more prophetic every year.

The sky lightened, the desert gave way to grasslands spotted with yurts, gullies of water shimmered. It had rained during the night, and when the sun came out between the scudding clouds the grass shone on the hills curving away from the tracks. I was thinking about how travel, like poetry and music and prayer, can make time tangible, lengthening the arc of an instant until it stands revealed in its terror and glory, a measureable thing beyond measure, like the solitary horse grazing by a long white yurt on the outskirts of Ulaanbaatar. What Perse explored in *Anabasis*, and what he must have experienced on his way to Mongolia, was the structure of time, the true subject of art and faith: how it seems to slow down in those moments destined to impress themselves upon our lives, for good or ill. And what I felt after a day and a night on the train was the immensity of physical space that Perse translated into an expansive poetic rhythm: his time signature.

Two Mongolian poets were waiting for us at the train station in Ulaanbaatar, a city described by a friend as a post-apocalyptic industrial wasteland, and as we drove along its potholed streets I saw that preparations for the celebration of the founding of the Mongol Empire could not mask the legacy of its Communist order, which had begun to unravel in the winter of 1990, in a democratic revolution marked by protests and hunger strikes. In the decrepit Soviet-style blocks of flats, weed-choked vacant lots, and overgrown parks, I recognized a familiar history of neglect from my travels in the Soviet Bloc. Much of Ulaanbaatar was built after World War II, on the ruins of Buddhist monasteries and temples razed in the name of progress: a monument to necessity, in the Land of the Blue Sky. And the only new development, it seemed, was the near ubiquitous presence of Genghis Khan, who drew the map of the modern world. *But we are all from the family of Genghis Khan,* Mongols say—although in the Communist era his name was erased from textbooks, his image banned, his exploits a forbidden topic of public discussion. Now his profile was everywhere—on billboards, in shop windows, on various denominations of the currency, on beer bottle labels, chiseled into the side of a mountain facing the city—as once it had filled the collective imagination of a hundred million subjects in an empire stretching from Korea to Kiev to Palestine, from the Pacific Ocean and the Asiatic steppes to the deserts of the Middle East: the largest land empire in human history.

How did he do it? By translating the defining features of nomadic life—mobility, social cohesion, adaptability—into a military doctrine and war machine lethal to standing armies and settled communities: fast, flexible, ruthless. Temüjin, for that was his name at birth, learned early the violent facts of life on the steppe. His father was poisoned, he killed a half-brother for refusing to share the spoils of a hunt, and after being captured in a raid he made a daring escape, which became the stuff of legend. His determination to unite the Mongol tribes and then to unify the world began with a case of wife stealing, a common practice on the steppe: when his wife was captured by a rival tribe, he enlisted a childhood friend, Jamuka, to help him win her back, and together these blood brothers changed the face of war, favoring merit over lineage, quickness over numbers, and the integration of the defeated tribes into a growing confederation—which in the end could not sustain two claimants to the throne. Jamuka broke with his friend, siding with another tribe, and boiled to death four of Temüjin's generals. Jamuka was then betrayed by his own men and handed over to Temüjin, who executed the generals for their disloyalty. Temüjin offered his continuing friendship to Jamuka, who refused, pleading instead to be put to death without bloodletting—and so Temüjin ordered his men to break his friend's back.

Temüjin renamed himself Chinggis Khan—a title, Jack Weatherford notes, derived from the Mongolian words *chin* ("strong") and *chino* ("wolf," the Mongolians' totem animal)—and the name by which he is known in the West, Genghis Khan, the Universal Ruler, reflects the success of his westward expansion, for this is its Persian spelling. His cavalrymen rode circles around his enemies, seizing lands and cities at heretofore unimagined speed, and from his first campaign, in northern China, until his death in 1227, Genghis Khan revolutionized warfare, governance, commerce, trade, communications, and culture: the way of the world. Believing himself to be ordained by the Eternal Blue Sky, the Golden Light of the Sun, and other natural deities to conquer the earth, he and his descendants left in their path a network of connections, which helped to bring the modern world into being. "In a flash, only thirty years, the Mongol warriors would defeat every army, capture every fort, and bring down the walls of every city they encountered," Weatherford writes. "Christians, Muslims, Buddhists, and Hindus would soon kneel before the dusty boots of illiterate young Mongol horsemen." What the horsemen carried with them, in rhymed messages containing orders and laws to complement the poems they sang of love and war, was an idea that today goes by the name of globalization—an international, and integrative, economic, political, and social order.

Terror was Genghis Khan's most potent weapon, which he skillfully deployed to subdue the cities upon which his army advanced, spelling out the dire consequences for those who did not submit to his will. The rules were simple: if a city surrendered without a fight, its citizens would become his subjects, entitled to the rights of any Mongol. But disaster awaited those who resisted. Take the siege of Beijing: first the Mongols rode around the Great Wall instead of attempting to penetrate it, and when they arrived at the city walls they did not attack at once but adopted new tactics, cutting supply lines to the capital (which reduced the trapped inhabitants to cannibalism), enlisting defecting Chinese engineers to build catapults and battering rams, waiting, waiting. When it came time to attack, Chinese prisoners were forced to lead the charge, bearing the brunt of their kinsmen's arrows; and when the Mongols breached the walls they showed no mercy, slaughtering every man, woman, and child, looting the buildings before setting them afire. The city burned for a month; a year later, a visitor reported that skulls were piled outside the walls and the streets were slick with human fat.

Wolves follow the wind, Mongolians also say, and if Genghis Khan's warriors, gathered like their totem animals into packs, followed a north wind into China, sowing terror in their path, they followed all the winds of the world in their campaigns to conquer Central Asia, Korea, the Caucasus, Russia and Eastern Europe, Persia and much of the Middle East. This storm from the East (the subtitle of a BBC series about the rise and fall of the Mongol Empire), a prototype of the Nazi blitzkrieg, dramatically reshaped the land, the Mongol hordes razing some cities in order to promote other cities which lay along more defensible trade routes, destroying irrigation systems to turn cultivated areas into grazing lands for the herds central to their war machine, clearing spaces for retreats and advances alike, which could be organized in no time at all.

The question remains: how did a million Mongols, the population of present-day Ulaanbaatar, rule over a hundred times as many subjects, in an empire six times the size of the Roman Empire? The answer: through propaganda. Genghis Khan used stories told by refugees fleeing for their lives to instill fear in his enemies; appropriated the natural resources and learning of the conquered lands—the Chinese art of medicine, Korean paper, Arab armaments, and so on; and then employed messengers to transfer that knowledge throughout the empire, building a network that made the mythical Khans seem indispensible to the wellbeing of people everywhere. That Mongolia, the least populated country on earth (more Mongols live in the Autonomous Region of Inner Mongolia than in Mongolia proper), resonates in our collective imagination is a testament not only to the terror that Genghis Khan unleashed but to the system of connections that he devised, which carried around the globe a wealth of stories and ideas, dreams and beliefs.

Call it the triumph of the nomadic spirit, which in another flash, less than two centuries, lost its political impress, the horsemen retreating to the steppe, falling under the dominion

of the Chinese; like a river, it went underground, resurfac-
ing in the accounts of explorers and soldiers and missionaries,
in the articulation of conflicts between settled and nomadic
peoples, in the yearning of individuals to be on the move—a
recurring literary theme. This summer, for example, a novel
trumpeting Mongolian nomadic ways over the agrarian values
central to Chinese identity had become the most widely read
book in China after *The Sayings of Chairman Mao. Wolf Totem*
was the work of Jiang Rong, the pen name of an economics
professor and Chinese historian who had been sent to Inner
Mongolia during the Cultural Revolution; his time with the
herders had instilled in him love for the freedom and strength
embodied by a people schooled in the ways of the wolf and
contempt for what he deemed to be the sheeplike Han, who
could neither fend off foreign invaders nor rise against their
own tyrants. Their weakness he blamed on Confucianism, the
essence of which, he argued, "is the suppression of freedom."
And his romantic vision of the herders, coupled with his harsh
critique of the Han, had found a ready audience, with millions
of pirated copies in circulation, despite criticism in literary
quarters of his didactic methods and message.

Not that the reform-minded author seemed to care.

"This book is not only a warning to the Chinese," he said. "It
should also serve as a warning to the West. I believe that the
West is weakening. I believe that China will overtake the West,
because the West is losing its spirit of freedom. It has become
too comfortable."

He had touched a nerve, I thought, because his fulsome
descriptions of nomadic life—hunting parties, feasts, and the
like—fed the imagination, and because he offered a simple
explanation for contemporary Chinese malaise, which could
account for problems ranging from the advancing deserts (a
consequence of agricultural methods destructive of the natural

order) to the continuing lack of political freedom (a function of a societal preference for material gain). I preferred the more complicated expressions of freedom available in poetry, which I had come to think of as a nomadic undertaking—a quest into the heart of things, with language as the guide. Perse believed that "poetry is, above all else, movement," and in poems like "Rains," "Snows," *Winds, Seamarks,* and "Drought" he evoked the elements in order to explore different forms of movement in the Book of Nature, movement that also stands for the human desire to merge with something beyond the individual self—a merging that, paradoxically, can become a liberation: in the Other we may experience our truest, our freest, self. "Let the sap, unweaned, burst from the stem!" he writes in "Drought," which in the end celebrates not death but life:

> Love spreads everywhere, and runs even
> beneath the bone, beneath the horn. Earth
> itself changes crust. Let the rutting season
> come, the season of troating stags! and man
> too, everywhere abyss, leans unresentful over
> the darkness of his own heart. Listen, O loyal
> heart, listen to that underground beating of
> an inexorable wing. . . .

In a letter dating from 1956, Perse spells out his methods by way of praising the virtues of modern French poetry over what he rather simplistically takes to be the abstract and discursive reasoning of English verse:

> Modern French poetry, on the other hand, feels
> it is not really poetry unless it merges with its
> living object in a live embrace, unless it informs
> the object entirely and even becomes a part

of its very substance, to the point of complete
identity and unity of subject and object, of
poet and poem. Seeking to do much more than
point out or designate, it actually becomes the
thing which it "apprehends," which it evokes
or calls forth. Going far beyond any mimetic
action, it finally *is* the thing itself, in that thing's
own movement and duration. This poetry lives
the thing and "animates" it totally and must
scrupulously and with infinite variation submit
to the thing's own measure and rhythm.

Perse embraces the elements, finding in the textures and
tonalities of the language measures for "the very movement of
Being": the flash and pulse of lightning, the curling force of
waves, the incitements of drought. Syllable by syllable, verset
by verset, the poet interrogates his experience, knowledge, and
imagination, leaving on the page traces of his escape routes
from the prison of the self: "the great Itineraries of action and
dream," as he wrote in *Winds.* And the itinerary of his nomads
in *Anabasis*—the settling of the city, the march across the desert, the prospect of further journeys—calls to mind the expeditions of restless spirits through the ages: merchants avid for
riches, missionaries ablaze with holy secrets, soldiers fighting
and dying for a new world order, and scribes to record it all—
dreamers burning for something just beyond their grasp.

I once went hiking with a friend in a canyon near Santa Fe,
in search of Apache tears, the polished pieces of obsidian or vol-
canic glass said to be the petrified tears of Apache wives whose
husbands leapt from a cliff to avoid capture by an enemy tribe.
My friend carried into the wild only a canteen of water and a
winding board—a fish hook, line, and sinker wound around a
piece of wood notched at either end. He liked to travel light,

he said, convinced that if he got lost or injured he had what he needed to stay alive. I felt foolish to have packed a Windbreaker, a notebook, and a book of poems in my rucksack, which seemed to grow heavier at every bend in the stream meandering through stands of ponderosa pine and juniper. I envied my friend for the spring in his step, his knowledge of nature, his love of Native American lore. From time to time he cast his line into the water, and while he waited for a nibble he joked about his inability to attract a buyer for his failing bookstore, relieved, it seemed, to be returning to his nomadic ways. I was the caretaker of a small estate, the owner of nothing, and though I had every reason to feel more lighthearted than my friend, who was about to lose his livelihood and maybe his house, I was as anxious as any writer, fearful of failure. I walked through the wild in a cloud of oblivion. My friend spotted Apache tears everywhere. How I coveted the small black stones that turned clear when he held them up to the light.

Lunch was heavy on mutton, the main food group of the steppe. Mutton cooked in different ways—in a hot pot, roasted, boiled. Mutton soup. Mutton dumplings. Deep-fried dough stuffed with mutton. Also potatoes and bread and beer. It is said that on his way home from conquering Central Asia and the Middle East Genghis Khan organized a hunt to entertain his troops and mark the end of a successful campaign. His men cordoned off thousands of acres, drove herds of antelopes, gazelles, and mules toward the middle, and over the coming months slaughtered them, along with rabbits and birds and anything that moved: a blood-drenched celebration designed to reconcile his sons whose ill will toward one another would lay the groundwork for the destruction of his empire.

What we know of Genghis Khan is derived mainly from *The Secret History of the Mongols*, the first Mongolian literary work, a ten-volume verse epic composed sometime after his death. The original Uyghur version no longer exists, and the Chinese transliteration has provided scholars with no end of questions. A Mongolian poet had just published a biography of Genghis Khan's father—an exercise in speculation praised by our host, Ayurzana Gun Aajav, an openhearted poet and novelist. *The Secret History of the Mongols,* which he had read ten times, was the source of his creative work. He had also written a series of books on various world religions, and he had a correspondingly large view of life, summed up, perhaps, in a deceptively simple poem:

> The sound of rain falling on the roof
> The sound of rain striking the roof
> The sound of rain striking the roof
> Repeat the unrepeatable

Then the stanza is repeated—a Buddhist poem that hardly reflected his training at the Maxim Gorky Institute in Moscow. He was, like most of his countrymen, favorably disposed toward Russia, despite the privations of the Soviet era, and he despised China with all his heart. The Gobi Desert divides Inner and Outer Mongolia, and Ayur spoke at length about the plight of Mongols trapped behind the border that was the starting point of Genghis Khan's imperial quest. Three centuries of Chinese occupation had hardened Mongolian hearts more than the poverty of the recent past.

After lunch we drove south of the city to go for a walk on a trail that took us past a shamanistic shrine, a golden statue of the Buddha, and a Soviet tank from the Battle for Berlin in 1945. Then we climbed three hundred steps to Zaisan Memorial, a circular monument, the interior of which was covered with murals commemorating, in vintage socialist realist style, all things Soviet: Soviet support for Mongolian independence in 1921, Soviet victories over Japan and Germany, the Soviet space program, and so on. Taking in the view of the river, the city stretching to the distant hills, the smokestacks etching the skyline in black, I realized that something had upset my stomach—which did not improve as we were whisked from one thing to another. We glanced through the car window at bronze statues of Genghis, Ogedei, and Kublai Khan; toured the national museum which consisted mainly of display cases featuring manikins in colorful *deels* made of sheepskin, felt, or silk; and attended a performance of traditional dance and music on the *morin khuur*, a two-stringed horse-headed violin whose melodies brought to mind the spike fiddling that I had heard in Malaysia. Our last stop was in a yurt to drink a bowl of *airak*, fermented mare's milk, poured from a leather sack hung from the wooden latticework near the entrance. It had a slightly sour taste, strong enough to mask poison, according to *The Secret History of the Mongols*. After dinner at a trendy bar, I went to bed feeling queasy.

I was no better in the morning, when Ayurzana and his bespectacled wife, also a poet, took us to Gandantecchenling monastery—which had a much different atmosphere than the Tibetan lamasery I had visited in Beijing. This was less a tourist site than a place of worship and study, where monks chanted prayers, Ayurzana's wife made devotions at a shrine, and boys seated cross-legged at low desks ran their fingers over the words in their books, reciting sutras formulated long ago. Perse said that although no man in the lamasery has seen the sea "the whole liturgy is based on an evocation of the sea; conch shells are part of the cult; coral and mother of pearl are altar ornaments; and the long, deep-sounding horns mounted on the corner terraces of the temples are used during the morning prayers to supply the distant rumble of the ocean." In the chanting of the monks I heard the "the sea-murmur" that sounds in Perse's poems.

Every third man in Mongolia was a monk by the time of independence, a legacy of the Khan's conquest of Tibet in 1240 and the gradual conversion of large numbers of followers of shamanism. Genghis Khan's decree of religious freedom, which was integral to an empire encompassing Buddhist, Christian, Confucian, and Muslim lands, vanished under the Communists, who executed monks and destroyed monasteries with zeal. Here in Gandantecchenling, for example, five temples were burned down; the rest were used to house Russian officials and horses until some of the surviving monks petitioned to have the monastery reopened, albeit under the scrutiny of the government.

But the fall of Communism brought Tibetan Buddhism back to the center of Mongolian spiritual life. Tens of thousands of people had greeted the Dalai Lama on his ceremonial visit to Ulaanbaatar, in 2002, during which he met with students in this monastery, and he would make another visit later this summer, riling Chinese authorities, which accused him of attempting to rally Mongolians to the Tibetan cause. They would not suspend train service to Mongolia, as they had four years earlier, but their message would remain the same: "The Dalai Lama is not merely a religious figure, but a political exile who over a lengthy period has engaged in splittist activities and hurt national unity. China is resolutely opposed to any country offering him a stage to engage in the above-mentioned activities."

Mongolia had thus inserted itself into a centuries-old dispute, the latest chapter of which dated back to 1959, when three hundred thousand Tibetans surrounded the Dalai Lama's palace in Llasa in the failed uprising that sent him and his followers into exile. The implications of his visit to Ulaanbaatar were clear to China's rulers, who called him a wolf in monk's robes: his plea for Tibetan autonomy was but a step on the road to independence, which might tempt China's Mongolian population to reunite with Mongolia proper and Muslims in the western provinces to join their coreligionists in Central Asia. The breakup of the country unified by Genghis Khan and his descendants was not outside the realm of possibility, at least in the minds of the Chinese leadership.

How does a man of the spirit undo what a man of the sword created? A question for the ages. The Dalai Lama took the view of poets and divines, not politicians: that truth will inevitably be revealed—in this case, the truth that no occupation lasts forever. Nor was this truth lost on members of the Chinese Politburo, who knew in their hearts that single-party rule, and the prosperity they had lately engineered, might not endure. The Party could lose the Mandate of Heaven. The Dalai Lama, or an incarnation of his spirit, might lead Tibetans to freedom. And His Holiness's equanimity in the face of Chinese intimidation had earned him worldwide admiration.

One of his admirers was the American poet W. S. Merwin, who in the early 1990s used to let me take care of his place on Maui while he gave readings on the mainland. Two decades before, on eighteen acres of land once intensively farmed for pineapples, he had build a house with solar panels, a rain catchment system, and an outdoor shower, and there above the sea he brought the depleted soil back to life, planting thousands of palms endangered or extinct in the wild—a botanical preserve, bounded on one side by a stand of ironwood trees and on the other by a dry streambed, which in the rainy season overflowed its banks. I tended the palm seedlings in the nursery; harvested bunches of strawberry bananas, which ripened on the lanai facing the sea; and listened at night to the swaying of the palm fronds in the trade winds.

"A dirty job," I joked to friends, "but someone has to do it."

I liked to travel to Maui a few days before William left so that I could spend time in his company. He was the purest poet I knew, a thoroughly independent man, and from him I came to appreciate poetry as the ultimate expression of freedom. "No one has any claims on it," he wrote, "no one deserves it, no one knows where it goes."

His claim to be descended from Merlin was not entirely facetious: he had Welsh blood, like the wizard of Arthurian legend, and there was evidence, he said, that Merwin was a New World corruption of Merlin. He had a sorcerer's impish air, with his twinkling blue eyes and ready laugh, and he dispensed wisdom freely, gently chiding me, for instance, for running in the morning while he meditated in his zendo; manual labor, he insisted, was better exercise. His work in the garden had definitely made him fit; and on our tours of his place he would recite the Latin names of his palms, occasionally raising a bushy eyebrow at my taxonomic ignorance—which was but the start of my education. At dinner, drinking wine made by a neighbor in the south of France, where he owned another house, he would recite passages from the poems of the British modernist David Jones. His every word and gesture pointed to the seriousness of the poetic vocation, his conversation was a continuing lesson in literature from around the world. Once I said of a well-known American poet that perhaps she was too intelligent to be great.

"You wouldn't say that about Dante," he shot back.

"Point taken," I conceded.

He recounted his visit, when he was a student at Princeton, to Ezra Pound, during his confinement at Saint Elizabeth's. The poet gave him two invaluable pieces of advice: to write seventy-five lines a day and to translate.

"Can you write that much every day?" I asked.

"No," he said. "But you can always translate."

Read seeds, not twigs: this was what Pound wrote to William on a postcard. And his house was filled with such seeds. First I read all of his books, then I picked through the boxes of books wrapped in plastic in the guest room, lately retrieved from the freezer to which they had been consigned to kill the silverfish feeding on their pages, and then I turned to the religious texts on the shelf between his study and the zendo. William was a serious student of Zen, had considered becoming a priest, and his stories often contained a kernel of Buddhist wisdom. For example, the story of the translator who brought a bag of books on a retreat to a Buddhist monastery, stacking them by his cushion before beginning his meditation. The Zen master kicked them over, instructing him to give up his attachment to books—a story to keep in mind, William seemed to suggest, as I devoured his books.

On the shelf by his study was a well-thumbed copy of *The Tibetan Book of the Dead*, which I kept on the rough-hewn table in the living room where I wrote one spring, flipping through its pages when I got stuck. Certain lines stayed with me concerning the *bardo*, or between—the transitional states that mark a life, of birth and dream and death, in every moment of which we may choose between remaining attached to our suffering, our fear, and liberating our true nature; we can become pure light, if we recognize that each breath may be our last. This text is also known as *The Great Book of Liberation through Understanding in the Between*—monks chant its verses over the dying and the dead, preparing their souls to return to earth—and I came to think of house-sitting as a form of the between: between the excitement that I experienced reporting from the war zones of the former Yugoslavia and the clock of ordinariness that I heard ticking at home. William's house was a good place for me to reflect on the poles of my existence, between wakefulness and oblivion, and I remember gazing at the wall of palms that had grown tall enough to block the view of the sea, praying for something to open in my soul.

The next year, after months of traveling in the Balkans, I arrived in Maui with my nerves frayed, and on the day of William's departure I offered to prepare lunch as much to allay my anxiety over the war as to spare him the trouble. (Before leaving to visit her sons on the mainland, his wife had left him instructions in the tiny kitchen for cooking white rice; the poverty of cabinets suggested that William had designed his house with little thought for the culinary arts.) While chopping onions for a salad I cut my finger, but thought nothing of it, and went on rinsing lettuce from the garden, slicing tomatoes, shredding tuna. Capers were what I needed, but a search of the cupboard yielded only a puddle of water. When I mentioned this to William, he stuck his finger in the puddle and licked it. I did the same, and when I tasted blood from my cut I thought to trace the liquid to its source—a hole in a swollen can of lychees.

"We all have to die someday," he said calmly.

He gathered plates, glasses, and silverware to set the table on the lanai. I followed with the salad and a bottle of white wine, we sat down to eat, all seemed well. An owl hooted, the palms swayed in the wind, and when, as often happened, our conversation turned to the environmental crisis, which William had taken to calling the Final Solution, I wondered how he managed to avoid despair.

"Look," he said, "if you're driving down the road and you see a terrible accident, you don't stop to ask whether anyone will live. You get out of your car and do what you can to save them."

This was the spirit of activism that coursed through some of his most memorable poems, including "Witness," which had become for me a sort of charm:

I want to tell what the forests
were like

I will have to speak
in a forgotten language

William was my tutor in that forgotten language; his sense
of a poet's obligations in the face of catastrophe surely influ-
enced my own. Yes, he admitted, like other poets of his generation he had written his share of bad political poems during
the Vietnam War—which did not lead him to shirk political
themes in his subsequent work. The fouling of the air, earth,
and water; the destruction of wilderness; the extinction of
flora and fauna—these were the consequences of mankind's
greed and hubris, subjects that enflamed his imagination, his
voice rising in some poems to the pitch of Jeremiah, his denunciations of those who would ruin nature growing more
pointed at lunch with each glass of wine.

His passion set off a new train of thought about the poet's
role in society. There is no formula for the right relationship
between poetry and politics. In some of his poems William belonged to the school of engagé literature that included poets like
Milton and Whitman, Pound and Neruda, in others to a medi-
tative tradition stretching from Tang poets to Wordsworth.
He conceived of the poetic enterprise in an altogether different fashion from Perse, who treated political subjects from an
oblique angle, if at all, and yet I considered them both to be tutelary spirits. Each believed that poetry was a way of life, each
turned to nature for inspiration and instruction, each sought to
render in pure tones the totality of their experience. William's
disparagement of Perse's rhetorical gifts and ceremonial style
I took to be a reflection of his own distrust of ornament; his
spare phrasing, plain diction, and lack of punctuation, the

antithesis of Perse's practice, seemed to me to address the same problem: how to cultivate awareness, as Perse wrote, of those "great forces that create us, use us, and control us"—history and the elements—and then describe them memorably. They were united in my mind in their solitude, which was a source of their strength, and in their determination to find a language adequate to the largest possible understanding of the human condition. But William dismissed Perse's claim in his final poem to disdain "the scarlet muck of language"—language used to falsify experience, that is. Like Pound, he would clear the dead wood of rhetoric from the field of poetry. My defense of Perse fell on deaf ears.

Now it occurred to me that poets work either by subtraction or addition, through sparseness or abundance—drawn, metaphorically speaking, either to the desert or the sea. In my own work I seemed to oscillate from one way of proceeding to the other, following a word, image, or rhythm into the vast of emptiness or plenitude, depending on my frame of mind, now practicing an economy of means, now giving myself over to extravagance. The desert and the sea—these were the poles of my imagination, and I recognized the anchorite and the mariner as congenial figures in my poetic explorations. Perse heard "the sea-murmur" in a liturgy performed in the desert, I was thinking, and I sought—what? For some reason I could not understand what William was saying. His words swirled over my head, the sky and palms spun wildly around me, I felt sick to my stomach. Fearing that I would faint, I rose from my chair to retrieve the bloated can of lychees from the trash.

"Maybe we should go to the hospital," I said, alarmed.

"It's forty-five minutes away," William replied. "It will be too late."

But then my sickness passed as abruptly as it had overcome me, and I returned to my seat, lightheaded. William said that my face had turned seven shades of green before going completely white. My appetite had vanished, and after lunch I was too weak to help him in the garden. On the drive to the airport he suggested that I see a doctor, but by then I had convinced myself that I was fine, and so I returned to his house, where for the next four days and nights I lay in bed, drenched in sweat, every bone in my body aching, my eyes sensitive to the light, hallucinations arising between bouts of nausea, scenes derived from the carnage that I had witnessed in the Balkans: a razed church, an iron rod piercing a coffin. How strange, I thought, to survive a war only to die in paradise.

To be released from suffering and the cycles of rebirth—this is what the Buddha holds out as a possibility to his followers, whose practice of meditation, mindfulness, and compassion for every living thing, reinforced by ceremonies and curing rituals, may lead them to the pure realm of light. For my part I was mindful only of pain, and longed for my soul to be freed from my body. In another life someone might read *The Tibetan Book of the Dead* by my deathbed, praying for my release from the between—and from the images afflicting me, what the Buddha might call the wrathful deities that I would have to come to terms with before my rebirth. But in this life I tossed and turned until one night, miracle of miracles, my fever broke, my pain dissolved, something lifted from my soul. The palms, the sky, the sea—everything took on a different sheen. This was not the pure realm of light, but a function of my heightened attention to the here and now, and it was splendid. And I understood that my wandering was not over.

The prospect of visiting the International Museum of Wisdom, otherwise known as the Mongolian Toy Museum, was not exactly thrilling. But what delights awaited me in what my Mongolian friends called the Intellectual Museum, which had opened on the 750th anniversary of the composition of *The Secret History of the Mongols.*

For forty years, Zandraa Tulmem-Ulzii had built and collected mechanical toys, chess sets, and puzzles, and in his private museum, a pink four-story building behind the East Center, were more than five thousand exquisite objects, puzzles, and games from around the world. His assistant, who led us from room to room, said that Tulmen-Ulzii's interest in puzzles dated to his childhood, when he found four dowels in his father's trunk. His mother told him that they were a toy, which he could not figure out how to assemble until he carved two more dowels for it. He went on to build puzzles that with each year grew more elaborate—and beautiful. One puzzle took more than fifty thousand moves to complete, and of the hundreds of chess sets, one of which contained over twenty-seven thousand interlocking pieces, the most interesting set featured historical figures for pieces: Genghis Khan, Marco Polo. East versus West, said the guide.

There were puzzles shaped like temples and pyramids and the Eiffel Tower, dolls in colorful native dress from many lands, elaborate carvings in wood and stone; the paintings displayed on the walls documented Mongolian ways as assiduously as the cave art in Dunhuang preserved a vision of life on the Silk Road; the yurt set up in the corner of one room made me think that Tumen-Ilzii had revived Genghis Khan's dream of gathering under a single tent all the knowledge in the world—rituals and ceremonies, histories and beliefs, the names of islands, the rules of war, the course of love, victory speeches, concessions, the last words of the wise and the condemned, tracts on the nature of God, recommendations for the treatment of diseases, musical scores, exercises in style, dictionaries, encyclopedias, maps, charts, guides to the heavens, innovations, equations, formulas. . . . Impossible to put it all together. But these exhibits suggested the variety of ways in which we puzzle out our existence. And for intimations of the vastness of creation there was the poetic device of the catalogue: Homer's list of ships, Whitman's inventory of things. Human ingenuity was what the International Museum of Wisdom celebrated, and in the puzzle master's hymn to creativity was a reminder that the desire to render the whole of the known world is ancient—think of the necropolis in Xi'an, biblical genealogies. The products of homo faber cut either way. "Plough-land of dream!" Perse wrote: the land on which history is inscribed.

Thus Genghis Khan had come and gone, and what remained was the record of his deeds in *The Secret History of the Mongols*. My friend Ayurzana was fond of quoting a speech attributed to a soldier on the death of the conqueror—lines that juxtapose images of a bird's wing and a funeral cortege, as if to unite the sky and the earth:

> You went as the wing of a soaring hawk, oh my
> Lord!
> You went as a load in a jangling cart, oh my Lord!
> You went as the wing of a frolicking martin, oh
> my Lord!
> You went as a load in a circling cart, oh my Lord!
> You went as the wing of a chirping bird, oh
> my Lord!
> You went as the load in the squeaking cart, oh
> my Lord!

At the doorway to another room of the museum was a photograph of George W. Bush taken during a flying visit to Ulaanbaatar. Bush had stopped off at the end of an Asian tour to thank the Mongolian people for supporting the war on terror. (A small contingent of Mongolian soldiers served in Iraq, as part of the so-called Coalition of the Willing, funded largely by the US government.) In the picture, the Mongolian president was handing him a puzzle created by Tulmen-Ulzii—*The Puzzle of Liberty,* our guide said without irony. But the puzzle master did not expect Bush to keep this loan from his museum. As a matter of fact he was quite upset not to have been paid for a puzzle valued at ten thousand dollars!

Our tour ended in the gift shop, with the guide spreading locks on a glass tabletop for us to open. How simple it looked to unlock them—but how difficult in actuality. I tried without success to pry one apart, unable to master the basic moves required to open it, which to me seemed intricate in the extreme. And I wish that I had paid attention when the guide took apart and then reassembled his gift to me—a wooden puzzle in the form of a rooster, marking the year of my birth, which now lies in pieces on my desk.

In his first cabinet meeting George W. Bush said that force can sometimes clarify matters. He was explaining his decision to allow Israeli prime minister Ariel Sharon free reign in using his military to solve problems with the Palestinians, though it soon became clear that he preferred force to diplomacy. The inconclusive wars in Afghanistan and Iraq illustrate the poverty of such thinking, for history suggests that peace, like freedom, is a puzzle solved not with force but with patience and intelligence. "Freedom," said Octavio Paz upon receiving the Alexis de Tocqueville Prize, "is not a philosophy, nor is it even an idea. It is a movement of consciousness that leads us, at certain moments, to utter one of two monosyllables: Yes or No. In their brevity," he continues, "lasting but an instant, like a flash of lightning, the contradictory character of human nature stands revealed."

What better emblem of this contradiction than the double life of Aléxis Léger and Saint-John Perse. Yes or no? This question animated his diplomatic service and poetics (the key image of *Exile* is the lightning flash dividing night into a before and an after); his answers shaped the international order, the French language, poetry: the world, that is, and our interpretations of it. "I have halted my horse by the tree of the doves": thus begins the closing song of *Anabasis*. The narrator stops to rest, to have a look around, to reflect on what he has seen. Just so, Perse gazed into the past and future, vistas within and without, and bestowed a blessing on his readers: "Peace to the dying who have not seen this day." Perhaps these lines returned to him in his final months, as he readied for publication a quartet of poems titled *Song for an Equinox*, which measures the coming darkness and what light remains—a work of the spirit whose governing metaphor is the moment when the earth tilts neither toward nor away from the sun and the hours of daylight match those of the night: the coda to a life of difficult balances. Perse died on September 20, 1975, three days before the autumn equinox. How clearly he saw.

PART III

WAR

WAR

I

The doctor was looking for the medieval hospital, and as she walked along the narrow lanes of the *souk*, under stone archways draped with banners, stopping merchants to ask for directions, she fretted about losing her way so close to the street owned by her family for generations. There were more than thirty kilometers of stalls, courtyards, and *khans* or caravansaries to navigate in this covered market, and it was hard to keep your bearings among so many people and distractions. It seemed that everything was for sale—carpets and jewelry, silk scarves and wooden boxes, mirrors, miniature editions of the Koran, twigs such as the one used by the Prophet to brush his teeth. A tea seller with a handlebar mustache clacked tiny ceramic cups, two men in a spice stall smoked water pipes while a third weighed cumin for a woman in a burka, a boy gazed at a cart heaped with mounds of brightly colored sweets. The doctor pulled me from the path of a man tugging the reins of a donkey with an infected eye, then led us along a slick tile floor through a public bath, where one old naked man was soaping the back of another, their flaccid skin dull in the afternoon light. Through the lanes sounded the muezzin's call to prayer, and while most men disappeared into the mosques some stayed behind to mind their stalls—and to flirt with tourists, male and female alike. There was the spirit of carnival in the air.

"Are you Scottish?" one young man called to me. "Irish?"

He sidled up to another man in our group.

"Do you know the name of this store?" he said, pointing to a display of carpets. "We call it 'Oscar Wilde,' because we are of the same persuasion." Then he winked at him. "Vegetarian!"

The Aleppo *souk*, the largest in the Middle East, has long been a meeting place, in a city strategically located between the Mediterranean and Mesopotamia. It is one of the oldest inhabited cities on earth, dating to the eleventh millennium BC (Abraham is said to have provided milk to travelers), and for generations of traders the *souk* was the last stop on the Silk Road before they set sail for Europe. Nor did its dominant economic position diminish until the seventeenth century, when Europeans began to use the sea route to India, around the Cape of Good Hope—though under Ottoman rule it maintained its hold on the Western imagination as a site of mystery, if not of economic opportunity. Shakespeare mentions the Syrian city twice in his dramas, in the first act of *Macbeth*—"Her husband's to Aleppo gone," says a witch—and in Othello's final speech:

> in Aleppo once,
> Where a malignant and a turban'd Turk
> Beat a Venetian and traduced the state,
> I took by th' throat the circumcisèd dog,
> And smote him—thus!

Then Othello stabs himself—an act that links his noble younger persona to the lost soul, transfigured by jealousy, whose murder of his beloved Desdemona is likewise a betrayal of Venice. For in Shakespeare's cosmology, in which personal deeds often carry political consequences, the Moor recognizes that he deserves the same punishment for his crime as he once dealt a Turkish cur: believing that he has been betrayed, Othello betrays everything that he loves; at the climax of the play his past merges with the present, and he sees both ways, registering the full dimensions of his loss. His is a form of double vision, if you will, which mirrors the dual nature of Aleppo, a crossroads of the East and West, where collisions of modern and ancient ways of being are commonplace. The city had lost its allure in the Western imagination before the collapse of the caliphate in 1924, but some modern visitors recognized its importance.

"Aleppo," T. E. Lawrence wrote, "was a great city in Syria, but not of it, nor of Anatolia, nor of Mesopotamia. There the races, creeds, and tongues of the Ottoman Empire met and knew one another in a spirit of compromise. The clash of characteristics, which made its streets a kaleidoscope, imbued the Aleppine with a lewd thoughtfulness which corrected in him what was blatant in the Damascene."

The "lewd thoughtfulness" of the merchants who stayed in the *souk* during evening prayers was the first surprise of my Levantine journey in the spring of 2007, on the eve of the fortieth anniversary of the Six Days' War. I knew that the civil war in Iraq would complicate my itinerary, but I had not taken into account the extent to which the looming Israeli celebration of its victory and occupation of Gaza, the West Bank, and East Jerusalem made Arabs seethe. Traveling through Syria, Jordan, Israel and the West Bank, Greece, Turkey, and Lebanon, sometimes in the company of other writers, sometimes alone, I could not escape the sensation that I had entered the world of the betrayed, in which occupier and occupied alike were doomed.

Aleppo was crowded with Iraqi refugees—men talking on street corners, clicking prayer beads in their *djebellas* and red-and-white checked *kaffiyehs*, which were available in the *souk*. The doctor suggested that I try one on, and when I balked at that she changed the subject: how the chaos in Iraq had made it impossible for her pro-democracy friends to speak out in favor of a system that anyone could see led only to murder and mayhem. She also blamed the war for all the women dressing in burkas—a new development, she sneered. She herself radiated health in her low-cut white blouse, tight black jeans, and gold hoop earrings—a fashion statement that carried political overtones in a repressive society.

Through an archway we came to an empty lane, in the middle of which stood the *bimaristan,* a mansion transformed into a hospital in 1254, during the Ayyubid dynasty, which had operated for nearly eight centuries, under Arab and then Ottoman rule; now it was being renovated into a museum. Inside its high cool walls was a courtyard of stone rooms, each displaying a *tableau vivant*: of an apothecary mixing medicine out of lapis lazuli; of a lecturer in the healing arts; of Ibn al-Nafis, the discoverer of the circulatory system, examining a woman draped in a blue blanket. There were four seated figures on a mat by the space in which whirling dervishes performed, and as we continued down a dark corridor the doctor explained why the dervishes did not suffer from vertigo: how they found equilibrium spinning around a fixed point, how they shed the trappings of desire, how the music haunted her: *Allah, Allah,* the mystics sing.

We entered a courtyard reserved for psychiatric patients, where small barred cells surrounded a fountain under a circular opening in the roof, through which poured the last light of the day. Birdsong, the sound of water trickling from the fountain, Sufi musicians playing through the night, readings from the Koran—these were elements of a healing regimen that included herbal therapies and liberal doses of opium.

"Very humane," said the doctor.

This place was for her a reminder of the greatness of a civilization gone to seed—which now produced only nostalgia and fanaticism. The women in burkas, for example: in her medical

opinion, the lack of sunlight on their skin—of vitamin D—was
bad for their bones and their minds. In the old days, when
houses like this mansion were built around interior courtyards,
women could lounge in the sun in casual clothes, without fear
of being seen by strange men. But there was no place to sun-
bathe in a modern apartment building, where most people
now lived; with so many families taking in Iraqi refugees, in
the midst of such economic and political turmoil, the doctor
was not surprised that religious codes of conduct were replacing her cherished secular values. More and more women were
thus covering themselves from head to toe. No wonder the region had gone mad.

Her fellowship to Radcliffe seemed like a cruel joke. Iraqi passports were now invalid outside the Middle East, and if the scholar
traveled from her home in Mosul to Baghdad to apply for a new
one she expected to be killed, since she was Sunni. (It seemed
that the post-invasion plans for Iraq had not included furnishing
passports to the citizens of the new democracy.) How was she to
get to Cambridge? Two million Iraqis had fled to Syria and Jordan
(an exodus larger than the forced migration of Palestinians from
their homeland in 1948, with the founding of the state of Israel),
sectarian strife had displaced two million more within the country, and though less than a thousand US visas had been issued
to Iraqis the scholar paid a middleman two thousand dollars (almost a year's salary) to get her a passport. One day, awaiting his
return, she took her advanced poetry students for a picnic on the
grounds of the University of Mosul, when her dean sent for her
in a panic: a letter had arrived from the *mujahideen* warning that
they would shoot her if her teaching did not improve; a bullet was
enclosed. In its campaign to drive professionals out of Iraq, Sunni
insurgents had killed or kidnapped more than three hundred
professors, including several of the scholar's closest colleagues;

in a frantic e-mail to some American poets concerned for her welfare she said her time was up. We urged her to flee. I hoped to meet her in Aleppo, if she could get a passport.

My involvement in her cause belonged to an American tradition of high-minded intervention in the region; so did this literary tour. It is true that from the beginning of the republic the US military has played a decisive role in shaping the history of the Middle East, from its very first war waged, in 1801, against the Barbary States of North Africa (to safeguard American shipping from pirates) to the invasion of Iraq two centuries later. It is also true that from the end of the second Barbary War, in 1815, American merchants and entrepreneurs have sought their fortunes in these desert lands, offering all manner of goods and services ranging from the sale of armaments and textiles to the development of oil fields. But this story involves more than guns and butter. American adventurers and missionaries, diplomats and writers, visionaries and realists—all have added to the fabric of life in what for a long time was known as the Orient.

Some nineteenth-century Protestant ministers, for example, projecting onto the Holy Land their millennial hopes, convinced their followers that the Second Coming of Christ depended upon the restoration of the Jews to Palestine. Hundreds and thousands of men and women heeded the call to prepare the ground for his return, making the difficult journey to Jerusalem, where they evangelized to Jews and Orthodox Christians with little success. (Proselytizing to Muslims in the caliphate was a capital offense.) All was not lost, though; for along the way they built clinics; established universities in Beirut, Cairo, and Istanbul, introducing generations of students to Western educational methods and ideas; recorded impressions of life in the last days of the Ottoman Empire; mustered support for the Zionist movement, which in the fullness of time would lead to the creation of the state of Israel—the original sin, in the eyes of the Arabs.

This escaped the notice of the majority of the innocents abroad, in Mark Twain's memorable phrase. Like their Puritan ancestors, who regarded the New World as another Zion, they were guided more by biblical maps and stories than facts on the ground; their zeal in Palestine to make contact with the origins of their faith and open Arab hearts and minds to the Protestant wonders of Christ all but closed off the possibility of registering the true lay of the land—which did not dissuade others from following in their footsteps. Indeed it became fashionable for antebellum Americans to travel to the Holy Land as pilgrims and tourists; published accounts of their journeys reinforced the idea that America's destiny was linked to the prospect of the Jews returning to their homeland—an idea sanctified by the report that on the last evening of his life, just before he was cut down by an assassin's bullet, Abraham Lincoln told his wife that he wished to go to Jerusalem.

Which was our final destination; and though our journey was literary it had its own missionary aspect, our charge from the State Department being to foster better relations with literati in the Levant. Creativity had replaced Christ as the currency of our mission, and in my darker moments I feared that in our ardor to connect with Arab and Israeli writers we would suffer from the same kinds of shortsightedness as our forebears. But then there was the Iraqi scholar, whose life might yet be spared.

Thus between meetings with administrators, faculty, and graduate students at the University of Aleppo and then with the vestry of the Orthodox cathedral, I tried in vain to reach the Iraqi scholar on her mobile phone, with mounting anxiety. Her decision to leave Iraq—she vowed not to return, if she made it to Cambridge—was a symbol not only of American disregard for the Geneva Conventions, which oblige an occupying authority to safeguard citizens, but of the region's largest catastrophe since the founding of the Jewish state; the question now was whether she could escape before the *mujahideen* killed her. But when I returned that night to my hotel there were no messages from her.

"Men of religion, of all religions, and also politicians, have played on the idea of the nation state and the religious state," the Grand Mufti of Syria said through an interpreter. He was a soft-spoken man in a white turban and grey *jubah,* and in his sitting room in Damascus he was the voice of moderation: a stay against conservative Islamic clerics, based in Saudi Arabia, whose teachings broadcast on satellite TV and jihadist Web sites resonated with more and more Syrian Muslims—to the consternation of Syria's secular government and its minority Alawite, Christian, and Druze communities.

"But there is no such thing as a religious state—there shouldn't be," insisted the Mufti. "There is no religious homeland, only a human homeland. And so the concept of a religious state and religious parties is a danger to all of us."

Writers, politicians, and clerics have pondered the nature of a Syrian homeland from time immemorial. If at various points in history it has encompassed a considerable expanse of territory, including parts of Jordan, Lebanon, Israel, Palestine, and Turkey, it has also endured enough foreign rulers—Canaanites, Phoenicians, Arameans, Egyptians, Sumerians, Assyrians, Babylonians, Hittites, Persians, Greeks, Romans, Byzantines, Arabs, Crusaders, Mongols, Ottomans, and the French—to guarantee that the merits and flaws of every conceivable governing structure have been debated. And its rich religious history—Paul was converted to Christianity on the road to Damascus, which in the seventh century became the seat of the first Islamic caliphate—established a tradition of political decision making entwined with spiritual concerns, which continues to this day. Thus in a new world order shaped by the war on terror, with the Bush administration advocating the overthrow of Syrian president Beshar al-Assad for his support of the insurgency in Iraq, the Mufti was keen to present a vision of Syria as home to a moderate version of Islam—a counter to al-Qaeda, if not to Hezbollah, the radical Islamic group operating in Lebanon with Syria's blessing. The US State Department had designated Syria as a state sponsor of terrorism in every global survey since 1979, but the government-appointed Mufti contended that terrorism was a product solely of religious fundamentalism.

"This is why we reject the idea of building a state based on religion: a religious state excludes the Other," he explained. "The state should be built on a civic rather than a religious basis. This is something that Christ, Muhammad, and Moses each called for. A homeland should be a civic state. Religion is not a state, it is a spiritual relationship. This is why we shouldn't confuse the two, as sometimes happens in Israel, in some Arab countries, in some European countries. We must refuse the idea of a religious state."

The spiritual relationship he described, the political vision he presented, recalled another history, when Damascus was a center of learning that drew the likes of Rumi, the thirteenth-century Sufi teacher regarded as Islam's greatest mystical poet. He was born in Afghanistan, and when he was a young man Mongol invaders forced him and his family to flee to Turkey, where a wandering dervish inspired his vocation. He traveled to Baghdad, Mecca, and Damascus before settling back in Anatolia, preaching and writing thousands of poems, frequently in a trance. His work is indeed ecstatic: in every encounter he sought divinity—for him friendship was spelled with a capital F—and his revelations about the nature of existence had made him the most popular poet in America. One short poem had become particularly important to me after 9/11:

> Inside the Great Mystery that is,
> we don't really own anything.
> What is this competition we feel then,
> before we go, one at a time, through the same
>   gate?

His followers founded the Sufi order, which spread throughout the Islamic world, inspiring poets and philosophers and scientists, drawing the ire of certain clerics. And no wonder. "I am neither Muslim nor Christian, Jew nor Zoroastrian," Rumi said; "I am neither of the earth nor of the heavens, I am neither body nor soul." Such a view of the human condition unsettled some of the faithful, even as it helped to usher in the golden age of Islamic civilization dear to the Mufti's heart. Rumi's vision was surely larger than he could embrace, and yet perhaps it informed at least some of this thinking.

What would become of Syria? An autocratic state ruled by the Baath Party, whose extensive security apparatus called to mind the totalitarian order that Saddam Hussein had created in Iraq—this was the kind of regime that had no place in George W. Bush's vision of the Middle East. The Mufti had his own ideas about Syria's future.

"There should not be twenty million Syrians divided into different confessions," he said, "but twenty million Sunnis, twenty million Shias, twenty million Christians."

It seemed that there was no place for Jews in the Mufti's vision of Syria—and yet in a matter of weeks he would announce that Syrian-born Jews who had fled after the creation of Israel in 1948 could return to their homeland and reclaim their property: a bold move in a country unreconciled to the loss of its Golan Heights in the Six Days' War. But it was very difficult to imagine Jews resettling in Syria, with Iraqi refugees straining society, pro-democracy activists being jailed, and American officials discussing plans to invade the country. The time for inter-communal gestures had passed.

The Bedouin bagpipers playing in the ancient amphitheater of Jerash, in northern Jordan, inherited the tradition from a Highland regiment, during the British Mandate for Palestine (1920–48)—the quasi-colonial territory carved out of the Ottoman Empire and sanctioned by the League of Nations. The excavation of Jerash, one of the best-preserved Roman ruins in the Levant, also began during the Mandate, which lay between the French Mandates for Lebanon and Syria and adjacent to the British Mandate for Mesopotamia—a map, that is, destined to be redrawn. Thus on an overcast afternoon, while a film crew shooting a documentary for the Discovery Channel packed up its equipment and my fellow writers explored the colonnaded streets and plazas, monuments and fountains, I climbed to the top row of stone seats to reflect on a history of shifting borders. A hot, dusty wind from the south blew over this valley in the mountains of Gilead, the homeland of the prophet Elijah. An Egyptian crow squawked overhead. The bagpipers marched back and forth in front of the stage in their kilts and tall hats. What a strange place to be.

The earliest settlements discovered within the city walls date from the Stone Age, and for millennia Semitic peoples inhabited the fertile area, which began to flourish with the arrival of Alexander the Great, in the fourth century BC. Under Roman rule, trade expanded throughout Arabia, the town grew into a city, a triumphal arch was raised to celebrate the visit of Emperor Hadrian in 129 AD. Shipping replaced land routes, and yet Jerash apparently continued to thrive. Constantine Christianized it in the fourth century, churches decorated with colorful mosaics were built with stones taken from the pagan temples, and every year the miracle of Jesus turning water into wine was celebrated. The Byzantine order held until the Persians invaded, in 614, and then the Arabs conquered the region in 636. An earthquake in 747 may have prompted an exodus from Jerash, which was abandoned by 800 (Crusaders arriving three centuries later reported it uninhabited), and for a thousand years its gates and columns, theaters and bathhouses—all disappeared under sand. It was not until 1806 that a German traveler recognized the archaeological significance of some exposed ruins, and excavations in the Mandate began to uncover one of the cities of the Decapolis, a league of Roman outposts responsible for defending the empire's eastern frontier—Palestine, that is, where Jesus taught.

Jerash lay between Philadelphia (present-day Amman) and Gadara, and it was in the country of the Gadarenes—a Gentile territory, near the Sea of Galilee—that Jesus performed one of his most mysterious miracles. In the Gospel accounts he and his disciples set sail across the sea one evening, and when a windstorm arises his frightened followers wake him from a nap, crying, "Teacher, do You not care that we are perishing?" He stills the winds and water, then rebukes the men for their lack of faith. "Who can this be," they wonder, "that even the wind and the sea obey Him?" When they make landfall a man possessed by demons emerges from a tomb to worship him.

"Come out of the man, unclean spirit!" Jesus commands.

The demons, which have pulled apart the chains and broken the shackles used to bind the man, recognize the Messiah; when he asks the man who he is, they answer: "My name is Legion, for we are many." And they implore him not to cast them back down to hell, but to send them into a herd of swine grazing near the mountains. This he does, and two thousand swine run downhill into the sea and drown.

The goatherds flee to the city to spread the news of this miracle, and when Legion begs Jesus to accept him as a disciple he is instructed instead to go home and tell his friends, "what great things the Lord has done for you, and how He has had compassion for you." This was the first messianic secret that Jesus allowed to be publicized, perhaps because Gentiles were unfamiliar with his ministry—and with the danger posed to Jews who proclaimed him to be the Messiah. The miracle story may also have had a political dimension: a legion was a phalanx of Roman soldiers, and some Biblical scholars read the expulsion of Legion's demons in anti-Roman terms, the spirits embodying the same army that in the fullness of time would crucify Jesus as a threat to the existing order. Did this healing prophesy Rome's expulsion from the Holy Land? Perhaps revolts against the occupation were common at the edge of an empire defined by its cruelty. Debt and dispossession marked the lives of Jews and gentiles alike, insurgents hung from crosses lining the roads, villages and cities from Sepphoris to Jerusalem were reduced to smoking ruins. Rome could not sustain such a cruel political order indefinitely.

The wind had a gritty taste—outside the amphitheater a colleague had noted that the black millipedes emerging from a sand hill presaged rain—and my thoughts drifted to the millennial silence of a vanished city, broken in the end by archaeological excavations, an international arts festival inaugurated by Queen Noor, and a large influx of tourists, for whom these bagpipers performed. A circle closed in my imagination: this Middle Eastern musical tradition, brought by Roman legions to the British Isles fifteen hundred or more years ago and then returned during the

Mandate, added strange notes to the place, like the call of the hoopoe from its nest atop a nearby lighting stand: *oop, oop, oop.*

Now it was the Americans' turn to send their legions to Mesopotamia—the latest in a long line of attempts to reorder the region, most of which had ended badly. Take the mandates carved out of the remains of the Ottoman Empire: they seemed like a good idea at the Paris Peace Conference, in 1919, when Woodrow Wilson and his counterparts from Britain, France, and Italy were redrawing the map of the world. The American president's Fourteen Points, introduced in a wartime speech as necessary preconditions for a lasting peace, had outlined a lofty set of principles, including a commitment to open agreements, free trade, democracy, and self-determination, inspiring people everywhere to imagine that a new day was at hand. "The very foundations have been shaken and loosened, and things are again fluid," a South African participant observed. "The tents have been struck, and the great caravan of humanity is once more on the march."

For the people of the Levant, judged to be unprepared to govern themselves after centuries of Ottoman rule, the Supreme Council (as Wilson and his colleagues came to be known) determined that mandates, or trusteeships, sanctioned by the League of Nations and administered by other powers, offered them the best route to self-governance. France thus assumed responsibility for Syria and Lebanon, Britain occupied Mesopotamia and Palestine (including the Emirate of Transjordan, which in 1946 became the Kingdom of Jordan), and another colonial order was created, destined to be shaped by sectarian strife. For the men hovering over their maps in the state rooms of the Quai d'Orsay took little notice of the political, religious, and tribal affiliations of the various peoples in their charge; hence a League of Nations report in 1925 on Mesopotamia warned that "serious difficulties may arise out of the differences which in some cases exist in regard to political ideas between the Shiites of the South and the Sunnites of the North, the racial differences between Arabs and Kurds, and the necessity of keeping the turbulent tribes under control." The warning held for the current American occupation of Iraq.

This was a familiar story to me. In the 1990s, the democratic revolutions in Eastern and Central Europe inspired violent factionalism in Yugoslavia, another successor state to the Ottoman Empire created at the Paris Peace Conference. As long as Marshal Tito wielded dictatorial power over the Serbs, Croats, Slovenians, Macedonians, Albanians, and Montenegrins, an uneasy peace reigned in the land of the South Slavs. But with his death in 1980, competing nationalisms, long suppressed by a skilful mixture of subsidies and security measures, returned with a vengeance. Elections reinforced sectarian divisions: fear of the Other led most Yugoslavs to vote along ethnic or confessional lines; outside powers meddled in the disintegrating political process; with no strongman to keep people from cutting their neighbors' throats, it was not long before war was on. What haunted me as I covered that war was the hatred unleashed by the advent of freedom: some two hundred fifty thousand people lost their lives in the Yugoslav wars of succession, millions more were displaced, and the NATO mission to enforce the peace in Bosnia and Kosovo might last for a generation.

The American occupation of Iraq set in motion a similar dynamic, with more horrific consequences. The fighting between Shias and Sunnis, between rival militias from the same confession, and between Arabs and Kurds put to rest George W. Bush's grand talk of freedom. The fact remained that the instruments of civil society required for the peaceful resolution of conflicts had neither existed before the invasion nor been established in the occupation; the overstretched American military's inability to stop the car bombings, the detonation of improvised explosive devices, and the gruesome work of the death squads—these exacerbated tensions between Iraqis suffering from shortages of electricity, gasoline, and jobs. A sober assessment of the situation suggested that Iraq was a failed state—no different, perhaps, from the ancient city-states that had risen and fallen in Mesopotamia, from Sumer to Ur to Babylon. Buried in these sands was the bloody record of who we are and where we came from.

In these exquisitely preserved ruins my thoughts turned to the careless destruction of archaeological sites in Iraq, thousands of which had been looted during the war. Before the invasion, archaeologists had pleaded with Bush administration officials to make every effort to preserve the heritage of the cradle of civilization, many sites of which remained unexcavated. But the plundering of the National Museum of its artifacts, which Secretary of Defense Donald Rumsfeld dismissed as the cost of freedom—"Stuff happens," he said—set the tone for what was to follow. Archaeologists formerly employed by Saddam Hussein were stealing bowls, sculptures, and frescoes to sell on the international art market; Babylon was crumbling under the weight of American tanks; the foundations of Western civilization were disappearing before our eyes.

"Freedom is untidy," Rumsfeld said. But the new political order that he and his cohorts were creating in the Middle East looked much different to those on whose behalf they claimed to be acting—a common theme in our discussions with government officials and writers, professors and students, merchants and refugees. The catastrophic fallout from the American decision to break up the old order was the subtext of nearly every conversation we had in Syria and Jordan; and if most of the people that we met, students excepted, refused to call us out on the consequences of what history would record as a disaster—a gamble, as the writer Thomas Powers notes, "of the sort that

makes or breaks empires"—the bagpipers showed no such restraint. The last song they played as I made my way out of the
amphitheater was "Yankee Doodle Dandy"—a song first sung
by British soldiers to taunt the ragtag forces of the American
Revolution.

The professor explained that one condition of her employ-
ment in the English department at the University of Jordan in
Amman was that she could teach any novel she wanted as long
as it contained no references to politics, religion, or sex—which,
as one writer noted, did not leave her much to choose from. But
her students, almost all of whom were female, refused to read
the books she assigned—not because they found them boring,
she insisted, but because they were studying English only to get
a good job. Each student was required to ask us a literary question. But first they had to rise to their feet, tell us their name,
and then translate it into English. Layla, said one woman, which
means born at night. Iman, said another, which means faith.
Alyah, said a third, which means transcendent. Heaven, the
professor corrected her. Transcendent, the student repeated.

The argument was not insignificant. Just as Adam named
the animals, so we name the world—children and deities, cities
and streets, wars and books. Naming is integral to poetry, and
as a colleague fielded a question about a poem's origins, explaining that her imagination could take flight over the various
meanings of a single word, I thought of the different names attached to the wars in the region, beginning with the 1948 Arab-
Israeli War, which was for Israelis their War of Independence
and for Arabs, al-Nakba (the Catastrophe). The Second Arab-
Israeli War was the Suez Crisis or Sinai War, in 1956, when
a British-French-Israeli operation was undone by the United
States, the looming power in the Middle East; the Third, in
1967, was the Six Days' War (after the Six Days of Creation),

which Arabs call an-Naksah (the Setback); and the Fourth, in 1973, was both the Yom Kippur War and the Ramadan War, since the surprise attack launched against Israel by Egypt and Syria coincided with the Jewish and Muslim holidays. It was true that Egypt, the Palestinian Authority, and Jordan had negotiated separate peaces with Israel—with the Camp David Accords in 1979, the Oslo Accords in 1993, and the Israel-Jordan Treaty of Peace in 1994, respectively—but much of the Arab world remained at war with the Jewish state, since the underlying issue—the Israeli settlement or occupation of Palestine, depending on your point of view—had never been resolved.

The Israeli-Lebanese conflict, for example, which began with the Israeli invasion of southern Lebanon in 1978 and included three major Israeli operations—Peace for Galilee in 1982 (the First Lebanon War, or Fifth Arab-Israeli War), Accountability in 1993 (which was for Lebanese the Seven-Day War), and Grapes of Wrath in 1996. The Sixth Arab-Israeli War, in 2006, which Israelis called the Second Lebanon War, and Lebanese the July War, was a likely prelude to another regional war, the main battlefield of which for three decades had been Lebanon. So much blood shed in so many names, which amounted to a single name: the Sixty Years' War, and counting.

Add to this the Bush administration's War on Terror, also known as the Global War on Terror, the Global Struggle Against Violent Extremism, the Long War, or World War IV, and the groundwork was laid for what James Madison dreaded: perpetual war. "No nation could preserve its freedom in the midst of continual warfare," the Founding Father wrote. For security trumps liberty in times of war, and Bush had expertly played on American fears after 9/11 to consolidate his power, citing vague terrorist threats to justify unprecedented levels of governmental secrecy, violations of international treaties, and restrictions on civil liberties, not to mention the Iraq War. The

traditional checks and balances built into the American system
of governance—the separation of powers, a vigorous media, an
informed electorate—had failed, Congress, much of the press,
and a majority of the citizens having refused to question mis-
leading administration statements; hence the disaster unfolding in the Middle East—and at home.

Some constitutional lawyers and commentators had drawn
attention to the ways in which the administration's actions
were raveling the fabric of the republic. The crisis lay deeper,
in the perversions of language practiced at the highest level of
government. Poets play a marginal role in American society, but
their efforts to give the right names to the things of the world
remind us that when language becomes so debased that it is
no longer possible to recognize reality, poetry, as Robert Frost
wrote, can provide "a momentary stay against confusion"—
the first step toward a realistic vision of our predicament. The
administration's falsehoods about the Iraq War, from the case
made for the invasion to its changing rationale for the occupation to its relentless promotion of any sign of progress, had led
to mayhem—which was to be expected. Good policy depends
upon an accurate description of the situation; anything short
of a precise rendering is a recipe for ruin. The Iraq War thus
represented, among other things, a failure of language. Our collective failure to articulate an appropriate response to the administration's Orwellian uses of language had left us paralyzed,
like bystanders to a terrible collision.

Bush's fabled inability to speak clearly was a potent symbol of the debasement of the language. Likewise his stubborn
refusal to call the sectarian strife in Iraq a civil war, which it
patently was, and the names devised by his military planners
for the proliferating doctrines and operations that defined our
engagement in Iraq, from Shock and Awe to Operation Hoplite
to the Surge. What the poet Paul Celan said of the German language after World War II—that it would have to "pass through

a thousand darknesses of deathbringing speech"—might apply to American English after Bush exited the stage.

The journalist Mark Danner named the Iraq War the War of the Imagination. In fact the plan to topple Saddam Hussein, which issued from the fervid imaginings of a coterie of neoconservative thinkers in Washington, might have remained on the shelf if not for 9/11. War is the most ambitious imaginative act in the political arena, since it seeks to reshape the world; and if it was true that Bush had set his sights on Iraq from the first days of his presidency, still he could not have launched his war without 9/11—and a campaign to stoke fears of another large-scale terrorist act. Joseph Goebbels, the Nazi propaganda chief, said that the case for war is easily made, in any political system, by appealing to fear—the means by which the Bush administration built its public argument to invade Iraq. But it was instructive that after four years of fighting no one could say for sure what the war was all about. Weapons of mass destruction? A new political order in the Middle East? Oil? What seemed clear, though, was that the Long War, also known as the Perpetual War, could have grave consequences for the republic.

The poet was explaining that her poems began when her world fractured into a before and an after—a method, I thought, that in the Levant might produce countless poems, each attempting to describe some portion of experience, to find the right name for every sort of experience, to honor that name's various meanings. How a Sunni interpreted the name Iman, for example—faith—made all the difference to a Shia: a critical fact that George W. Bush and his advisors either ignored or misunderstood when they decided to invade Iraq. The teacher looked around the room, impatiently.

"Next question, please," she said.

Up and down corkscrewing canyons etched with dry terraces we drove toward the Jordan River Valley, through the land in which God first revealed himself to Abraham, Job, and Moses, and then, in the new covenant heralded by John the Baptist, incarnated himself in Jesus Christ. It was a spare landscape, with dust swirling into an overcast sky, and in this place of visions and revelations I reflected on its history as a safe haven. That tradition began with the apocryphal story of Cain seeking refuge here after murdering his brother Abel, continued in al-Naqba, when Jordan took in the bulk of Palestinians fleeing the new Jewish state (they now make up nearly half of the population of the kingdom), and with up to a million Iraqi refugees (in a country of less than six million) King Abdullah could see history repeating itself. He had just closed the border to Iraqis.

One victim of the new decree was the Iraqi scholar whose difficulties in taking up a fellowship at Radcliffe had inspired me to try to help her. Against all odds, the middleman to whom she had paid a year's salary showed up one day with her new passport. She took the next bus from Mosul to Aleppo, where she spent the night before continuing to Damascus, arriving just after we had left for Amman. She had no luck in arranging a consular interview at the American Embassy, so she traveled to Jordan, where she was stopped at the border for so long that by the time she bribed a guard to let her take a taxi to Amman we were gone. Nor could she arrange a consular interview at that American Embassy, so she took one bus back to Damascus and then another to Aleppo. On the day that we drove to Israel she arrived in Mosul, without a visa.

Exodus was the theme. Scholars debate whether Moses actually received the Law, parted the waters of the Red Sea, and so on, but if the stories recorded about him are only etiological their importance is hardly diminished, since they provided the imaginative and moral scaffolding for a region defined by exile. The Old Testament is among other things an essay on migration, which is what frequently happens when one political order gives way to another. My conversations in

Syria and Jordan inevitably turned to the order inaugurated by the creation of Israel, with its displacements and despair. The conveners of the Paris Peace Conference but dimly understood the complications of carving a Jewish homeland out of Arab territory, to say nothing of the growing importance of oil; the centerpiece of Woodrow Wilson's global order, the League of Nations, collapsed before the founding of the Jewish state, but the ideas articulated by the Zionist movement endured. In no time another chapter in the ancient story of exile was being written.

Into the Jordan Valley we drove. On one side of the road were green fields as far as the eye could see, and on the other, dusty towns populated largely by Palestinian refugees and their descendants. The stark juxtaposition brought to mind what an Israeli Arab had said to me, with a sardonic grin: "God taught the Israelis to build terraces."

Entering Israel at the Sheik Hussein crossing was no easy matter. After clearing customs on the Jordanian side, we took a bus across the Jordan River, which was no wider than an irrigation ditch, and when we disembarked on the Israeli side we waited for two hours while our passports were checked and rechecked. The pair of Israeli expeditors sent by the embassy to ease our way had no influence over the female soldiers, who seemed to take pleasure in making trouble for us. Finally we were waved toward the door.

Thus we entered the promised land.

The Donkeys of Nazareth was the title of the human rights lawyer's latest book about his hometown. He was regaling us with stories in the early evening, our dinner party with several Israeli and Arab poets having fallen apart at the last minute, when one had gotten sick, another had crashed his car, and a third had taken his wife to the hospital. On short

notice, American diplomats had rounded up four Arab artists to meet with us in a convent that doubled as a hotel. In a
room near the kitchen were two young filmmakers who kept
their counsel, a dozing painter who woke from time to time
to shuffle into the next room, not to partake of the refresh-
ments laid out for us, but to belch loudly, and the lawyer, who
did all the talking. He said the donkeys had been brought
from Crete three thousand years before, that you could learn
everything you needed to know about Jesus's childhood home
by observing the donkeys, that he had long since solved the
riddle of identity for himself: he was Arab by tribal affiliation,
Palestinian by national origin, Israeli by citizenship, a lawyer
by profession, a writer by calling. The filmmakers stared at
him contemptuously. The painter went into the next room to
belch. It sounded like he might throw up.

The poet I really missed at this gathering was Taha
Muhammad Ali, whose work I had come to know during his
last reading tour in the United States. A gentle, soft-spoken
man, he dramatized, on the page and in person, the experience
of exile, transforming his memories of Saffuriya, the Galilee
village of his birth, razed in the first Arab-Israeli War in 1948,
into a magnetic field of language. In *Never Mind*, a collection
of twenty poems and a story translated into English, he con-
jures up the daily life of Saffuriya (which in the Bible is called
Sepphoris, the traditional site of the Virgin Mary's birth), dem-
onstrating the capacity of literature to render what has long
since disappeared from the earth—its people and customs and
lore. Ali was self-taught, his formal education having ended
before he fled with his family to Lebanon; after a year in a
refugee camp he snuck back across the border only to discover
that nothing remained of Saffuriya. So he settled in Nazareth,
opened a souvenir shop, and served a lengthy literary apprenticeship, reading and writing and selling trinkets to Christian

pilgrims, learning by fits and starts how to restore through literature the vanished world of his childhood.

"No vein can bleed / more than it already has," he wrote in "Exodus," which dates from the first Lebanon War, in 1982—and yet recent history suggested that unhealed wounds continue to bleed, even if they are sometimes momentarily stanched in a poem.

His translator, Gabriel Levin, recounts a story that Ali told one night at a poetry reading in Jerusalem: how when he was ten years old his mother, discovering a mouse, sent him to a shopkeeper in Saffuriya to buy a trap. The one he brought home clicked shut at exactly five o'clock, catching what he called "the most beautiful mouse, with green eyes and a belly white as cotton." Fast forward fifty years: his wife, spotting a mouse in their kitchen in Nazareth, sent him off to buy a trap. The one he wanted was no longer available, though someone thought it might still be made in Hebron. As it happened, he was in Hebron the next week for a reading, after which he was taken to a shop where the old-fashioned traps were sold.

> "Did you make these traps?" he asked the
> owner of the shop. "No," the man answered,
> "they were made by my father, Ziab Al-
> Shantawi." Ali paused, and then said to the
> Jerusalem crowd, "That was the very same
> name as the shopkeeper in Saffuriya." And so
> he returned home with a new-old mousetrap,
> and the next day, he added, at exactly five
> o'clock the mousetrap clicked shut, and once
> more he saw "the same beautiful mouse, with
> green eyes and a belly white as cotton . . ."

Levin remarks on the dislocation felt by Ali's audience, the poet having "caught them in the snare of his words, though it was hard to know just how." Indeed the snares of history and poetry operate with the same ruthless logic.

The protest against Prime Minister Ehhud Olmert had broken up by the time we checked into our hotel in Tel Aviv. What brought more than one hundred thousand Israelis into the streets was a state commission of inquiry's preliminary report blaming Olmert for his mismanagement of the 2006 Lebanon War; the catalogue of his government's failures—from inadequate preparation to insufficient support for civilians in northern Israel to tactical, operational, and logistical shortcomings by the military—helped to explain the decline in his approval rating from over 90 percent during the war to 3 percent, which was within the margin of error—that is, it was entirely possible that no one liked him.

The war, which began with Hezbollah paramilitary forces capturing two Israeli soldiers in a bid to force the release of Lebanese political prisoners in Israel, triggered instead an Israeli assault against Lebanon, which led to hundreds of deaths, extensive damage to the civilian infrastructure, and enough unexploded cluster bombs (supplied by the United States) to render the southern part of the country uninhabitable (thirty-six million square meters). It was difficult to fathom Hezbollah's claims of victory after such destruction—its leader, Sayyed Hassan Nasrallah, even apologized to his countrymen for their suffering, admitting that he had miscalculated the fury of the Israeli response—and yet because its militia, backed by Iran and Syria, had fired hundreds of Katyusha rockets into northern Israel, inflicting casualties on a military machine that had heretofore easily mastered its foes, Arabs likened the Party of God to David toppling Goliath. Israelis, too, understood that in this proxy war between the United States and Iran no one had won—which was the real message of the demonstration. If it was too soon to foretell the fall of the Olmert government, which was also plagued by scandal, it was still refreshing to be in a place where citizens could voice their dissent.

After a long day, I but dimly noticed the spare decor of the swank seaside hotel, and in the elevator I had two thoughts: that I needed sleep, and that the American body politic needed inquiries into the fabrications and failures of the Bush administration—on everything from its rationale for the invasion of Iraq to its bungled occupation, from its attack on civil liberties to its response to Hurricane Katrina. It was Mark Twain who said that a lie can travel halfway around the world while the truth is still putting on its shoes. In the end the truth would likely emerge—though not before irrevocable damage was done to the republic. Democratic gains in the 2006 congressional elections had restored some oversight to the political system, but the administration continued to flout the law, domestic and international opinion, even reality itself. I entered my room overlooking the promenade, and the sea wind blowing through the open windows carried the tang of salt. When I inserted my key into the outlet to switch on the power, mood lights came up, synthesized music filled the air, and on the large flat-screen television was a video of a beautiful woman sauntering on a beach, naked. The show on the Fashion Network was *Midnight Hot*. Clearly, I was no longer in an Arab culture—and I was wide awake.

The writers gathered around the table in a seminar room of the Helicon School of Poetry were discussing the revival of Hebrew: how elastic the language chosen for the Jewish state had proved to be; how new words to fit the changing society were being coined; how easily biblical phrases mixed with slang, Yiddish, and English; how one man's father refused to curse in Hebrew; how television and film had accelerated the introduction of the vernacular; how writers brought this evolving language to the page; how Arabic had to undergo the same transformation. They spoke with rising passion, seemingly oblivious to their American guests, and as they argued over the consequences—cultural, literary, political—of what one poet called the relativism of Hebrew I recalled a conversation, in Cairo, with an Egyptian writer who described himself as a victim of religious extremism. An Egyptian parliamentarian was trying to ban his latest book, in which he argued that the reform of the Arab mindset must begin in the language. Arabic had not changed in fifteen hundred years, he declared, because it was the language of the Koran. But the Arab world had to open itself to ideas from abroad, because it was facing a wave of intolerance. Still he did not believe that change could be imposed from without. Psychologically speaking, he said, we cannot accept orders from without to reform. That can only come from within.

The Israeli argument took another turn. Without a fixed point, a moral center, the poet cried, all is lost—which prompted another poet, who had remained silent throughout the discussion, to tell a joke: a mouse escaping from a cat scurries into a hole, and when after a little while he hears the barking of a dog he assumes that the cat has run away. But when he emerges from his hole the cat is waiting for him. Wait! the mouse cries. I know you'll eat me up, but before you do please tell me how you learned to bark like a dog. The cat replies: you have to know two languages to survive in these times.

The gallows humor made me think of a poem by Dan Pagis, a Holocaust survivor who escaped Europe to make a new life in Israel, teaching medieval Hebrew literature at Hebrew University in Jerusalem until his untimely death from cancer in 1986. In "written in pencil in the sealed railway car" Pagis explores, in telegraphic style, the limits of what can be said in extremis, discovering in the biblical story of Cain and Abel a way to bear witness to the incomprehensibility of the Final Solution. The poem, in Stephen Mitchell's translation:

> here in this carload
> I am eve
> with abel my son
> if you see my older son
> cain son of adam
> tell him I

What does she want to tell the first murderer in the Old Testament, the son condemned to wander the earth? Western history hangs on what remains unwritten.

A silence fell over the room as the Israeli writers gathered themselves for the next round of their argument. The eyes of the Americans glazed over.

The restaurant had set an elegant table for twenty guests in a separate room on its second floor, with American and Palestinian flags propped crosswise in a centerpiece of flowers. Our luncheon in Ramallah with alumni of the International Writing Program (IWP) was to be a reunion, and I looked forward to seeing old friends—poets, novelists, and filmmakers, whose haunting portraits of life in the Occupied Territories had given me insight into the repercussions of al-Nakba: "news that stays news," as Ezra Pound argued.

I was particularly eager to see Ghassan Zaqtan. Born in Beit Jala, a Christian town near Bethlehem, he came of age during the civil war in Beirut, editing a literary journal for the Palestinian Liberation Army (PLO), and by the time we met, in August 2001, he had published several volumes of poetry and a novel. He also directed documentary films and the House of Poetry in Ramallah, which an Israeli tank leveled soon after he arrived in Iowa City—the third attack in a year on the cultural center, which the Israelis called a terrorist institution. The editorial offices, library, archives—everything was destroyed. Ghassan shrugged if off, as if to suggest that he had seen it all, as perhaps he had, having fought against Maronite militias and Israeli forces in Beirut, fled with the PLO to Tunisia, and survived two *intifadas* and several marriages. He brought to our discussions a levelheaded perspective, balancing the animus that some of his fellow writers harbored toward the United States in the weeks after 9/11 as the nation prepared for war in Afghanistan, and he seemed to revel in the absurdities visited upon him. During the IWP travels around the country, for example, he was the only writer whose one-way plane tickets did not attract the attention of security personnel at every airport. Unaccountably this former PLO fighter was never taken aside for additional screening.

No doubt he saw the absurdity in the fact that we could not meet. For after the recent Palestinian parliamentary elections, in which Hamas, a militant Islamist group listed as a terrorist organization by Israel, the United States, and the European Union, had swept to a surprising victory, the Bush administration instituted a no-contact policy with the Palestinian Authority—an edict that covered all public employees, including Ghassan, who had just accepted a position with the Ministry of Culture. As it happened, his new wife, who directed an NGO, had contracted with the US Consulate in Jerusalem to organize our meeting with IWP alumni, and while she was quite upset that Ghassan could not join us—it was her birthday, too—she continued making preparations until the eve of our journey to Ramallah, when she abruptly ordered the writers to boycott the lunch. (Ironically, one month later, after Hamas took control of the Gaza Strip, its militias routing the forces of Fatah, the mainstay of the PLO, the Bush administration reversed its no-contact policy with Fatah, hoping to strengthen its tenuous hold on the West Bank.)

The next morning, during a class at Bir Zeit University, where a blind English professor and her students listened politely to our discussion of writing and literature, I held out hope that friendship would trump politics. But after the session, when I walked out into the blinding sunlight, my heart sank. The white walls of the engineering building were plastered with posters announcing the agenda of the Hamas-led Islamic Bloc, which had just won the student council elections. Their message was unambiguous: We have a solid plan to kidnap Zionist soldiers, and our elite Mujahideen are ready to act. And: One of our women in prison was attacked by three Zionists. And: We have captured a group plotting to kill our children. Groups of students studied the texts, nodding in agreement. How to compete with *that*? I wondered. On the drive past the compound in which Yasser Arafat had lived under Israeli siege for two years until his death in 2005, I resigned myself to not seeing my friends. And in the restaurant we stood around the table, in an uncomfortable silence, until it became clear that I should ask the *maitre d'* to seat us in the main part of the restaurant, without the centerpiece.

Presently we were joined by the blind English professor who had hosted us at the university and a Sorbonne-educated translator. When the waiter brought food to the table, the professor asked the translator to teach her the secret of making stuffed grape leaves. The translator folded a piece of pita bread into the blind woman's hands, then cupped them in her own, explaining how to measure the filling for each leaf. The professor applauded her vivid description, and said that she should host a cooking show on television—an idea that the translator found preposterous. She had given up her professorship because of the army checkpoint near the entrance to the university—she lived in daily fear of being arrested and deported to the Gaza Strip, the residence listed on her identity card, which made no mention of her marriage. Indeed it had taken her eight years of pleading with the Israeli authorities to add her children's names to her identity card—which simply meant that if she was deported she could take them with her. She looked at me.

"The Israelis are very generous," she said, deadpan.

She had met her husband in Canada, and in the first flush of hope after the signing of the Oslo Peace Accords they returned to Palestine, settling in the West Bank—a better place to find jobs and start a family, they thought, than in her native Gaza. But then her mother took sick, her father had to hire a taxi from Gaza to visit her in the hospital in Jerusalem, no one was with her when she died. It took a full day to retrieve her body—and this was as nothing compared to what happened when her father died. He never met his grandchildren, and she could not attend his funeral, for the second *intifada* had closed everything down. It was a wonder that she had convinced the authorities to add her children's names to her identification card. They still refused to recognize her marriage.

"Very generous," the translator repeated.

Our conversation turned to the security wall built to protect Jewish settlements on the West Bank—hundreds of kilometers of concrete barriers snaking through Palestinian land, dividing families and farms. Palestinians viewed the wall as another land grab, in violation of the Geneva Convention prohibiting an occupying power from settling land under its control. Israelis argued that it prevented suicide bombings. Both were true. At this table everyone had a story to tell: how a woman accustomed to crossing the street several times a day to check on her elderly mother had to drive for forty-five minutes to a checkpoint where she might wait for an hour or more, depending on the guard's mood, before learning whether she could even continue her journey; how a muralist was turning his portion of the wall into a rural scene, all trees and fields, until an army patrol ordered him to paint it over; when he argued that the Israeli side of the wall was decorated in a similar fashion, the soldiers aimed their guns at him; and so on.

The muralist's response to the new constructions was of a piece with the wartime efforts of some inspired men and women in Sarajevo who tried to lift the siege through acts of the imagination. They staged plays in unheated theaters, arranged concerts, published books; on the wall raised to defend civilians against snipers, a makeshift barricade of shipping containers, dumpsters, burned-out cars and buses, cement blocks and sheets of plywood lining the streets and sidewalks, artists took advantage of dense fog one night to paint on the side facing the Serbian soldiers who had taken up positions in the Jewish Cemetery portraits of Slobodan Milošević and Radovan Karadžić, the orchestrators of the siege: to fire through the wall the soldiers had to aim at their own leaders—a symbolic way of forcing them to think before they shot. Thus art can turn the world upside down.

Not this day, though. The mood of the table grew darker yet. None of us could find the words to change the atmosphere.

It's a time of walls, someone said, noting that American contractors were erecting walls around Sunni parts of Baghdad, accelerating the division of a city known for its rich mixture of people into separate confessions. Another mentioned the administration's plan to build a wall along the Mexican border to prevent illegal immigration. And on the drive back to Jerusalem a South African-born novelist remarked that the wall reminded him of his childhood experience of apartheid. I mentioned the ire that President Jimmy Carter's best-selling book, *Palestine Peace Not Apartheid,* had provoked in some political circles. The title alone was enough for several critics to accuse him of anti-Semitism.

"Looks like apartheid to me," said the novelist.

For some the wall offered contrasting visions of Israel—a law-abiding democracy protecting its citizens or an imperial power encroaching on occupied lands in defiance of international law. Israel or Greater Israel? The grievous divide between Arabs and Jews brought to mind an afternoon in Tel Aviv, when from the esplanade I saw dozens of kayakers paddling around a jetty, racing to shore, where a beach party was in full swing, and then, beyond the next jetty, a circle of women in burkas, holding hands in the waves. The two peoples were inextricably linked, as they always had been—and might always be, regardless of what form the wall took, imaginary or concrete. Now it kept out suicide bombers, a terror tactic brought from Beirut by the PLO upon its return to Ramallah, and protected the settlers, who often took the law into their own hands. Put it another way: the wall faced in both directions, as in the old joke. A woman tells the rabbi that her marriage is failing because her husband is mean. You're right, says the rabbi, and sends her home. The next day the husband tells the rabbi that his marriage is failing because his wife is mean. You're right, says the rabbi, and sends him home. The beadle cannot believe his ears. How can both be right? he asks. You're right! says the rabbi.

Perhaps the true meaning of the wall was to be found in Kafka's story "The Great Wall of China," which is at its heart a meditation on empire, an enterprise defined by the limits it draws on imagination and geography, the walls it erects in defense of—what? A political idea? A belief system? Access to natural resources? The Qing dynasty had fallen by the time Kafka wrote this story, in the winter of 1917, and with the Austro-Hungarian, Ottoman, and Russian imperial orders in their last throes he must have felt it was a propitious moment to explore the meaning of a timeless imperial image. His narrator, a mason who began his career working on one section of the wall, five hundred yards long, before being sent to a different neighborhood to build another section, is compiling a historical report on its piecemeal construction, in order to determine its role in preserving the Chinese empire. He admits that the empire's origin is cloaked in mystery—which may explain the strange tone of his report: his language is precise, measured, befitting his trade, and yet his narrative meanders in a dreamy fashion, images and ideas emerging with the clarity of a set of ruins encountered in an otherwise empty desert. There is no way to read these ruins, he suggests, except to wonder who built them, and when, and why.

"But how can a wall protect if it is not a continuous structure?" the mason asks—a question that remains unanswered, like most of his questions. For example, he recalls that in the first years of construction a scholar argued that the Great Wall would provide the foundation for a new Tower of Babel, the original having failed to reach heaven, in this view, not because God toppled it to restrain his children, confounding their languages so that they could not communicate, but because its foundation was too weak to support the structure. "How could the wall, which did not form a circle, but only a sort of quarter- or half-circle, provide the foundation for a tower?" the mason wonders—another unanswered question highlighting the inexplicable fact that at a critical moment in history an entire people joined forces to build the Great Wall.

On whose order, though? The narrator cautions against speculating about imperial decrees, and then proceeds to do just that, reflecting that the high command may have "existed from all eternity, and the decision to build the wall likewise." He concedes that the empire is immortal, but what of the emperor, perhaps the only one who understands the purpose of the Great Wall? Is he even alive? The mason explains the situation in a parable, published separately as "A Message from the Emperor" (the complete story did not appear in print until after Kafka's death), which points to the fundamental enigma of our walk in the sun: we never learn what it was all about.

The parable, then: the emperor has a message for you, dictated on his deathbed, and so his messenger, "a powerful, an indefatigable man," sets out on a journey, wading through the crowds in the inner chambers of the palace, the symbol of the sun glittering on his chest. But there are too many people, thousands of years pass and still he has not reached the outer gate, beyond which he will have to fight through the sediment of the imperial capital, the center of the world—an impossibility. "But you sit at your window when evening falls and dream it to yourself," the mason concludes.

The message remains a dream, haunting and inscrutable, like all the fictional dreams that Kafka consigned to the dustbin. ("The Great Wall of China" was among the writings that he instructed his literary executor, Max Brod, to burn—an order that, fortunately, Brod ignored.) About one thing the mason is chillingly clear: "Human nature, essentially changeable, unstable as the dust, can endure no restraint. If it binds itself it soon begins to tear madly at its bonds, until it rends everything asunder, the wall, the bonds, and its very self." Such was the feeling in the Occupied Territories: the Palestinians might take matters into their own hands at any moment, tearing off their bonds, with incalculable consequences.

Walls, walls, walls. I did not travel much before the Berlin Wall came down—the event that inspired my wanderlust, my urge to chronicle life abroad—and in my years on the road I had come to regard the construction of any wall, piecemeal or systematic, in personal or political realms, as a sign of decay. Thus I marked the beginning of the end of the occupation of

Palestine. No telling how long it would take. "Against whom was the Great Wall to serve as a protection?" Kafka asks. There is no answer.

Our Palestinian driver sped down the road built for the settlements, which with Israeli military bases occupy more than half of the West Bank; the walls surrounding them were topped with barbed wire. There were no other cars on the road.

"Paid for with your tax dollars," he joked.

The diplomat had to be out of the Old City by dusk, and as she led us down narrow lanes seeking a familiar landmark I recalled the Syrian doctor's request to portray Jerusalem for her in an e-mail—without mentioning the name of the city that she was forbidden to visit. It was a request suited to Italo Calvino's *Invisible Cities*, a marvelous fiction in which Marco Polo tells Kublai Khan stories about the cities that he has visited in the Tartar's empire—fantastic cities that he calls thin cities, trading cities, cities and memory, cities and desire, cities and the dead, continuous cities, hidden cities. The aging emperor, seeking a pattern in the explorer's tales, realizes that each city is the same. What will remain of the city after he and his empire are gone? Fifty years after Saint-John Perse celebrated the founding of a mythical Central Asian city, reviving the epic tradition in order to explore the mechanism by which civilizations rise and fall, Calvino discovered that just as the structures of empire and belief differ only in particulars so the essence of a city is everywhere the same. What Calvino and Perse knew was that different ways of being in the world may look remarkably similar from a distance.

As the diplomat described the security situation—she would be a prize catch for Islamic militants—I sought a pattern in our journey from Syria to Jordan to Israel and the West Bank, through cities that in memory were blending together—cities that from the beginning of civilization had belonged to a succession of political empires and orders, the births and deaths of which were usually violent. How to describe a walled city, less than a half square mile, with arguably the most contested history of any place on earth—a city razed and rebuilt, razed and rebuilt? Some of the holiest sites of Judaism, Christianity, and Islam are located here, and to recite their names—the Temple Mount, the Church of the Holy Sepulchre, the Dome of the Rock—is to rehearse monotheism's tangled history. Archaeology in the Old City is thus never pure science: excavations are political events in a place in which even a walk can carry political meaning. All it took to set off the second Palestinian *intifada,* for example, was for an Israeli politician, Ariel Sharon, to stroll to the Temple Mount and declare that it would always remain under Israeli control.

There is no more contentious holy site than the Temple Mount, a complex set on a hill, which remains largely unexcavated. This is where the Jewish temple, God's earthly dwelling place, was twice built and twice destroyed, first by the Babylonians in 586 BC, then by the Romans in 70 AD; it is said that the third and final temple will be raised here when the Messiah prophesied in the Old Testament comes to bring peace on earth; Jews gather at the Western Wall, an exposed section of the ancient wall, to praise God, pray for mercy, commemorate the temple's destruction. Christians meantime believe that the Messiah has already appeared, in the figure of Christ Jesus: on his visit to the temple he overturned the tables of the money changers, accusing them of converting the sanctuary into a den of thieves. "Destroy this temple," he told his fellow Jews, who mistakenly believed that he was referring to the temple built by Herod, "and in three days I will raise it up." Indeed he was prophesying his resurrection: just as he was raised from the dead, so his followers, the living stones of the church, make of their own flesh a temple, in preparation for his Second Coming. And the Temple Mount is Islam's third holiest site, after Mecca and Medina. It was from here that Muhammad ascended into heaven on a flying white horse with the archangel Gabriel during a night journey in 621. It is said that the Prophet knelt in the ruins of the temple built by King Solomon in the tenth century BC to replace the tabernacles central to Jewish worship, and received a revelation to pray five times a day; hence the construction of the Al-Aqsa Mosque, the Farthest Mosque, after the Muslims conquered Byzantine Jerusalem in 638; the Dome of the Rock, the oldest Islamic shrine, modeled after the Church of the Holy Sepulchre, is said to contain the foundation stone of the temple—and on it goes.

Mark the progression from the Jewish temple built to provide a permanent home for the tabernacle, the portable dwelling place of the divine, to the Christian vision of the body as a temple housing the spirit, to the Islamic veneration of Muhammad's ascent into heaven. Three different ways of conceiving of salvation, each tracing a route from the visible world to the invisible. The ceremonies, rituals, and wisdom guiding the faithful on their earthly journeys have more in common among the Abrahamic faiths than we might imagine. In fact more binds together these monotheistic faiths rooted in the desert (traditions of prophets and revelations, of ethics and eschatology) than divides them—and yet what blood flows from the differences. Thus some rabbis called on the Israeli authorities to erase signs of Islamic presence on the Temple Mount after Israel conquered Jerusalem in the Six Days' War: every army in the Holy Land must decide whether to cut the Gordian knot of its common past; a history of razed synagogues, churches, and mosques suggests that many conquerors prefer to start anew rather than find common ground. But in 1967 Israel chose to preserve the holy places under its control, renovating them regardless of how they were damaged. And while extremists on all sides wished to rid the Old City of their enemies I retained through the darkening lanes an image of a Jewish settler that I had seen earlier in the day. He was packing a pistol outside his jacket, leaning over the rail above an excavated section of the Cardo Maximus—the Byzantine Road, a line of marble pillars and wooden roof planks leading to a modern shopping mall, which gives way to the Arab bazaar, in the middle of which a band of Japanese Christians was following their guitar-playing pastor, singing hymns in English.

It was dizzying.

Every stone in the Old City is a symbol of division, the full force of which came home to me in the Church of the Holy Sepulchre, in the press of tourists wending through the chapels. Saint Helena's journey to the Holy Land in 326, at the behest of her son, Emperor Constantine, had both religious and political implications: the churches that she built on sites commemorating the life of Jesus served as imperial outposts, none more important than the one raised near the hill that generations of Christians had venerated as Golgotha, where Jesus was crucified. Constantine's relationship to Christianity remains unclear—the story goes that he waited until he was on his deathbed to convert—though his pious mother sanctified his marriage of faith and power, claiming to discover Christ's tomb, which became the centerpiece of the church, as well as the True Cross—which was stolen in a Persian raid three centuries later, recovered, and then distributed, in splinters, throughout the empire. Politics was thus inscribed in the very stones of the Church of the Holy Sepulchre, which over the centuries was repeatedly attacked. When Jerusalem fell to the Muslims, though, the caliph vowed to preserve the holy places—a policy that did not hold. Indeed the razing of the Church of the Holy Sepulchre, in 1009, laid some of the groundwork for the Crusades, the fallout from which continues to shape the region.

Just as the Abrahamic faiths are defined by division, within and from one another, so Christendom's divisions are mirrored in this church, the custodianship of which is shared by the Greek Orthodox, Roman Catholic, and Armenian Apostolic Churches, with Coptic, Ethiopian, and Syrian Orthodox monks caring for some of the shrines. The legacy of the schism in 1054, which divided Eastern and Western Christendom, Constantinople and Rome, suffuses the dank corridors and chapels of the darkening church, the walls of which have been stained by centuries of burning incense. Under Ottoman rule, Franciscan and Orthodox monks fought for control of the church; hence the keys were given to two Muslim families who to this day lock the monks inside at dark and unlock the doors again at dawn. No denomination, it seems, can abide another. A monk keeping watch from the roof moves his chair into the shade, and fists are raised. The Benedictine monks singing vespers during my visit, processing through the Greek Orthodox chapel, were courting disaster.

Near the entrance to the church was a wooden ladder, which had been leaning against the wall, in the same position, for over a hundred and fifty years. No one dared to move what had become an emblem of the *status quo*, the nineteenth-century diplomatic term applied to the custodianship of Christian holy sites in Palestine in the waning years of the Ottoman era. The existing state of affairs has special meaning in the Church of the Holy Sepulchre, where the different denominations argue regularly over who should take care of what in the common area. The result is that no one takes care of anything; hence the dilapidated air of Christianity's holiest site—the soot-stained murals, the dust, the piles of debris in the corners. Which is to be expected: the status quo invariably leads to a hardening of attitudes—and neglect. The church is badly in need of restoration, and no one can agree on a course of action to save it from falling into further disrepair. The ladder brought to mind the imperative of the seventh-century saint, Isaac of Syria: "The ladder that leads to the Kingdom is hidden within your soul. Flee from sin, dive into yourself, and in your soul you will discover the stairs by which to ascend." But those steps were difficult for many Christians to divine in such a politically charged atmosphere.

It is ever thus. There was a moment after 9/11 when much of the world seemed to unite in its rejection of al-Qaeda: an opportunity squandered by the Bush administration. What skilful diplomacy might have produced at that turning point in history will never be known. But what if the White House had attempted to lead people in a common effort to defeat terrorists instead of dismissing its allies, questioning the patriotism of Americans who disagreed with its tactics, and driving a wedge between us and the rest of the world? It may be politically expedient to appeal to the public's fears rather than to encourage (*en* + *courage*) brave deeds for the larger good. And surely the history of Christianity suggests the difficulty of uniting even in the service of a common faith. But grave threats can clarify what needs to be done, for individuals and nations alike, if sufficient courage can be mustered. Leadership consists in summoning every one of us to a larger vision of what we can make of our lives. This George W. Bush did not do—although it must be said that whatever else he hoped to accomplish by invading and occupying Iraq he had surely upset the status quo, as the unrest throughout the region illustrated. Thus the increased level of risk faced by the diplomat who was escorting us through the Old City.

She stopped at the end of an alley and suggested that we retrace our footsteps to the Via Dolorosa, the Way of Grief, the route that Jesus took to his crucifixion, which Christian pilgrims have followed for centuries. Halfway up a hill, not far from the Church of the Holy Sepulchre, there was an Arab boy on a bicycle parked sideways in the middle of the street. He was singing Queen's hit song, "We Will Rock You," though it was not until we came face to face with him that I heard how he had twisted the refrain.

"We will, we will fuck you," he sang. "Fuck you." Then he smiled.

A few steps farther on the diplomat met an Arab acquaintance, who escorted us to the Damascus Gate. Muezzins were calling the faithful to prayer, church bells rang, the end of *shabbat* triggered a pilgrimage to the Western Wall—an eerie cacophony that seemed to presage the end of the world, as it always does in Jerusalem.

II

What a luxury it was to talk about justice in the House of Literature, on the Greek island of Paros, with fifteen writers from around the world. We convened *The New Symposium* one spring morning around a low glass table covered with papers and books, coffee mugs and carafes of water, with the light streaming in through the windows, and the first figure for justice to emerge from our discussions was of the blindfolded goddess holding a sword and scales—an American poet imagined the scales trembling. But when a Russian essayist invoked Dostoyevsky's image of a newborn needing food and shelter to describe the idea, a Greek writer recalled the retribution that his family had suffered during the civil war; an Algerian novelist, ignoring the civil strife in his country, railed against the forces of globalization; a Bengali's poem praising a group of mothers stripping off their clothes to protest a rape-murder committed by Indian paramilitaries prompted a Burmese woman to describe how she had survived a prison sentence by practicing Buddhism—and so it went.

One afternoon I walked from the hill village of Lefkes down to the sea, along paving stones worn smooth by a thousand years of use, between stone walls and terraces of gnarled olive trees growing since the time of Christ. From the dove house near the Church of the Holy Trinity came the sound of cooing, and from the far side of the ravine the gravelly voice of a man on a megaphone, offering *horta*—greens—from a pickup truck. I was seeking my own image for justice—an idea that in the American prosecution of the war on terror had lost meaning. The prison scandals at Abu Ghraib, Bagram, and Guantánamo Bay; the "extraordinary rendition" of terrorist suspects; the "disappeared"; the Justice Department memoranda condoning torture; the violations of the Geneva Conventions; the illegal wiretapping of domestic telecommunications; the suspension of habeas corpus—the bill of complaint was long. Can an imperial power mete out justice impartially? This was the unspoken question of our symposium, which the foreign writers were too polite to raise in front of their American hosts. Nor did they remind us of the moral authority squandered in our war of aggression ("the supreme international crime," according to the Nuremberg Tribunal) and occupation of Iraq. The ancient Greeks had a name for the sin, *hubris*, and if Congress would not hold the White House to account for its actions, a writer could record the costs and casualties, corrosion of liberty, decline of influence. In Greek tragedy there is always a reckoning for individuals contemptuous of the moral order. The same holds for overreaching states and empires.

The Byzantine trail was lined with poppies, thistles, and morning glories, and in the brilliant sunlight of the Cyclades I picked thyme, and sage, and oregano, rubbing the oily leaves between my fingers to smell their fragrances. Beyond a ruined sheepfold, by a stand of gorse, I stopped to gauge the distance to the windmill on the ridge, an excursion to save for another day, then turned to look at the hillside thick with pines, poplars, and the whitewashed houses characteristic of the Greek islands—a legacy of the Metaxas dictatorship (1936–1941). The decree to whitewash every building issued from the regime's ideological center, the Under-Ministry of Press and Tourism, to which the poet-diplomat, George Seferis, was attached. Even as Saint-John Perse navigated the corridors of power in the Quay D'Orsay, Seferis toiled in a press office modeled on Goebbels's Ministry for Public Enlightenment and Propaganda. He had taken the position to be near the woman who would become his wife.

"Wherever I travel Greece wounds me," Seferis wrote after sailing around Paros early in the dictatorship, in a poem that, in his biographer's words, elaborates "a bleak vision of Greece as a ship without a helmsman, bound on a voyage that has left citizens and political leaders alike behind." This was a story he knew well. He was studying law at the Sorbonne in 1922 when Turkish forces recaptured Smyrna, his childhood home in Asia Minor, and expelled his family; exile became his theme. His adulthood was defined by dictatorships (he began his diplomatic career under Metaxas and died during the junta created by the right-wing colonels who seized power in 1967) and departures. When Nazi forces invaded Greece, he served the government-in-exile in Crete, Egypt, South Africa, and Italy, bitterly noting that "Whether the entire population of my country is wiped out, or only half of it, will now depend upon the idiocies of the British generals." After the war, he held diplomatic posts in Ankara and London; served as minister to four countries at once—Lebanon, Syria, Jordan, and Iraq;

and made several trips to Cyprus to attempt to mediate what
he called "the mechanism of catastrophe" governing relations
between Greece and Turkey. His last posting was as the royal
Greek ambassador to the United Kingdom. He did not move
into his own house in Athens until he retired from the foreign
ministry in 1963; home was for him thus a matter of his relationship to the language, which for much of his working life
was constrained by his diplomatic obligations—reports and
briefings, meetings and receptions. There was so little time for
reflection that he feared he would turn into a machine.

"In order to speak at all, in a debased age," he wrote, "it's perhaps necessary—perhaps you can't do otherwise—to speak in
its language. This doesn't mean that you accept it." Commerce,
politics, the media—these are the chief means by which language is debased in the modern world, and Seferis's refusal in
his literary work to accept the ways in which it can be used
to falsify experience earned him the Nobel Prize in 1963—the
third diplomat-writer to win the award in four years, after Perse
and the Yugoslav novelist Ivo Andrić. His banquet speech in
Stockholm concluded with these prophetic lines:

> In our gradually shrinking world, everyone is
> in need of all the others. We must look for man
> wherever we can find him. When on his way to
> Thebes Oedipus encountered the Sphinx, his
> answer to its riddle was: "Man." That simple
> word destroyed the monster. We have many
> monsters to destroy. Let us think of the answer
> of Oedipus.

Global problems, Seferis argued, cannot be resolved without
a general recognition of the commonality of human experience.

More binds us together than divides us ("everyone is in need of all the others"), even if it is sometimes easier to define oneself against the Other than to look for Man—a vision, that is, rooted in our common destiny, with which to destroy the monsters that threaten on all sides, in every age.

And this vision can only be cultivated by finding the right names for things. How else to analyze a problem than to accurately describe it? For example, the monster unleashed on 9/11, which George W. Bush had misnamed the War on Terror. The United States could not slay it alone; and since power is as much a matter of perception as of economic and military might the fact that in Iraq some well-aimed stones, in the form of improvised explosive devices, had stopped the American Goliath in its tracks was not lost on anyone inclined to wage asymmetrical warfare, the phrase du jour in foreign policy circles. Every occupation produces a David capable of bringing down a great power.

If an empire collapses from within, its decline may well become apparent first on its periphery; and as I continued down the trail, with lizards scattering into the brush and swallowtail butterflies alighting in the trees, I recalled how Arab, Persian, and Ottoman armies had nibbled away at the Byzantine Empire in the Holy Land and Anatolia, until Constantinople fell in 1453. But it was the Latin Church that delivered the decisive blow to Eastern Christendom when in 1204 the Venetian armies of the Fourth Crusade sacked Constantinople instead of liberating Jerusalem from Muslim control. The Great Schism of 1054 between Rome and Constantinople was sealed in blood, the Byzantine order fatally weakened, the way cleared for the arrival of the conquering Turks.

In Parikia, the capital of Paros, in the Byzantine Church of One Hundred Doors, I had stood under the dome, gazing at a silver-plated icon of the Madonna, marveling at the survival of this beautiful church. It was built on Saint Helena's promise to the Parians, on her journey to the Holy Land, that if she discovered the True Cross she would raise on the site of their pagan temple a church with a hundred doors—though only ninety-nine have been found; legend has it that the missing door will not be revealed until Constantinople is returned to the Greeks. And it occurred to me that just as monastics devote themselves to prayer and fasting, seeking to unite their wills with God in order to find the doorway to eternity, so the missing door of this church might serve as a figure for justice—which may not be found on earth, as Seferis well knew.

For Holy Week in 1954 he traveled to Jerusalem, which was then part of Jordan, and on Good Friday, in the monastery of Saint Sabba, in the dry hills west of the Dead Sea, where it seemed to him that Greek Orthodoxy was dying and only Byzantium survived, the service disappointed him. "Impossible to imagine the human capacity for making a mess of things," he wrote. "Here in these holy places, we've turned the burial of Christ into an excuse for bombast." Then he remembered the acts of devotion performed by old women staying there, one of whom had passed away that very morning. The abbot who told him about it was joyful, and the other pilgrims "experienced this death as though it had been a blessing. I don't know why one might say that it wasn't."

There is in fact a religious element in Seferis's work. The Orthodox faith in which he was raised, his love of the Greek landscape, his grasp of the continuity between the prophecies of the Delphic Oracle and the lines of thought traced in modern poetry—these gave him a large view of religion's role in life. "The gods are born immortal," he said, "but they die." What replace them are orders of understanding—religious, philosophical, political—in which poets search for a language adequate to experience. Like T. S. Eliot, with whom he was in poetic dialogue for decades, Seferis explored not only the vitality of various literary traditions but also the connection between the sacred and the secular.

"The end point to which the poet reaches out," he wrote, "is to be able to say, 'Let there be light,' and for there to be light."

But the light that he made in the fall of 1966, with the publication of his most devotional works, a translation of the last book of the New Testament, Revelation, and *Three Secret Poems*, was for many Greeks extinguished by the coup d'état the following spring. Seferis remained silent for the first two years of the dictatorship, declining on two decisive occasions to raise his voice on behalf of artists persecuted by the colonels. In the first instance the composer Mikis Theodorakis brought Seferis a tape of his poems, which he had set to music while in prison, and asked him to join the protest against the ban on his music—a pointless gesture, in the poet's eyes. Then friends of the poet Yannis Ritsos, who was under house arrest and about to undergo surgery, sought his help in securing permission from the authorities for Ritsos's wife to visit him in the hospital. Seferis was, in his biographer's words, "both moved and embarrassed by the request, soon afterwards withdrawn." His diplomatic silence spoke volumes.

He spent the fall of 1968 at Princeton, translating Plato, and at a reading in New York he was asked to comment on the political situation in Greece. He refused, to the audience's dismay. He would not criticize the junta from abroad, he later explained, and thus condemn himself to exile. But when he returned to Athens in the spring he began to consider speaking out, inspired perhaps by the freedom that he had witnessed in America and by his sense that the next generation would be destroyed by the regime's debasement of language. *Greece of Christian Hellenes*, the slogan displayed on signs everywhere, signaled for the poet the death of the three most important words in his lexicon, and he was moved to record a statement for the BBC, which was then smuggled out of Greece to be broadcast on the World Service and printed separately for inclusion in the newspapers.

"This anomaly must end," he told his countrymen.

The effect was dramatic. The regime eased its censorship laws, creating a space in which artists and writers could breathe again. What was for Seferis a personal liberation helped to spell the end of the dictatorship—although he would die before it collapsed in 1974, after a failed attempt to annex Cyprus led to the Turkish invasion and occupation of the island. His funeral in 1971 brought one hundred thousand people into the streets of Athens, in defiance of the junta, and as they followed the hearse bearing his coffin from the church to the cemetery they sang a forbidden song based on one of his poems, "Denial," set to music by Theodorakis, with the police looking on—a poem of renunciation for the love of his youth, which concludes: "And so we changed our lives."

At the base of the canyon was a bridge over a dry streambed, where I paused for a drink of water, and then I climbed up the trail, which the Parians once used as an escape route from pirates. From the next rise, where the wall had crumbled into a stand of gorse, I could see in the distance a steep hill overlooking the Aegean, Kephalos, atop which was an abandoned monastery surrounded by the ruins of a medieval castle. There was a story of a Turkish soldier dressing up as a pregnant woman to gain entrance to the castle; that night he opened the gate to let in his fellow soldiers, who sacked and pillaged it with their customary ardor; the queen threw herself off the cliff to avoid being taken prisoner.

I reached carefully into the bushes to pick from among the sharp thorns a coconut-scented flower—the subject of Seferis's final poem, "Across Gorse," written in the spring of 1971. On the day of the Annunciation, which that year coincided with Independence Day, the poet, his wife, and two friends escaped the crowds in Athens to drive to Cape Sounion, at the tip of Attica. On a hike to the ruins of a spectacular temple of Poseidon—the last sign of civilization for ancient mariners sailing away from their homeland—the poet recalls that the name of the shrub with the yellow blossoms has not changed since Plato's retelling of the Myth of Er, in which he introduced the idea (destined to become central to Christianity) that in the afterlife the just and unjust will be treated accordingly; hence Ardiaios, the tyrant of Pamphylia, pays for his sins, including the murders of his father and brother. He is bound hand and foot, thrown down, flayed, dragged across thorns of gorse, and then hurled into the abyss, "a tattered rag." This coded attack on the colonels, which layers a classical text over the feast celebrating the archangel Gabriel's revelation to Mary that she will give birth to the Son of God, compresses centuries of religious, philosophical, and political thought on the nature of justice into a crucial poetic act: the naming of things. Seferis reserved his last words as a poet—"Ardiaios of Pamphylia, the wretched tyrant"—to giving evil its proper name.

Plato settled the "old quarrel between philosophy and poetry" by banishing poets from his Republic. In the famous Socratic allegory, prisoners are chained deep in a cave from childhood with their eyes fixed in one direction, condemned to mistake the shadows projected on the wall for reality; the intelligible world lies outside the cave, from which one man escapes, the philosopher, who comes to see that the sun is the cause of all things, and then returns underground to try to free the captives of their delusions—in vain. For as his eyes adjust to the darkness they say that his ascent into the light destroyed his vision. He should never have left in the first place, and if he encourages others to follow him upward he will be put to death. Socrates concludes his allegory about the journey of the soul from the prison house of sight into the intelligible world, the dire consequences of which point to his own fate, with a memorable definition of epistemology:

> In the world of knowledge the Form of the
> Good appears last of all, and is seen only with
> an effort. When seen, however, it can only lead
> us to the conclusion that it is the universal
> author of all things beautiful and right, that it
> is the origin of the source of light in the visible
> world, and the immediate source of reason
> and truth in the intelligible world. Without
> having seen the Form of the Good and having
> fixed his eye upon it, one will not be able to act
> wisely either in public affairs or in private life.

Philosophers are in Plato's view best suited to grasping the Form or Idea of the Good, which makes them the ideal rulers of the utopian city-state sketched out in *The Republic*. Their education, then, is critical to the welfare of all; poetry must be avoided at all costs, since it represents things at third-hand, mere shadows of reality. This is not what literature offers, though, in its kindling of the imagination. Plato's mistake, as scholars have noted, was to think that a work of art can add nothing new to the available store of reality. But what Seferis reveals through the act of naming a shrub aright is a heretofore unknown connection between contemporary dictators and a mythical tyrant, which spurs readers to reflect on the endurance of evil and the elusiveness of justice.

Socrates invokes two figures for justice, which is for him a matter of establishing harmonious relations among the three parts of the soul (rational, irrational, passionate) and of the city (rulers, guardians, workers): for individuals, a rational charioteer driving a pair of horses; for the ship of state, a philosopher-navigator charting a course into port. A charioteer who cannot control his horses is doomed no less than the ship of state with the drunken captain at the helm—a common figure for America in the new millennium.

Plato disdained politicians because they tried to please people, and sophists because they had ceased to dispense wisdom (the definition of *sofia*) and instead employed their rhetorical skills not to discover the truth but to seek advantage over their rivals. Aristophanes satirized Socrates as a sophist in his play *The Clouds*, though the peripatetic philosopher understood the danger of using rhetoric to deceive. The noble lies told by the neoconservative thinkers (schooled in Plato) who dreamed up the invasion of Iraq; the distortions of language issuing from the White House—"unlawful combatants," "extraordinary rendition"; the rhetorical sleights-of-hand employed by administration officials to justify torture and circumvent the Geneva Conventions on the treatment of prisoners of war—these were exquisite examples of sophistry.

Take the August 1, 2002 Justice Department memorandum, the so-called "torture memo" prepared by Jay S. Bybee and John Yoo, which buttressed the argument made by the president's lawyer, Alberto Gonzalez, that the war on terror "renders obsolete Geneva's strict limitations on questioning of enemy prisoners"—a line condemned the world over. The memo was eventually withdrawn, but not before the damage was done—to countless innocent individuals and to the reputation of the United States. From Bush's decision to defy international law it was but a step to the prisoner abuse scandals at Abu Ghraib. Nor were the authors of the memo held to account—Bybee was awarded a federal judgeship, Yoo returned to his tenured position in the law school at the University of California, Berkeley. But what is needed in the face of an existential threat, such as the one posed by al-Qaeda and its sympathizers, is not obfuscation or sophistry, but a clear-eyed view of the matter, without which the ship of state is certain to founder.

Before me lay the eastern plain of the island (vineyards, olive trees, a scattering of houses) and then the sea, where I planned to swim. In addition to exile, diplomacy, and the Nobel Prize, Seferis and Saint-John Perse shared a love of the sea, and it was the union of a maritime sensibility and clarity of vision that made them my tutelary spirits: they inscribed into every line vast experience of the world, like sailors taking soundings. (Seferis titled three volumes *Logbook.*) No doubt their wisdom was hard-won. Their long hours devoted to the affairs of state cut into their writing time, and yet what glories issued from their pens, perhaps because they witnessed the making of history from the inside and then translated into verse some of the oceanic rhythms of their separate languages—the images and insights that crest in the fortuitous marriage of one word to another, the swells and waves of meaning that arrive as if from a great distance.

Two entries in Seferis's journals, read at a decisive moment in my apprenticeship, profoundly altered my understanding of the stakes involved in writing. On Palm Sunday, 1947, Seferis wrote "Yesterday I had the most humiliating idea I may ever have had in my life: to stop writing for a period of time—five or ten years, I don't know—to find a job that would allow me to save a little money, and then do what I want. A ridiculous thought; for living things there's no deferment." I resolved then and there not to defer writing, regardless of how complicated my life might become; for living things, no matter how insignificant they might appear to be (and what at first glance is more insignificant than the work of an apprentice writer?), must be cultivated at any cost.

Then there was this: impressed by a young supporting actress who reckoned that it would take her twenty-five years of hard work to become a good tragic actress, Seferis recalled a visit, during his student days in Paris, to the apartment of a violin bow maker:

> It was on the top floor of a house in the vicinity
> of the Gare du Nord. To the right, as I entered,
> an orderly pile of unplaned wood. "All this," I
> asked, "will you make it into bows?" "Not I," he
> replied. "It will be made into bows by my son;
> the wood has not dried yet." I was impressed
> by this consciousness of continuity. How many
> know to wait for the wood to dry.

That the respective poetic personae of Seferis and Perse seem fully developed from the first pages of their collected works is a testament to their good sense not to twist green wood into forms likely to crack. How to conduct a writing life complicated by work and travel? There were few better guides than these diplomat-poets.

Now in the rising heat I recalled an excursion on the first day of our symposium. The American photographer John Pack took us into an abandoned marble quarry, every shaft of which he had explored during twenty-five years of residence on Paros. Sculptors in antiquity had favored Parian marble, the most translucent in the world, and here were the slick white veins mined for statues, columns, temples, and the Acropolis. The air was cooler, and as we descended in silence, lest we trigger movement in the earth—though if it came to that, John said, there were worse ways to die than under a ton of marble—I ran my fingers along the dank walls and ceiling, bending lower and lower with each step. We were walking toward the center of the earth, and at the bottom of the quarry John instructed us to sit in silence for several minutes, in absolute darkness.

I kept expecting my eyes to adjust, but the darkness was so complete that I could only hear the breathing of my fellow writers. Deep in the earth, as on the mountaintop, we seek truth, the handmaiden of justice, and from the depths of the unconscious arise visions and myths: the stuff of our cultural inheritance. What came to me in the dark was an image of three Iraqi men on a street corner in Damascus.

"Now turn toward me," said John.

And then there was light. He had placed over his flashlight a thick piece of marble through which shone yellow light; and as we murmured our amazement at the stone's translucence, in what John called "the language of light" spoken by artists through the ages, I recalled Seferis's tribute to the special light of the Greek islands: "Today I understood why Homer was blind; if he had had eyes he wouldn't have written anything. He saw once, for a limited period of time, then saw no more."

We took another route out of the cave, stopping along the way to collect pieces of marble, and after climbing for some time there appeared far above us an opening in the earth, a circle of light, which for a religiously-minded poet like me pointed to God: a means of orienting myself in the darkness of my days and nights, like the light shining through the marble. When we emerged into the blinding sunlight, John suggested that we carry a chip of Parian marble with us wherever we traveled—which I do.

III

"The Lord Jesus passed forty days on earth after his Resurrection from the dead," begins the reading for the Feast of the Ascension, which I attended at the Church of Saint George, in the Phanar district of Istanbul. Commemorating Christ's ascension into heaven, on the fortieth day after Easter, the feast marks the completion of his earthly ministry. This is for the apostles the moment of truth: for weeks Jesus has told them about the kingdom of God, explaining that the promise of the Father is not to restore the earthly kingdom, nor to free them from the Roman yoke, but for them to "be baptized with the Holy Spirit not many days from now." And after he is taken up in a cloud they wallow in their grief until two men dressed in white admonish them to stop gazing skyward; they must prepare for his return, preaching the good news of his resurrection. That strangers must recall them to their mission reinforces the idea that the future of Christianity lies in the hands of men subject to the same doubts as anyone. Jesus will not return until the Day of Judgment; and yet the apostles, transformed by the gift of the Holy Spirit, will testify in his name, in the expectation that their faith will be rewarded, even if it costs them their lives. The Feast of the Ascension thus offers Christians a window onto the origins of the church, when for believers the leap of faith was the greatest.

In the rush-hour traffic winding around the Golden Horn I feared that we would miss the service. And when our taxi driver got lost in the narrow streets of the historically Greek district overlooking the harbor (*Phanar* means "lighthouse") a Turkish friend and I decided to walk to the church, past a succession of boarded-up buildings, some of which seemed to be on the verge of crumbling into dust. The population of Greeks in the city that they call Constantinople has declined steadily since the founding of the Turkish state in 1923, and as we hurried along silent empty sidewalks it felt as though we had entered a neighborhood of ghosts. Outside the small church, which for over four centuries has been the seat of the ecumenical patriarchate, Eastern Christendom's equivalent of the Vatican, my friend pointed to a video camera affixed to the top of the wall.

"Now the Turkish security knows who we are," he said.

If in the Byzantine era relations between the ecumenical patriarch, first among equals among Orthodox bishops, and the state (read: emperor) were complicated, then the gulf between religious and civil powers only widened after the fall of Constantinople in 1453. Nowhere was this more apparent than in the history of the Church of Saint George. Twice in the eighteenth century it was heavily damaged by fire, and twice the Ottoman authorities waited decades before allowing its reconstruction; when it was burned again in 1941, fifty years passed before the Turkish government authorized its restoration; in 1997, a bomb damaged its neoclassical façade, injuring a deacon; the list of indignities has steadily lengthened. Indeed the ecumenical patriarch occupies a precarious position. He must be chosen from Turkey's dwindling Greek population, which can no longer send prospective candidates for training to the patriarchal theological school, on the island of of Halki, the government having closed it down in 1971. The question of succession has thus taken on new importance, with the current head of the faith, Bartholomew I, in his seventh decade. And there was an air of resignation among the handful of parishioners, mostly elderly, awaiting his procession into the church—or so it seemed to me, though perhaps I was just tired. But I also knew that church history is defined in part by such congregations standing at the edge of the abyss, praying to be delivered to the other side. Somehow it seemed appropriate that the treasures in this church included the marble column on which Jesus was tied and whipped: out of his suffering came a new covenant between God and man, strengthened by prayer, vigil, and the Holy Mysteries.

Greeks were not the only threatened minority in Turkey. My visits to the editorial offices of the country's largest daily newspaper, *Zaman,* and an Armenian weekly, *Agos* (circulation, five thousand), revealed a major fault line in the republic

built on the ruins of the Ottoman Empire. Turkey is a big laboratory, the editor of *Zaman*'s cultural section said through an
interpreter. And after 9/11 there were plenty of politicians and
pundits who argued that the Islamic democracy straddling Asia
and Europe might become a theocratic state like Iran. He had
no patience for their exaggerations.

The Iraq War had caused serious problems for Turkey. First,
the parliament had voted down a bill allowing American forces
to invade Iraq from its soil, souring relations with Washington,
and now the fracturing of Iraq along Kurdish, Shia, and Sunni
lines had given Turkey's restive Kurdish population renewed
hope of acquiring a land of their own—a sensitive issue for
Turks, said the editor. Militants from the Kurdistan Workers
Party (PKK), a political or terrorist organization (depending on
your point of view) trying to carve an independent Kurdish
state out of the border region of Turkey, Iraq, Iran, and Syria,
had found refuge among their kinsmen in the Kurdish province of Iraq, where they could train and plan attacks on Turkish
positions. Turkish troops were thus massing along the border,
lobbing shells into an area protected by American forces. They
might even have to fight against their NATO ally—which did
not seem to faze the editor.

"Can we say that your terror is more important than our
terror?" he asked.

The main division in his country, he continued, was not
between Islamists and secularists, as outsiders seemed to
think, but between those who wanted democracy and those
who wanted to maintain the status quo. A history of military
coups to enforce a secular vision of the state had in this telling
left most Turks wary of the elites—Western-educated men and
women who aligned themselves with the generals to protect
Turkey from fundamentalists. But freedom of religion does not
mean freedom *from* religion, he argued. It was incredible for

him to think that Turkish accession into the European Union might depend upon whether girls could wear head scarves to school.

"This is a war of symbols," he declared.

There was no more prominent symbol than the Nobel laureate Orhan Pamuk. The novelist had been charged with "insulting Turkishness," a crime punishable by up to three years in prison, after condemning his countrymen for refusing to acknowledge the genocide committed in the last years of the Ottoman Empire. "Thirty thousand Kurds and a million Armenians were killed in these lands, and nobody but me dares to talk about it," Pamuk told a Swiss newspaper, provoking a swift reaction. Turkish lawmakers passed legislation forbidding such "insults," right-wing columnists said he should be silenced, and with his arrest more questions were raised about Turkey's suitability for EU membership. His trial in December 2005 was quickly adjourned, and the charges against him were dropped the next month—three days after the editor-in-chief of *Agos*, Hrant Dink, convicted of the same crime, was gunned down in front of his office, prompting another international outcry.

Not an exceptional assassination, was the cultural editor's verdict. Scores of writers and journalists had been killed in the previous twenty years, in what he called a kind of social engineering. He did not know which elements of the state or so-called deep state—a shadowy, anti-democratic security apparatus tied to the military—were involved in Dink's murder. But he did know that the mourners at his funeral, one hundred thousand strong, were trying to solve a problem that sprang from a dark source—which I took to mean Turkey's inability to come to grips with its past crimes against humanity.

"I personally do not accept that there was an Armenian genocide," he countered, his voice rising. "There was suffering on both sides. Armenians massacred Turks. The Turkish people have pride in their history. They gave safe haven to the Jews five hundred years ago. So how could they decide to get rid of Armenians?"

He could not stop himself, and so began a monologue, which went something like this: Some Armenian documents make claims on Turkish soil. Remember that Armenia is already occupying another Turkish state, Azerbaijan. But if Turkey is admitted to the EU it may have the courage to face its past. In fact for twenty years it has debated whether there even was genocide, despite Armenian efforts to block the discussion, supported by their lobby in Washington. And everyone knows how strong their lobby is.

"This is an ontological issue for Armenians," he said. "It's very difficult for them to leave aside their suffering and come to a point where they can have a debate."

What to say? Debating the historical record is an essential part of denying crimes against humanity, as is blaming the victims. Our meeting drew to a close.

On to Harbia, the upscale neighborhood in which *Agos* was located: an unlikely setting, it seemed to me, for an execution-style murder. But one winter morning a young man from the provinces, who had never visited Istanbul, was delivered to the entrance of the Armenian weekly, where he shot Dink in cold blood, then made his escape. The guard posted at the door was new, and as I climbed the stairs to a suite of narrow rooms, which in their clutter resembled the offices of a literary journal, to meet the new editor-in-chief, Etyen Mahçupyan, I wondered if he worried about meeting the same fate as his friend. But this was not what he wished to discuss. He was a lanky, bearded man surrounded by papers and books, an academic (his doctorate was in international relations) wreathed in cigarette smoke, and he wanted to talk about living in a country ruled by an Islamic party. As a member of the

Armenian community (the first nation to adopt Christianity), it was his duty to speak to Turks about Armenia, human rights, and their obligations to deal fairly with their fellow citizens, irrespective of their nationality or beliefs, reminding them that in the Ottoman era they were instructed to treat Christians and Jews respectfully, as fellow members of the Book, second-class citizens though they were. But chaos had ruled in this changing land.

"No one is secure," he said. "If someone wants to harm you, they do it. Security is a mentality. If Turks want to live with others not like them, then there will be security. But the state is afraid to solve any problem, because if it solves one problem it will have to solve the others—Armenian genocide, Kurds, head scarves.

"We have become experts at postponing," he said with a flourish. "Most empires decline quickly. But it took the Ottomans two hundred years. Maybe it's still going on."

The argument that the Sick Man of Europe—the Ottoman Empire's moniker in its waning days—infected not only na-tionalists within its borders (Greeks, Serbs, and others seek-ing independence, Turks hoping to reform a corrupt political system), precipitating its demise, but also present-day jihad-ists around the world, rang true; for it was Osama bin Laden's dream of restoring the caliphate, abolished by the Turkish state in 1924, that ushered in the Age of Terror. If al-Qaeda's state-ments on the virtues of Islamic theocracy sounded like fevered babbling to the uncomprehending West, it seemed to me that their rejection of modern secular society was traceable to a common sensation—the vertigo induced by the fall of one civi-lization and the rise of another. I experienced a minor version of it myself later that day, in Hagia Sofia, the sixth-century pa-triarchal church converted by Sultan Mehmed II into a mosque and then by the Turkish Republic into a museum. From the second floor I peered over the railing into the nave of what was once the center of Byzantium, the New Rome, feeling light-headed and very sad. What bin Laden and his associates mourned was the loss of a glorious center—something that Greeks in Constantinople had felt since the Fourth Crusade.

It was true that the Greeks took back their city sixty years after the Crusaders had sacked and pillaged it, stripped Hagia Sofia of its most precious icons and relics (which were shipped to Venice and then distributed to churches in the West), and ruined any chance of reuniting Christendom. But the damage to the Greek soul eased the way for the Ottoman Turks, who made the Church of Holy Wisdom their symbol of conquest, plastering over most of its remaining frescoes and raising a minaret. The mosaics located high enough to be spared the whitewasher's brush—of the Virgin Mother and Child, of Saint John Chrysostom, of various emperors and empresses—hovered over the blank walls. And perhaps it was my own faith that attuned me to the power of these holy things lying just beyond reach. On pilgrimages to Mount Athos, in Greece, I had acquired a handful of icons—windows onto eternity, in the words of one theologian—to nourish my prayer life. All I could think about were the laborers assigned the task of gouging out mosaics, burning icons, obliterating the past.

Synagogues, churches, mosques—wherever I traveled I saw holy places razed in the name of another name for God; what haunted me was the sheer ordinariness of the work of annihilation. It takes nothing to lay waste to the sacred: from the destruction of Byzantine icons and frescoes by Iconoclasts, Crusaders, Ottomans, and Communists, to the mosques leveled throughout Bosnia, to the Taliban decision to do away with the pair of monumental statues of the Buddha carved into a cliff in the Bamyan valley of Afghanistan, there are always some prepared to destroy that which matters most to others.

To pack dynamite around statues labored over for decades, to set the timers, and then to step back and watch the stone subjects of more than a millennium of proper veneration crumble into dust—this is a timeless theme of history.

The monks processed before us into the church, chanting in deep, resonant voices, followed by His All Holiness in his ceremonial vestments. Known as the Green Patriarch for his interest in environmental matters, Bartholomew was also at the forefront of the ecumenical movement to reunify Christendom, divided since the Great Schism, splintered by the Reformation and Counter-Reformation, and subject to seemingly endless arguments, battles, and wars over the right way to worship God. The Turkish government did not recognize his Ecumenical title—which did not stop his reconciliation talks with the Vatican. Indeed he had recently received Pope Benedict XVI, only the third papal visit since 1054 (all in the last forty years), when the bull or decree issued to cast Eastern Christendom to the winds had split the church, hastening the dissolution of Byzantium.

Around the patriarch the monks took their places to celebrate the revelation that Christ is both human and divine—the central issue of the seven ecumenical councils, the only ones recognized by the Orthodox Church, whose spiritual leader stood among the faithful with a regal bearing. Orthodoxy means "right worship," and it was difficult for me to imagine a more complicated position than his: how to govern a worldwide communion of three hundred million people—how to discern the right path for the church, that is, based on his life of prayer and sacrifice, his knowledge of scripture and tradition, and his attention to the political realities of the modern world—from the margins of a society growing ever more hostile to his faith? The Greeks of Constantinople were almost gone, and there was talk of moving the patriarchate to the Greek island of Patmos, where tradition holds that the apostle John had recorded the Revelation, or to the monastic republic of Athos.

"O Christ our God," the monks chanted, praising his ascension, which united the earthly and the heavenly. "You were never separate but remained inseparable, and cried out to those who love You, 'I am with you and no one is against you.'"

It was comforting to be among believers, whose faith was perhaps no sturdier than my own. At the conclusion of the service, the Greeks approached His All Holiness to kiss his hand and receive his blessing and a small gold cross. He had a flight to catch, so he did not tarry afterwards, and as he hurried to his residence I turned to my friend.

"What will happen after he dies?" I said.

'Thanks God he has a long, long life," my friend replied.

IV

So this is how it ends, I thought, kneeling in the dust on a dirt road behind a mosque, with four Lebanese Army soldiers aiming their rifles at me. The noon sun beat down on my bare back, arms, and legs, a short, rough-talking major having ordered me to strip to my underwear, and as he scrutinized my passport his men went through my notes and papers, which included receipts for hotels in Tel Aviv and Jerusalem and a second passport acquired in the event that an Israeli border official stamped my first one, thus preventing me from entering Lebanon. (The two countries were technically still at war.) I lacked a press pass, which made my presence in the war zone suspicious. And my problems would be compounded once the soldiers discovered that I had also gone to Syria, another enemy of Lebanon's. How to explain the pair of laminated posters bought for my daughters at a convent near Damascus, the first showing translations of the Lord's Prayer into French,

Aramaic, and Arabic, the second a table of ancient alphabets titled *Syria Cradle of Civilizations*? Why had I not left them in my hotel room?

"Are you out of your fucking mind?" the major shouted. "Keep your hands up!"

"Mistake," I said. "Mistake."

"You're telling me," he said. "A big fucking mistake!"

My mistake had been to leave the apartment building from the rooftop of which British, French, and Lebanese journalists were covering the standoff at the Nahr al-Bared refugee camp, a few hundred meters away. Television cameras were pointed at the camp—a city, really, of thirty thousand—that borders on the Mediterranean north of Tripoli, and all morning ambulances had raced to its entrance to remove the dead and wounded. But there was little else to record beyond the occasional crackle of small-arms fire. *Relative calm*—this was how the journalists described the confrontation between the Lebanese Army and Fatah al-Islam, a Sunni insurgent group linked to al-Qaeda and, perhaps, to Syrian intelligence services. The insurgents had taken up residence in Nahr al-Bared eight months before, and then, one week ago, attacked army positions around the camp, killing several soldiers. Thousands of Palestinians fled the camp, and when car bombings resumed in Beirut and its environs the fear took hold that Lebanon's worst crisis since its civil war (1975–90), which claimed one hundred fifty thousand lives, might spark another conflagration. But today it was calm enough for a barber from the apartment building to give journalists haircuts. I needed a shave, but as I circled the roof, surveying our position—the white façades of the camp to the northwest, from which plumes of smoke would rise again once the shelling resumed; the orchard and gardens that lay between this building and the sea; the dirt road past the mosque to the west—the barber packed up his tools and left.

. The leader of Fatah al-Islam, Shaker al-Absi, had the usual terrorist pedigree—a history of dislocation, intelligence, and ruthlessness—to make him known in counterterrorist circles. Yet he remained a shadowy figure. News accounts suggested that he was born in a Palestinian refugee camp on the West Bank, immigrated with his family to Jordan after the Six Days' War, and left medical school in Tunis to join Yassar Arafat's Fatah Brigade. He was sent to Libya to train as a fighter pilot; flew bombing raids on Chad in a Russian MIG-23; helped the Sandinistas in Nicaragua. He rejoined Fatah in 1982, when Israel invaded Lebanon, and fought in the Bekaa Valley—from which he fled at some point to Libya, then to Yemen, and then to Damascus, where in 2002 he was arrested for plotting against the Syrian regime. In the same year a Jordanian military court sentenced him to death in absentia, along with the late al-Qaeda in Iraq leader, Abu Musab al-Zarqawi, for the murder of an American official in Amman. Unaccountably he was released after three years in a Syrian prison, and went on to found Fatah al-Islam.

Those who saw Syria's hand in the crisis at Nahr al-Bared, in a land just starting to recover from the previous summer's war with Israel, thought there was a connection to the impending UN vote to convene a tribunal to examine Syria's role in the assassination of Lebanon's former prime minister, Rafiq al-Hariri. This assassination had precipitated the Cedar Revolution—the series of demonstrations, hailed by the Bush administration as another hopeful sign in the democratization of the Middle East, that led to the Syrian withdrawal from Lebanon. The revolution had run its course, though, before the war with Israel, which Secretary of State Condoleezza Rice had dismissed as "the birth pangs of the new Middle East." And now it seemed that Syria was causing mischief again in its backyard. When a Lebanese novelist moonlighting as a television producer offered me a ride to Tripoli, I leapt at the chance to see what the mischief was all about.

From the roof of the apartment building it looked easy—to follow the dirt road behind the mosque down to the sea—and since nothing much seemed to be happening in the camp I decided to go for a walk. I had not gone far when a brown sedan drove slowly past, and as it neared the mosque a crossbar was lowered from behind a tree. Soldiers swarmed around the car, shouting at the driver, waving their rifles. I thought it best to turn back—and that was when the shots rang out. It took me a moment to realize that I was the target, as bullets flew by my head, and longer yet to stop in my tracks, which must have riled the soldiers even more. For now they were running toward me, screaming; and when they shouldered their rifles, taking aim again, I raised my hands.

How in the hell had I gotten myself into such a mess?

In Thoreau's essay on the art of walking (or sauntering, as he preferred to call it, in the manner of the medieval vagabonds who sought charity under the pretense of going to the *saint-terre*, the holy land: a dubious etymology), he contrasts the "courage" of those who can sit at their desk for hours, with the so-called vagrancy of the saunterer, who is in fact "no more vagrant than the meandering river, which is all the while sedulously seeking the shortest course to the sea." I found sanction for my restlessness in Thoreau's imperative to wander—in my travels I like to take the measure of a place on foot—and one metaphor seemed particularly apt for my itinerary in the Levant: "every walk is a sort of crusade," he wrote, "preached by some Peter the Hermit in us, to go forth and reconquer this holy land from the hand of the Infidels." Thoreau's spirit of pilgrimage into nature was what guided my exploration of the lands shaped by the original Crusaders and Infidels.

Thus on my first morning in Beirut, a week before my journey to Tripoli, I set off on foot toward the sea, and within a block of my hotel a soldier stopped me to inspect my satchel. The sun was bright, the wind was rising, checkpoints were set up on every corner of the neighborhood. Troops at a roundabout climbed onto a truck draped in camouflage; an armored vehicle raced down a hill thick with billboards of Rafiq al-Hariri; at the sight of a pair of tanks guarding the last intersection before the waterfront it finally came to me that the city was on war footing. The sea was before me as I walked toward the Corniche, the promenade of palm trees that led to the Saint Georges Hotel, outside of which al-Hariri had been killed in a truck bombing on February 14, 2005. The protests that began a week later against the Syrian occupation, inspiring Hezbollah to organize pro-Syrian protests, culminated on March 14, when hundreds of thousands of Christians and Sunnis took to the streets—the Cedar Revolution, which soon forced Syria to withdraw its troops and intelligence agents from Lebanon, ending thirty years of occupation.

The protests gave rise to a political movement, the March 14 Alliance, which, led by al-Hariri's son, Saad, swept to power in parliamentary elections later that spring. And in the post-electoral euphoria some believed that the Cedar Revolution reinforced the democratic trends set by the elections in Iraq, flawed though they were. But it turned out that al-Hariri's assassination was just the first in a series of bombings, mainly targeting anti-Syrian politicians and journalists; by the next summer, when another war was on with Israel, hope for real change had faded. Lebanon was regularly invoked now as an example of what Iraq might become—a fractured society ruled by a weak central government, with competing blocs buttressed by their own militias.

War seemed far away on a Sunday morning by the sea, as

couples strolled by, teenage boys played soccer in the sand or gathered on an outcropping to smoke a hookah, and swimmers stood by the shore as if debating whether to enter the water glittering in the sunlight. Yet there were signs of it everywhere: in the military vehicles wheeling by, in the piles of rubble, in the oil-slicked rocks—black legacies of an environmental catastrophe dating from an Israeli attack on a fuel storage tank at the power plant south of Beirut last summer. Thousands of tons of oil had spilled over a hundred and fifty kilometers of coastline, contaminating harbors, beaches, and historic sites, including a port used since the time of the Phoenicians. In some places the oil seeped a meter or more into the sand, the fisheries and nesting sites of endangered sea turtles were threatened, and after months of cleanup it remained unclear how much of the damage done to the marine environment was irrevocable, not to mention the harm to the tourist trade.

Uphill I headed toward Raouché, a fashionable neighborhood at the western tip of the city, and from the guardrail overlooking a pair of tall rock formations rising from the sea I watched a motorboat, in rough water, try to steer close enough to the arch under the larger rock to unload the boy on its prow. But the waves kept carrying the boat toward the other Pigeon Rock, which was in fact shaped like a boot, and it was some time before the boy managed to jump onto a ledge by the arch and start to climb the steep cliff, slick with salt spray. He slipped once or twice nearing a cleft halfway up the rock, where it looked as if he could secure a better handhold, and there he stopped, paralyzed, it seemed. A wild expression came over his face, he hugged his knees to his chest, and long minutes passed before he inched back down to the ledge, where he signaled for the boat to return. But the waves were too high now for his friends to pick him up, so they circled the cove, between the shore and Pigeon Rocks, waiting for the wind to die down.

Suicides favored the spot where I was standing—the jagged rocks at the base of the bluff had claimed the lives of the lovelorn for generations—and when I stepped back from the guardrail I noticed that the boy on the rock had caught the attention of an older woman, who did not leave until she saw that he was safely aboard the boat.

Crisis averted, I thought, and continued walking.

"We have harsh experience with this sort of thing," the former prime minister said of the fighting at Nahr al-Bared. "And there is no visible way of resolving the problem."

This was for Selim al-Hoss a variation on an old theme. An avuncular man in a drab brown suit, he joked that he was the only prime minister twice defeated for reelection. But he had also served three terms, and survived (a mark of distinction for a Lebanese politician), and as he held forth in a sparsely furnished office next to his Beirut apartment, trying to puzzle out the insurgents' identity, his country's precarious position came into focus for me. Lebanon's complicated political system, a product of the French Mandate following the breakup of the Ottoman Empire, was supposed to reflect its demography, with parliamentary seats divided evenly between Christians and Muslims, and with high-ranking offices reserved for members of specific religious groups; hence the president was Maronite, the prime minister Sunni, the deputy prime minister Orthodox Christian, and the speaker of parliament Shia. But no census had been taken since 1932—the numbers would reveal that Christians were no longer in the majority—and it was hard to imagine how the necessary accommodations to changed circumstances could be made as long as larger countries (read Syria and Iran, Israel and the United States) continued to meddle in Lebanese affairs.

Terrorism was for many the preferred method of addressing the new facts on the ground. Menachem Begin, the paramilitary leader, Israeli prime minister, and Nobel Peace Prize
laureate, said that terror was a matter of "dirtying the face of
power," an insight derived from the success of the Jewish resistance in driving Britain out of its Mandate for Palestine. And
it was terrorism, al-Hoss admitted, not politics, that led Israel
to withdraw its forces from southern Lebanon in 2000, his last
year in office.

"All Arab-Israeli wars end in defeat for the Arabs," he said—
except for the one on his watch, which ended the Israeli occupation. But he took no credit for the resistance mounted by
Hezbollah (the "Party of God" founded after the Israeli invasion of southern Lebanon in 1982): a campaign of kidnap-
pings, assassinations, and suicide bombings that profoundly
altered the political environment. The 1983 Beirut barracks
bombing, for example, which had killed two hundred forty-
one American servicemen, led the United States to withdraw
its troops four months later—a precursor to the Israeli retreat
in 2000. Supplied with arms and matériel from Syria and Iran,
Hezbollah further dirtied the face of Israeli power in the 2006
war just by holding out against a greater military force, inspiring other insurgencies—Hamas firing rockets from Gaza into
Israel, Shia militia in Baghdad launching missiles at the Green
Zone. And now Hezbollah had raised a tent city in Riad Sohl
Square, in central Beirut, to try to bring down the government,
paralyzing the political process.

"If we had real democracy," said the former prime minister,
"we would not have so many crises"—the civil war, al-Hariri's
assassination, Nahr al-Bared. "Since 2004 we have been in a
crisis punctuated by explosions. Somehow Lebanon could not
translate its freedoms into democracy. We are very vulnerable,

very open to imported storms, like the Iraqi storm. And the question is, why did America invade Iraq, if not for WMD, or 9/11, or freedom and democracy? I'm inclined to say for Israel. Iraq would always have been a lump of power in a regional war. Now it's not. Now the focus has shifted to Iran."

He rose to his feet—representatives from the Palestinian community had arrived, seeking his help in defusing the crisis at Nahr al-Bared—and on his way to the door he stopped, remembering something.

"On the last day of the war," he said, "the fighting was in the border villages. They went back to where they started after thirty-four days of war. This was the first time that Arabs stood up to Israel in a full-scale war. So Hezbollah is highly respected in the Arab world. Why, it's even dreaded in Israel."

The Hezbollah spokesman refused to answer my questions. A balding, bearded professor of law and political science in a blue blazer, he droned on in the lobby of the Bristol Hotel, describing the squalor of his childhood in a refugee camp, the birth of the PLO, the savagery of the civil war—which in his telling was started when a Phalangist militia fired on a busload of Palestinians returning from a wedding, killing forty. The actual figure was thirty, and he neglected to mention the fact that on the same day gunmen killed four Christians at a church in East Beirut. His monologue brought to mind all the potted histories I had transcribed in the Balkans: politicians and poets, soldiers and refugees chronicling in numbing detail the perfidy of their enemies, which seemed to stretch back to the beginning of time. When I tried to change the subject—Hezbollah's relationship to Iran was uppermost on my mind—the professor retreated even further into history.

"Shias have always been revolutionaries, since they began with a revolution"—and here he rehearsed the biography of

Ali ibn Abu Talib, the first relative of the prophet Muhammad to convert to Islam, revered by Shias as the true inheritor of Islam—"and so they view themselves as martyrs."

I was not sure what this had to do with Iran, so I pressed him on the matter.

"Hezbollah's victory in 2000 gave Palestinians hope," he replied. "Remember that the second *intifada* began four months after the Israeli retreat. If the weakest country can defeat Israel, then there is hope for more. Hezbollah is not a party but a religious national movement for a place with no history of nation-states. The propaganda is that Hezbollah is an Iranian compound, but Hezbollah is first Lebanese, then Arab."

I tried again, but he began to talk about Iraq.

"The war is a curtain to block our view of other dark matters," he said—namely, that Americans were using profits from stolen Iraqi oil to finance Sunni guerrillas in their fight against Hezbollah. "There is no doubt that the Sunni-Shia violent divide, the design of America, is to be repeated here," he intoned. "It's the same as when America and the Saudis financed the *mujahideen* in Afghanistan."

"Is Hezbollah still committed to eradicating the state of Israel?" I asked.

"The best way to bleed the Palestinians is to pit Fatah against Hamas," he said.

I closed my notebook.

"They divided the Arab world into twenty-one countries," the Palestinian said as nearby a sheik in a white robe climbed out of a Lexus with a Dubai license plate, "and now these people from the Gulf do not think of themselves as one people. But they are. I know it was decadent in the Ottoman Empire, but at least we were one people."

The Palestinian had buttonholed me in front of my hotel,

and after he went on for some time about the success of the caliphate in forging a common Arab identity I asked him what he made of the car bombing in Beirut the night before, which had killed one person and wounded a dozen more, escalating the crisis in Lebanon.

"Every day is pregnant with things happening," he said excitedly. "Everybody wants everything, and you can't have peace like that. All the Israelis want to do is talk."

"What does Israel have to do with this?" I asked.

"The Jews lost their way when they were expelled from Spain," he replied, "and now they work for the Anglo-Saxon Corporation. The real massacre will take place when the Western powers decide to push them into the sea. Arabs would never do that."

"I'm not following you," I said.

"If the United States could be fair, then peace would come," he explained. "But these stupid people think the situation will last forever. It won't."

"Which people?" I said. "The Lebanese?"

He rubbed his hands together, joking that people from Hezbollah do not like to shake hands because they fear receiving an electric shock.

"A war between gods is absolutely nuts," he said.

I had no idea what he was talking about.

South Beirut, a Hezbollah stronghold, was shelled continuously during the war, and as a group of writers milled near a gaping hole in the ground where a skyscraper once stood, surveying the charred buildings, rubble, and rebar twisting out of concrete like strands of hair, a Hezbollah foot soldier emerged from a café to tell us that we were not safe here. A construction crane loomed above—Lebanon was called the world's largest construction site—and in the hammering you could hear the death knell of the government. For in the aftermath of the war it was Hezbollah, not the civil authorities, which aided victims of the Israeli bombardment, handing out thousands of dollars in cash to rebuild their apartments and businesses. Lebanon suffered grievously for Hezbollah's miscalculation over Israel's response to its cross-border attack, but the Islamists won a public relations battle, within and without. Into the van we climbed, and on the drive by downtown Beirut we passed the tent city raised by Hezbollah in protest against the government. A history of tent cities flashed through my mind, from the military camps built by Genghis Khan for his warriors to the quarters arranged in Mecca for pilgrims on the Hajj to the tents pitched in the line of fire for prisoners at Abu Ghraib—a history of nomadic life, that is, into which I had stumbled, as if into a family feud. Anything could set it off again.

The rooftop of the Bristol Hotel had a good view of the drama unfolding after the second car bombing in two days. A white sedan parked at an angle on the next street had caught the attention of two soldiers, who dragged barricades to either end of the block to close it off to traffic, then snuck up to the car to look inside, as if to peek into a haunted house, and then ran to hide behind a tree for a moment before returning to the car—a spectacle repeated several times before an officer arrived and ordered them to keep their distance. The latest car bombing, within blocks of the hotel, had wounded ten people.

An elderly Palestinian couple begged us to come inside. They had returned to Beirut after long residence abroad, and they were keen to introduce American writers to the deplorable living conditions in Lebanon's twelve refugee camps. But their nostalgia for the city they had fled during the civil war vanished with the bombing, along with their desire to show us what life was like for the four hundred thousand Palestinians confined to the camps—miniature Gazas, they called them.

They feared that we would be targets if we stayed in Beirut and, claiming responsibility for our welfare, hired a van to drive us to Damascus in the morning. I went to my room to pack, recalling a conversation with an older woman on the Corniche. We had been discussing the fighting at Nahr al-Bared.

"This happens every spring," she said. "The planes are full, and then Syria makes trouble so that the tourists will go there instead."

On the road to Damascus were scores of billboards of President Basher al-Assad looking upward, as if slightly bewildered. Despite his puzzled countenance, there was no uncertainty about the outcome of the upcoming referendum on his leadership. Indeed the headline in the *Syria Times* made me think that the election had already taken place: "People countrywide voice full support for president's national policy." Evidently Syrians one and all had pledged their loyalty to the dictator, who was running unopposed. But with a stagnant economy, Iraqi refugees straining social services, the looming UN tribunal on the al-Hariri assassination, saber rattling by the White House, and chaos in the region, not to mention the fact that he was judged to lack his father's political savvy—and ruthlessness—al-Assad's grip on power was hardly secure. Hafez al-Assad had ruled Syria with an iron fist for thirty years until his death in 2000, creating a police state like Iraq under Saddam Hussein (though the two Baathist dictators loathed each other); when the Muslim Brotherhood rose up against him in 1982, for example, he had at least ten thousand people (and perhaps as many as twenty-five thousand) massacred in the town of Hama—a rare instance in recent history in which the brutal suppression of an insurgency worked. (The Chinese crackdown at Tiananmen Square was another.) The constitution was amended after his death to maintain the line of succession, lowering the minimum age for presidential candidates from forty to thirty-four—the age of Bashar, who gave up his ophthalmology practice to offer Syrians a political vision little different from that of his father.

In the capital were more billboards, with images of old men, women, and children illustrating captions like "I Believe in Justice," "I Believe in History," "I Believe in Childhood," and "I Believe in Peace." The last billboard showed al-Assad, with the caption "I Believe in Syria." He would take 97 percent of the vote to win another seven-year term in office.

Saint Thekla, companion of Paul, was one of the first Christians tortured for her faith, and for her suffering she is venerated in the Orthodox Church as a proto-martyr—a guide to open the way "through every torment," as illustrated by her own history of miraculous escapes from death and defilement. Born into a wealthy pagan family in central Anatolia, at eighteen she was engaged to be married when in defiance of her mother she sat by her window for three days and nights, listening to Paul preach the Word of God. She heeded his call to chastity, vowing to give herself to Jesus, and the governor, heeding complaints from her mother and fiancé, had the apostle arrested. She secretly visited him in prison, infuriating her mother, and after he was expelled from the city she persisted in her belief in the Son of Man. In a rage her mother demanded that she be burned at the stake. The governor obliged. Thekla was brought to the arena, where she made the sign of the cross before her arms were tied to the stake, and just before the fire was lit she had a vision of the Savior, which strengthened her. Suddenly the heavens opened, torrential rain and hail extinguished the flames, and the chastened governor ordered her release.

Banished from her hometown, Thekla traveled with Paul to preach in Antioch, where a nobleman became smitten with her. (She was considered a great beauty.) When she refused his hand in marriage she was condemned again, this time to be ravaged by wild beasts. She was led into the arena, and to the astonishment of the crowd the lioness loosed upon her first sat at her feet, then killed a bear and a lion, sacrificing itself for her. The rest of the cages were opened, and as the animals charged her Thekla climbed into a pit of vipers, where her prayers saved her once more. But the nobleman was not finished. He had her tied to a pair of oxen, and when they ran off in opposite directions to tear her to pieces the ropes slipped from her arms. Once again she was freed.

In 45 AD, with Paul's blessing, she settled in Maaloula, a village on the eastern slope of the Anti-Lebanon Mountains, fifty kilometers from Damascus, to lead an ascetic life. One day a pagan youth discovered her praying in the canyon above the village and cornered her, intending to spoil her virginity. Thekla prayed for deliverance, and the rock wall split open, revealing a way out. This was the narrow gorge or defile down which my friends and I walked in the morning sunlight, crossing a trickle of a stream under cliffs rising thirty meters or more; where the canyon opened into an amphitheater, with swallows and pigeons contending for perches, we ascended a rock face to a ledge in which graves were cut. We were coming from the monastery of Saint Sergios, which dates from before the Nicene Council, in 325, when Constantine's bishops laid aside their differences to affirm the doctrine of Christ's divinity: *Light of Light, very God of very God.* . . . Inside was a semicircular pagan altar around which Christians living in nearby caves had built their stone church, on the cool limestone walls were portions of recently uncovered frescoes, and our guide, a young woman with a beautiful voice, recited for us the Lord's Prayer in Aramaic— the language in which Jesus had taught his disciples to pray.

Aramaic, the language of the Middle East before it was supplanted by Arabic, has less than twenty thousand speakers left in the world, many of them living in Maaloula, a popular destination for pilgrims. *Maaloula* means "entrance" in Aramaic, after the defile from which we entered the village, and at the entrance to the Convent of Saint Thekla, above an icon of her holding a cross and a scroll, was a photograph of Assad. The church was closed, so I climbed a flight of stairs carved into the cliff back of the convent to a grotto dominated by a grapevine supposedly growing since Thekla's day. By candle-light in a further recess a nun was braiding a prayer rope, se-cured with a blue bead; against the wall of the cave in which the saint is buried were abandoned crutches—proof of her cura-tive powers. Thekla is regarded as the Mother of the Sick—the water dripping from the ceiling is said to cure flatulence—and I followed an Indian pilgrim to drink from the shrine of a saint glorified as an equal to the apostles. Her faith was such that a canyon opened for her, as the Red Sea had parted for Moses. Or was it the case that she had not noticed the cleft in the rock until her life depended on it?

How we fail to see what is right before our eyes, refusing to heed the call to love and faith and truth—which depend upon our recognition of what lies in the here and now, in what the poet Wallace Stevens called "the plain sense of things." Routes from the visible to the invisible are discovered in acts of attention—to the beloved, to the things of the world, to the historical record—and in this grotto it seemed to me that I had lost sight of something crucial. In Damascus the day before, revisiting the citadel and the *souk* and the Umayyad Mosque, I noticed little, wondering why on earth I had agreed to leave Beirut. And what I realized now, gazing at the mountains in the distance, was that I had to return to Lebanon. So a friend and I hired a taxi to drive us back that very day.

There was a long line of trucks carrying building materials wait-ing to enter the country, and while I waited for my friend to sort out a visa issue on the Lebanese side of the border I talked with an Iraqi businessman. He had taken a taxi from Baghdad, and now he was waiting for his driver to hire a Lebanese taxi to take him to Beirut, where he would buy parts for his road-construction firm. I asked him how things were in Baghdad.

"Americans hate Muslims and Arabs," he said. "All they do is bomb, and then they hand out a little money. It is the worst."

He placed his hand over his heart, bowed, and walked away.

Presently my friend returned. On the drive to Beirut, which included several detours around bridges destroyed by Israeli air strikes, we saw the scars of war—piles of debris, gaping holes in the road. The destruction of Lebanon's infrastructure in 2006 was of a piece with the damage done during the Israeli invasion in 1982, which had inspired Osama bin Laden. "As I looked upon those crumpling towers in Lebanon," he said in a taped message in 2004, "I was struck by the idea of punishing the oppressor in kind by destroying towers in America—giving them a taste of their own medicine and deterring them from murdering our women and children."

Past another fallen bridge the weather changed abruptly, from brilliant sunshine to thick fog, which slowed our progress through the mountains and brought us to standstill in the Druze town of Aley. "The fog of war," we joked when the traffic eased. Only when we arrived in Beirut forty minutes later did we learn about the car bombing that had wounded sixteen people near the main government building in Aley.

The café, founded during the war to house refugees, was popular with the intelligentsia, and the panel discussion, in a dingy side room that served as a lending library for books in English (*The Crusades Through Arab Eyes*, *The State of the World*, *Running Linux*), drew a crowd. Samir Kassir, journalist, historian, and critic of the Syrian occupation, had been blown up in his car on

June 2, 2005, a victim of the Cedar Revolution, it seemed, and the posthumous publication of *Being Arab*, his essay on Arab malaise, was a call to action from the grave. The mood in the room was somber. No assassination in Lebanon had been solved since 1976, according to the British journalist Robert Fisk, whose foreword to *Being Arab* included a haunting refrain: *So who murdered Samir Kassir?* The answer was plain to everyone here: Syrian intelligence agents.

But at issue this evening was how the rise of Islamic fundamentalism and the Iraq War contributed to the malaise that, as Kassir wrote, had "hollowed out" Arab history. "What remains is a state of permanent powerlessness that renders any chance of a revival unthinkable." No wonder militant Islam was for many Arabs their only recourse.

Rami Khoury, editor-at-large of Beirut's leading English newspaper, *The Daily Star*, took up the theme. "You have three hundred million Arabs," he said, "asking only one thing: to be treated as human beings. We must not allow these historical traumas to turn us into animals. The Islamists must not allow victimhood to dominate the political process. They don't give us a blueprint for positive change."

But the Islamists had created the most powerful movement in the region, and Arab intellectuals had to engage them, not submit to their dictates.

"We are all challenged to speak truth to power," said Khoury.

This was what had distinguished Kassir, and his writings against Arab victimhood gave Khoury hope, like the Cedar Revolution, which was a kind of awakening—even though Lebanon remained hostage to regional and global conflicts.

"The first time the word 'freedom' was used was in Mesopotamia, in what we now call Iraq," he said. "We need one Lech Walesa, one Poland, one breakthrough in the Arab world to bring all the tyrants down."

Kassir had gone to his grave less sanguine about the future. "But there's no talk of optimism," he wrote. "The Arab world, the Levant in particular, remains the prisoner of a political and social system that may allow diversity to express itself, but never allows it to translate into any change in the decision-making processes." Lebanon escaped the prison of Israeli and Syrian occupation only to be drawn into another war, which ended with Hezbollah on the rise. The assassinations of intellectuals added to the malaise. And now there was no telling what the fighting at Nahr al-Bared might bring.

After the panel I walked to Verdun, a Sunni district, to see the storefronts and apartment buildings gutted in the second car bombing of the week. The sidewalks were empty, the street lights out. I noticed a woman cleaning up glass from a shattered display window in a clothing boutique. Beirut had been called the Paris of the Middle East before the civil war, and even in the debris Verdun looked posh. The speaker of parliament and the minister of information lived nearby, the restaurants and banks would reopen soon, and the Russian Cultural Center had survived the blast—a message (for those who detected a Syrian plot) to the UN Security Council member, which said it would not veto the resolution on the al-Hariri tribunal. Maybe the truth about the killing of the former prime minister would emerge from the investigation. Maybe someday the assassins would be brought to justice. But I had a feeling that even as the panel could not answer the real question of the evening—*Who murdered Samir Kassir?*—so the truth about the crime that touched off the Cedar Revolution would remain hidden, perhaps forever.

Relative Calm—the title of a popular drama during the civil war—turned into the rooftop refrain as the day wore on, even as a sniper in the camp shot dead a refugee attempting to leave, ambulances retrieved the dead and wounded, and rumors flew: that the insurgents had honed their fighting skills in Iraq, that on the first day of the standoff they had slit the soldiers' throats, that one or more suicide bombers had slipped into the orchard in front of our outpost. Word spread that the army was preparing to invade the camp. It's only a matter of time before the region goes up in smoke, said a journalist.

Relative calm: a good time to go for a walk.

The occupation of Iraq—a study of decisions seemingly taken lightly, from the military's refusal to protect ministry buildings and museums from looters, to the disbanding of the Iraqi Army, to the use of Saddam Hussein's prison at Abu Ghraib—had stoked the fires of an insurgency, which was burning out of control. And if the inevitability of our failure in Mesopotamia appeared obvious to many Americans only in retrospect, hardly anyone I met in the Levant claimed ever to have imagined a different outcome.

Michael Young was the exception. The greying columnist for *The Daily Star*, who described himself as a Lebanese libertarian (he was in fact half American, with a degree from the Johns Hopkins' School of Advanced International Studies), applauded Saddam's overthrow—and mourned our failure to create a pluralistic society in Iraq.

"The only thing that interests me is freedom in the Middle East—freedom from these tyrants," he said when we met in l'Antoine Café, in the ABC Mall—the site of the first car bombing of the week. He wore a blue blazer and jeans, smoked a cigar, identified with the American neoconservative writers who had promoted the invasion of Iraq.

"What was important to me," he said, "was that if you could get rid of one tyrant it would affect the whole region. But the Americans screwed it up big time."

Iraqis were the victims of what he termed the Bush administration's lack of unity of purpose about the final aim of the war—a "classic bureaucratic shambles," for which he blamed Condoleezza Rice. As national security advisor she had ignored her charge to serve as an honest broker of policy differences in order to preserve her friendship with President Bush. She told him only what he wanted to hear.

"She was a realist, then she was a utopian, and now she's a realist," the columnist said. "Nobody knows where she is."

And nobody knew what to do about Iraq. Young foresaw a massacre if American troops were withdrawn, and yet their presence guaranteed more bloodshed.

"You have separate conflicts that feed off each other," he explained, leaning back in his chair. "But if the Americans leave, what happens to Kurdistan, Saudi Arabia, here, Iran? America is stuck in a dilemma. Maybe it's better that way."

Meantime Lebanon had to be saved. He said that Syria was playing out its future here, noting the proximity of the bombing in Verdun to the Russian Cultural Center.

"That's what thuggish regimes do," he argued. "Intimidate and provoke a reaction contrary to their interests: the Security Council vote on the tribunal. The Syrians want to have a say in Lebanon—i.e., to regain control. In this crisis they have a veto."

He accused the Syrians of systematically eroding the possibility of an independent Lebanon emerging from thirty years of war by assassinating their opponents, arming their partisans, and supporting al-Qaeda and its affiliates.

"If it's the Syrians," he said, "it's not subtle."

Just look at what happened to his friend Samir Kassir, who had been killed down the street from the mall. Did he worry that he would meet the same fate?

Young smiled. "I hope to live a long life!" he said.

Then he turned serious. "Let's win here, and then look

elsewhere. Our societies are deeply wounded, and I'm afraid that in response to the suffering we've moved toward religion. We had a moment with America, but it passed. The tragedy in Iraq is that they failed. Our only hope now is if Iran becomes democratic."

And with that he went off to browse in the bookstore.

From the mall I walked down to Kassir's shrine—an olive tree planted in front of a supermarket where the historian's car had exploded when he switched on its ignition. I was copying the inscription on the plaque when a young man from the apartment building across the street demanded to know what I was doing. I said that I was a writer, which seemed to make no impression, so I showed him my book about the Balkan Wars, pointing to my photograph, which he studied for some time before he walked away, shaking his head.

In a televised address to the nation, on the seventh anniversary of the Israeli pullout from Lebanon, Prime Minister Fouad Siniora praised the warm relations between Lebanese and Palestinians, and promised to rebuild the country, to organize its defenses.

"We will not be afraid of explosions," he declared, glossing over the situation at Nahr al-Bared. "We will not allow Lebanon to become a playground for conflict."

But it was widely believed that there was already a proxy war on between America and Iran, with Hezbollah threading a fine line between the combatants: the elected government, Syrian intelligence agents, and Israel, which many feared would strike again at the least provocation.

That night I met friends for dinner in a Maronite district of Beirut. We were sitting at an outdoor restaurant, under a grape arbor, when the air suddenly filled with the sounds of fireworks and gunfire. Everyone around us looked up, startled.

"What are they celebrating?" my friend asked her husband.
"Independence Day," he replied.
'Oh,' she said.

If weddings in the Old Testament are considered to be signs of God's marriage to his chosen people, the Israelites, then the wedding at Cana, in Galilee, where Jesus turned water into wine, the first of his seven miracles recorded in the Gospel of John, proposes a different relationship between mankind and divinity: a form of union, in which both Jews and Gentiles can participate. In this new covenant Jesus traveled into Gentile territory to extend God's blessing, and just as marriage creates a new familial order, making two into one, so the new religious order inspired by faith in the Son of Man remade the region and the world. The transformation of water into wine—the precursor to the Last Supper and centerpiece of the Eucharist, when Jesus is present in the communion wine—reveals how faith can reorient one's entire being: to keep the sacraments, to be conscious of last things in the way that Jesus counsels, is to know that water can taste like wine.

The story of the wedding at Cana appears only in the Gospel of John, the most poetic and perhaps least reliable account of Jesus' ministry, and biblical scholars question the miracle's authenticity as well as its setting. Faith in Christ depends upon belief in the defining moments of his ministry, which in John's telling include feeding the multitudes and raising Lazarus from the dead. The archaeological record is a different matter. Three villages near Nazareth have been identified as possible locations of the marriage feast, including Kafr Kana, the traditional site of the biblical Cana, where the Greek Orthodox and Franciscan churches attract pilgrims from around the world. Some archaeologists think that the nearby ruins of Khirbet Qana may prove to be the true site—excavations have uncovered an important building complex there—while Lebanese Christians claim that on his way to Jerusalem Jesus stopped in Qana, now a predominately Shia village by the Israeli border, to give the first sign of his divinity.

Wherever the truth lay, one overcast morning I hired a taxi to take me to Qana. The driver, a retired Druze engineer from the Chouf Mountains, near the fabled cedars of Lebanon (most were cut down long ago), stopped first at the Ministry of Information in Beirut, and after my request for a press pass was denied we set off down the coast, past fallen bridges, gutted buildings, the power plant attacked by the Israelis, a tank destroyed in an air strike. On the waterfront in Sidon, close to the place where Jesus is said to have healed the demon-possessed daughter of a Canaanite woman, fishermen draped fraying *kilims* over their nets, under the bleary eyes of old men smoking hookahs. Paul sailed from here, in the custody of a Roman centurion, preaching the kingdom of God until his martyrdom, and for some along this coast little had changed since his departure. Across a causeway and a marble column laid on its side I came to an islet of ruins—a thirteenth-century castle built by the Crusaders. Three Lebanese soldiers armed with submachine guns were exploring the ground floor when I climbed the tower to the roof, from which I saw a freighter riding at anchor in the calm water. The soldiers' laughter announced their arrival soon after, which was my cue to return to the taxi.

Our next stop was Tyre, the Phoenician port that in the early days of the church offered sanctuary to persecuted Christians, and as he navigated checkpoints, passing palm trees, smoking rubble, and green houses, my driver grew reflective.

"Maybe Israel will attack Hezbollah," he said, "but it must wait for America to give the green light. Nobody knows when. Maybe today, maybe tomorrow."

He parked beyond a tank aimed at a Palestinian refugee camp, leaving me to stroll in the Roman ruins, and in the midday heat I got as far as the triumphal arch, bordered by the columns of the aqueduct, before returning to wake him from a nap—which did not make him happy.

We drove inland on a heavily cratered dirt road, and beyond the UN checkpoint at the emerald Litani River we passed tobacco fields, terraces of olive trees, banana groves, scorched apartment buildings crowned with Hezbollah flags (a green logo—the first letter of the word *Allah* clutching a Kalashnikov—on a yellow background), billboards of martyrs and Hassan Nasrallah, the Hezbollah leader. On one rooftop was a poster of the Supreme Leader of Iran, Ali Khamenei, with a banner proclaiming: "This is Hezbollah!" On another was a rocket launcher aimed at Israel, next to a poster of Nasrallah.

"Before the war," said my driver, "no one heard of Nasrallah. He's from Lebanon, but he takes everything from Syria and Iran." His greatest fear was that Hezbollah would convert Lebanon into a theocracy. And when we arrived in Qana he said, "Do something for Syria. They don't know anything about democracy. Let America do that."

In fact six US C-130s had just landed in Beirut to deliver ammunition, night-vision goggles, communications equipment, and armored cars to the government, while Iranian president Mahmoud Ahmadnejad was warning Israel not to repeat the mistake of the previous summer by attacking Lebanon, promising to "cut the root of the Zionist regime from its stem. Sixty years of invasions and assassinations is enough!"

There may be doubts about the setting and authenticity of Jesus' first miracle in the Gospel of John, but there is no disputing the fact that Qana, Lebanon was the scene of two devastating Israeli attacks, in 1996 and 2006, the first of which killed over a hundred civilians seeking refuge in a

UN peacekeeping compound, mostly children. The memorial commemorating the victims of the 1996 massacre, which occurred during what is known in Israel as Operation Grapes of Wrath and in Lebanon as the Seven-Day War, consisted of marble tombs laid like plinths by the deserted UN barracks. In the exhibition hall were photographs of the horror, and from an old man I bought a grainy videotape shot in the aftermath of the attack. The opening sequence was set in the hospital, where the wounded were arriving in cars and ambulances. There were burned and bleeding children, doctors and nurses running from room to room, a rescue worker searching for pulses in two boys wrapped in a single body bag, women shrieking, men throwing up their hands—and then the video cut away to the scene of the massacre, the UN dining hall, where the walls and roof were gone and the dead lay in a great pile. Some peacekeepers hauled the wounded to waiting cars, some dragged corpses from the rubble or covered them with blankets, one dumped a dead child out of a plastic bag, another carried off body parts.

The journalist Robert Fisk and investigators from the UN and Human Rights Watch have documented the events of April 18th, 1996, and while Israel disputes their findings there is no doubt that war crimes were committed, perhaps on both sides. As usual, the victims were innocent. What happened was this: after Hezbollah fighters in a cemetery three hundred meters from the UN base opened fire on Israeli soldiers laying mines along a Hezbollah infiltration trail, an Israeli artillery battery laid siege to the base, where eight hundred villagers from the surrounding area had taken refuge. For seventeen minutes antipersonnel shells rained down on peacekeepers and civilians alike, while a surveillance drone and an AWACS plane monitored the action from the sky. The United States and Israel accused Hezbollah of using civilians to shield its fighters—a charge that, if true, constituted a violation of the Geneva Conventions—but this did not absolve Israel of the crime of launching indiscriminate retaliatory strikes.

On this day the cement floor of the dining hall was covered with dishes, bits of clothing, bloodstains. There was a smear of oil on a rusted Israeli tank whose turret was aimed at the church on the next ridge. A plaque read: Your silence makes you an accessory.

When news broke of the massacre, I was in Barcelona for a UNESCO conference on the reconstruction of Bosnia's higher educational system. I remember thinking that history could not have ended, as an American scholar famously proposed, if we were still fighting over the maps drawn up after World War I. For even as peace took hold in the Balkans among the South Slavic successor states of the Ottoman Empire, war was breaking out again among its successor states in the Levant. The Bosnian delegation had survived the siege of Sarajevo, the terror and privations and war crimes, and the news from Qana, which we monitored from the hotel bar, brought back the darkest memories. One professor recalled watching a CNN report about a sniper attack down the street from his apartment in Sarajevo, which showed an ambulance delivering to the hospital a girl shot in the leg: his daughter.

The issue in Barcelona was memory—the artifacts, records, and multiple meanings of which scholars and academic institutions preserve, explore, and disseminate. And it became clear in our discussions that the reconstruction of Bosnia's higher educational system depended less on raising money to rebuild the libraries, museums, and universities damaged or destroyed in the war (although considerable funds would have to be earmarked for that) than on designing ways to ensure that scholars and students could pursue knowledge in a rigorous manner, unfettered by fear. The Bosnian delegates argued that truth could not be discovered without a proper knowledge of what happened in these lands and why—not just in the distant past but in the war that had torn their country apart—and that without the truth there could be no justice for the victims of Serbian crimes against humanity. Classrooms and book collections could be rebuilt, but if there was no honest reckoning of the Serbian-run concentration camps, ethnic cleansing campaigns, and massacres (notably of eight thousand men and boys in Srebrenica), the likely result would be generations of embittered, and potentially violent, Bosnian Muslims.

Just so, Qana had become a rallying point in the Middle East. Two months after the Israeli attack, Osama bin Laden declared jihad against America, citing the massacre as a reason for Muslims to rise against the infidels. And the Islamists' righteous anger was redoubled in the summer of 2006, when Israeli jets struck an apartment building in a village near Qana, killing two families. History was repeating itself, they said.

I came to another plaque with this inscription:

THE NEW HOLOCAUST
18 APRIL 1996
UNITED NATIONS HOSPITAL
UNITED NATIONS OFFICES

It was monstrous to compare what happened in Qana to the Shoah—and yet it was a commonplace in this part of the world. The silence of the marble tombs said more to me about the horror of the crime than any spurious conflation of it with the Final Solution. Likewise the verse, from the Sermon on the Mount, inscribed on the plaque celebrating the service of the Fijian peacekeepers in Qana: "Blesseth are the peacemakers for they shall be called the children of God."

My driver said nothing on the way to the shrine, which had

opened just before the April war in a bid to attract pilgrims to what might be the site of the marriage feast. It was also possible that Jesus came through here after his ministry in Tyre and Sidon, then walked up the valley to Capernaum before going on to Jerusalem, perhaps following the path that twenty centuries later became a Hezbollah infiltration trail. The sky had clouded over, the parking lot was empty, and there was not a soul in sight as I walked under a grape arbor to the ticket office. A corkscrewing path down the side of a hill took me to a cave filled with candles where, according to local tradition, Jesus, his disciples, and his mother rested. At the wedding, when Mary told Jesus that there was no wine, he replied, "Woman, what have I to do with thee? My hour is not yet come." So she told the servants to do whatever he said, which was to pour water into six stone pots, such as the jars excavated from this site, and then he turned the water into wine.

Then I saw something remarkable: inscribed in a rock wall was the figure of Mary holding the infant Jesus. Then thirteen figures—Jesus and his disciples—and a profile of him, all carved, so it is said, by early Christians fleeing persecution, determined to celebrate their rabbi. "Blessed are the merciful," he said, "for they shall obtain mercy."

The sun burned my neck and shoulders, the stones in the road bore into my knees, and the soldiers surrounding me kept waving their guns. Nevertheless I felt a strange sense of calm, as if I was floating a couple of meters above the ground, watching a ritual in which someone who looked like me knelt in his underwear, leaning forward like a penitent, with his hands behind his head and an army officer screaming at him.

"Do you know what these men do?" the officer cried. "If I wasn't here, my friend, you would be a dead man. Do you understand?"

I nodded.

'Don't you fucking understand?" the officer shouted. "You have a beard. You have dark glasses. You have a hat. You have a black bag, for God's sake! You could have been a suicide bomber. What am I going to do?"

He paced around in a little circle, flipping through the pages of my passport, then stepped away to make another call. When he returned, he looked even more agitated.

'This is a military zone, man," he said. "Do you know how tense it is here?"

Again I nodded.

"Do you understand?" he repeated.

"Yes," I said.

He ordered me to put my clothes on, and when I had dressed he paged through my passport again, carefully examining each visa, each entrance and exit stamp, as if he had missed something the first time through. Malaysia, China, Mongolia, Syria, Jordan, Israel and the West Bank, Greece, Turkey—these were the names of the places flashing before my eyes. And more: Cyprus, and all the new countries in the Balkans—Bosnia, Croatia, Montenegro, Serbia, and Slovenia. And Myanmar and the DMZ in Korea. And the Czech Republic and Slovakia, Poland and Ukraine, Germany and France, India and the United Kingdom. And Lebanon. Places marked by division and conflict.

I was standing between two walls, two gardens, with my hands raised and a siren wailing near the camp, as a soldier read my notes: *Our relationship with tomorrow is sick,* a Lebanese writer had told me. *The word "tomorrow" means something different here than in Europe or America, where it means tomorrow. Here it means "maybe."*

There's something funny in Lebanon, the writer said. *People go to war as if they were going to a movie. Why not do something*

*to stop it? Lebanon is like a fragile plant growing in harsh ter-
rain, with elephants stomping all around it.*

There were notes from a conversation with a French television journalist who had borrowed clothes from a Palestinian
woman to sneak into the camp, which she called a tomb. She was
a striking, sharp-tongued woman dressed this day all in black
(black sweat suit, black sneakers), and every hour she would pace
the roof, memorizing her dispatches, after the recording of which
she would stroll to the restaurant across the street to smoke a
hookah. *When I went out, she said, it was like I had been in the
dark for three days. It's a laboratory of terror. A big jail. It's the
same in every camp, and the international community won't do
anything about it. When they want to invade Iraq in one year,
one month, they do it. And the hard men of Fatah al-Islam, the
terrorists who came from different parts of the Middle East and
married women in the camp, are ready to die for their cause.
We are not against them, the civilians say, we are not for them.
We are against the army that bombs us indiscriminately.*

A crowd was gathering at the end of the road, including a
British camerawoman I recognized from the roof. I figured that
having witnesses reduced my chances of being killed, though
not of being arrested and perhaps beaten. The officer looked at
his soldiers, whose rifles were still trained on me, then tapped
my passport on his palm.

"My men are on high alert," he said. "They would have shot
you if I wasn't here. Do you understand?"

I nodded.

He shook his head. "You're a journalist, but you don't have
a press pass."

"I write books," I said.

"And you don't have a camera," he said.

"I take notes," I said.

He stared at me for a long time, shaking his head.

"Do you have any children?" he said finally.

I cannot say why, but I was certain that my fate depended upon my answer.

"Two daughters," I said. "Six and eleven. I would really like to see them again."

His eyes bored into mine for what seemed like a very long time.

"You are a lucky man," he said at last. "Do you understand?"

"Yes," I said.

"Believe me," he said, "you have been given another life today."

"Thank you," I said.

"Understand?" he said.

"Understood," I said.

He motioned to his men to put everything back into my bag and then to return it to me. "Check your papers," he said to me. "Make sure nothing is missing."

I hastily looked through my notebooks, passports, receipts.

"It's all here," I said.

"Then go in peace," he said.

And so I did.

Epilogue

The shore is rough with stones and crusted salt, which scrape the soles of my feet, and it is a relief to wade into the Dead Sea. Late on an autumn afternoon, with the full moon rising over the Judean Hills, I float on my back in warm water the color of lead, among men and women from around the world, searching the limestone cliffs overhead for caves like the ones that we drove past in Qumran, on the northwest shore, where the Dead Sea Scrolls were discovered just after World War II. The story goes that a Bedouin herder threw a stone into a cave to drive out a stray goat, and struck an ancient jar containing a scroll wrapped in linen—the first of thousands of fragments unearthed from caves in the area, including the oldest extant Hebrew Biblical texts. Written on leather parchment, the scrolls contain apocrypha, hymns, prayers, legal writings, a manual on communal living, prophesies of the coming apocalypse; what they reveal about Judaic beliefs and practices in the centuries before the Romans destroyed Jerusalem in 70 AD is a variety of religious experience, some of which courses through modern Judaism and Christianity. "Hear now what wisdom is," we read in the Book of Secrets, which has been reconstructed from fragments found in two different caves, and then the tantalizing text breaks off.

The scrolls belong to a turbulent moment in history—some date from the period when the first Gospels were written—and the discovery of the library brought to Qumran for safekeeping during the Jewish revolt unsettled conventional wisdom about Judaism and Christianity. "In their apocalyptic message," writes the scholar Neil Asher Silberman, "the scrolls give a voice to a group that felt dispossessed and disenfranchised in a world turned upside down. They express a rage against invaders and contempt for collaborators, who are only interested in personal gain." In this they resemble the writings of reformers in every age whose determination to recall the faithful to the divine origins of their belief has often altered the course of history. From Martin Luther's theses on papal indulgences, nailed to a church door in Wittenberg, Germany, to al-Qaeda's Internet postings on the danger that democracy poses to Islam, the tradition of writers taking aim at the corruptors of their faith has led to no end of change and conflict.

The scrolls were probably written by the Essenes, one of several ascetic groups of Jews who believed that the priests of the Second Temple were corrupt. They went into the desert to renew their faith, hoping to create the true Israel, as Christians and Muslims through the ages have sought to create truer visions of their faith. The desire for purity, a constant in Judaism, Christianity, and Islam, seems to emerge with particular force at moments of dramatic change, when as the poet William Wordsworth observed, it feels as if "The world is too much with us." From the Essenes to the Desert Fathers, the Puritans, and the Islamic Revolutionaries in Iran, believers have sought to cleanse the forms and practices of their religion, and there is perhaps no purer vision of faith than the Temple Scroll, displayed in the Shrine of the Book in Jerusalem, which contains plans for a magnificent temple, never realized, which would be free of worldly contamination. The scroll describes, in abundant detail, a tripartite structure, sixteen hundred cubits square, which exists only in the imagination: a temple for a city restricted to the purest in heart and soul, built around the Holy of Holies, the inner sanctuary of the Tabernacle, accessible only to the high priest on Yom Kippur—an eternal space, which Christianity and Islam adopted for their own houses of worship. In short, the dream of a civilization.

It is difficult to maintain my balance in the water, which is nine times saltier than the Mediterranean, and just to bob up and down I have to push myself forward, as if to somersault, careful not to splash water near my eyes or ears, for they will burn; a nick on my wrist feels as if it is scalded, so I keep my hand raised, as if to call for help, though I cannot possibly go under. But if I surrender to this strange medium, giving myself over to a natural suspension that feels anything but natural, letting the current carry me where it will, as the sky darkens above the cliffs, then I feel at peace.

David took refuge nearby, gathering his forces to fulfill his destiny as the King of the Jews, and since we do not know where the Psalms attributed to him were composed I comfort myself with the thought that some of them might have taken shape right here. For they are our common inheritance in the West, viewed by Jews, Christians, and Muslims as revelations from God: "Bless the Lord, O my soul!" I like to think that the music of the Psalms is what binds together descendants of the Abrahamic faiths: reading or chanting these praise songs and laments, prayers and hymns of thanksgiving, which transcend geography and history, we enter a timeless, borderless realm, the exploration of which can school the heart and mind. The Psalms are a source of wisdom and instruction, even for those who do not know them, for they have shaped the imagination of the West and live on in the language: "Yea, though I walk through the valley of the shadow of death, I will fear no evil." The Psalms cross every border of thought and feeling— which may explain why Walt Whitman, Saint-John Perse, and Czeslaw Milosz employed the form of the Psalms to write poems exploring their place in the universe.

If travel confirms anything, it is how little we know about

the world. And this ignorance is the starting point for some of the greatest works of the imagination. In her 1996 Nobel Lecture, the Polish poet Wisława Szymborska suggests that inspiration is born of curiosity about the limits of our knowledge. "This is why I value that little phrase 'I don't know' so highly," she writes. "It's small, but it flies on mighty wings.

> It expands our lives to include spaces within us
> as well as the outer expanses in which our tiny
> Earth hangs suspended. If Isaac Newton had
> never said to himself, "I don't know," the apples
> in his little orchard might have dropped to the
> ground like hailstones, and at best he would
> have stopped to pick them up and gobble them
> with gusto.

Newton's curiosity got the better of him, though, and from his discovery of the laws of gravitation came a new understanding of our place in the universe. He was one of those "restless, questing spirits" (Szymborska's phrase for her compatriot Marie Sklodowska-Curie) whose questions change the world. Poets, she argues, "if they're genuine, must also keep repeating 'I don't know.'" For each poem offers but a makeshift answer to the question that set the poet humming, and new questions may arise before the ink is dry—questions that cannot be ignored if the poet hopes to remain vital. "Hear now what wisdom is," we read, and then the text breaks off.

The experiences recorded in these pages are the fruits of encounters in which I learned how little I know about Malaysia, the Middle Kingdom, and the Middle East. My travels in the key of terror have brought me to the Dead Sea, with a band of poets from around the world, where I find myself recalling a question posed by a perceptive friend, who wondered why the dove released by Noah after the flood returned to the ark: it could just as well have stayed on dry land instead of hazarding another water crossing to lead the ark to safety—and a new covenant with God. What compels us to return to the sources of love, faith, and conflict, all journeys into the unknown?

Everyone is on war footing: the standoff at the Nahr al-Bared refugee camp in northern Lebanon ended, with the Lebanese Army killing dozens of militants—although Fatah al-Islam's leader, Shaker al-Abssi, may have escaped. But Christian militias are rearming, and civil war seems closer than ever. Hezbollah and Israel have just negotiated an exchange—one Hezbollah prisoner and the corpses of two fighters for the body of a drowned Israeli who washed up on the Lebanese coast three years earlier—but Hezbollah remains silent about the fate of the two Israeli reservists whose abduction set off the Second Lebanon War, in 2006; few doubt that a Third Lebanon War is in the offing. And war in the Gaza Strip is inevitable, Israeli defense officials are telling their American counterparts, arguing that Hamas cannot be destroyed otherwise, while in Tehran Russian president Vladimir Putin is warning American allies not to be dragged into a confrontation with Iran. Putin is the first Russian leader to visit that country since the Yalta Conference, in 1943, when Stalin, Churchill, and Roosevelt planned for the aftermath of World War II. But prospects for peace in the region seem more remote now than what most Europeans felt in the grim prelude to the Normandy invasion.

I got a taste of this on opening night of the Sha'ar International Poetry Festival, at a dance theater in Tel Aviv. After performances of Shakespeare's sonnets in Hebrew translation, readings in several languages, stand-up comedy, a silent video titled *Last Days*, and music by a band called Panic Ensemble, a poet from Gaza took the stage to deliver the final reading—a short poem, he promised (it was after midnight), which turned out to be a rant, several pages long, about the Israeli occupation. I listened to it in English translation, on headphones, until the interpreter said, "beware of a curse that may come," and then fell silent. The poet's voice boomed in the auditorium. I wondered if the interpreter was too offended to continue, or did not have the rest of the text to translate. All that could be heard was the poet raging on and on. And when a comedian came on stage to lighten our spirits before sending us back into what he called "the shit out there," I felt hopeless. But then the comedian and a singer joined forces to sing a nonsense song, which revolved around the word "guitar," and the mood in the theater brightened.

Taratina, tinatara, they sang.

The festival is a microcosm of society. Poets from a dozen countries have traveled here to give readings, make connections, see the sights. There are among us recognizable types: the arrogant and embittered, open-minded and gullible, ambitious and content. An Indian poet who has stirred audiences with his poems about the injustices of the caste system—he comes from the untouchable class—surprised me one day when he said that he was the president of the Buddhist Society: he seemed more interested in promoting his career, seeking invitations to other festivals, than in pursuing a spiritual discipline. But I was not surprised to hear an aging Polish poet, whose vitriol toward the other poets is impressive, announce on the drive to the Dead Sea that he had no wish to swim in what he called the "treacly water," because the current might carry him far from shore. There were probably some on the bus who wished devoutly for that to happen.

Then there is the Israeli poet who teaches the Alexander Technique, a form of alternative medicine designed to make people aware of their habits—the first step in the reunification of the body and mind, the poet told me one night on a bus ride to Jerusalem. He recited a history of the method: how Frederick Alexander, a nineteenth-century Shakespearean actor who had lost his voice, became convinced that his problems stemmed from the way he projected his words on stage; how he studied his movements in a set of mirrors until he learned to resolve the tensions in his body; how he not only regained his voice but relieved his asthma. In his books he said that physical ailments are connected to the mind, the poet explained in flawless English. And in my practice I guide pupils to discover those links, mirroring their actions until their routines become apparent to them. We're creatures of habit, he said, stretching his hand out in the dark. Usually we view everything as static, but in fact my finger emerges from my hand and flows into the space around it. We have to become aware of that, of the present moment, to get into the flow. This applies to writing, too. We use language in habitual ways until it fills with deadness. A writer has to hear the language at its most vital.

A book must be the axe for the frozen sea inside us, Kafka wrote. And while many books thicken the ice, as indeed many things in life deaden our senses, curiosity, and imagination, it is also the case that in our every encounter—with another person, with ourselves, with literature and film, in art and ceremony, in travel and at rest, in war and peace—we are presented with a chance, whether we realize it or not, to break up that ice.

Seismic evidence suggests that an earthquake, in the time of Abraham, destroyed the cities of Sodom and Gomorrah, which may lie under the waters at the southern end of the Dead Sea. A major fault line runs under the sea, and the region is long overdue for another earthquake. This knowledge adds a certain frisson to my reflections, as I float in the warm, calm water, giving myself over to the elements, oblivious to the tectonic shifts in the offing. A worldwide economic crisis, a presidential election in America, revolutions in the Middle East—these will reshape the global order, with far-reaching consequences. But for now I am content to bob in the water, aware only that at any moment the ground could shift, and then I might be riding an enormous wave into the afterlife.

Not far from here, in Nag Hammadi, in Upper Egypt, a cache of papyrus codices bound in leather was discovered in 1945, just before the Dead Sea Scrolls came to light—thirteen books that revolutionized scholarship on the early church. A farmer digging in a field struck an earthenware jar, and though he feared that it might contain a spirit he broke it open, hoping to find treasure. But the golden flecks floating into the sky were bits of papyrus, and when he brought the ancient manuscripts home his mother burned more papyrus to cook dinner. Some weeks later, he gave what remained of the books to a priest for safekeeping from the police, he and his brothers having hacked a neighbor to death to avenge their father's murder in a blood feud. The priest showed some of the books to a local history teacher, who sent them to Cairo, where antiquities dealers sold them on the black market. Eventually government officials confiscated them, and though they wound up in the Coptic Museum decades passed before scholars began to systematically examine the fifty-two texts known as the Gnostic Gospels—a body of work that upended conventional views of early Christianity. It turns out that followers of Christ had more diverse beliefs than anyone imagined.

Gnosis is the Greek word for knowledge, and the divine wisdom recorded in texts like the Secret Book of James, the Gospel of Thomas, and the Secret Book of John is of a different order than what most Christians consider to be the foundations of their faith. For these secret teachings of the Savior present a more radical vision of Jesus than what has been handed down for two millennia, with more complicated ideas about salvation.

"Be wanderers," he said, according to Thomas, the disciple who doubted his resurrection until he touched the flesh of the risen Lord, and tradition holds that Thomas went to India to spread the faith. Professor Elaine Pagels finds connections between Eastern and Western thought in his writings, and indeed his account of what the Savior said differs in profound respects from the Gospels of Matthew, Mark, Luke, and John:

> Jesus said, "I am not your master. Because you
> have drunk, you have become drunk from the
> bubbling stream which I have measured out. . . .
> He who will drink from my mouth will become
> as I am: I myself shall become he, and the
> things that are hidden will be revealed to him."

Which prompts Pagels to ask: "Does not such teaching—the identity of the divine and human, the concern with illusion and enlightenment, the founder who is presented not as Lord, but as spiritual guide—sound more Eastern than Western?" She goes on to posit that Eastern and Western religions were not nearly so distinct two thousand years ago as we have come to think of them, and perhaps Thomas established a link between them, which was strengthened by Mongol warriors and Sufi traders, and then largely forgotten.

What a strange coincidence that these secret texts and the Dead Sea Scrolls were discovered one after the other in the wake of a global catastrophe. The war was over, the losses were being tallied, and even as a new international order began to take shape, one grounded in multilateral organizations like the United Nations, the World Bank, and the International Monetary Fund, these finds challenged reigning views of the underpinnings of Judeo-Christian civilization. It is a commonplace to say that this postwar order began to pass on 9/11.

And after 9/11 many said that everything had changed. But in fact everything is always changing—our body's cells divide, day turns into night, seasons pass—although dramatic change is what we remember best. Births and deaths, of course, and the pivotal events that shape a life—a failed exam, a missed flight, the day you left work early to walk for hours through the snowy woods and decided to change your life. We say that nothing will ever be the same, but is this not true of every moment of our lives? What we learned after 9/11 was that the foundations of our belief are never as secure as we think. For this book I visited cities that once were central to the imagination (Xi'an, Damascus) and now are not, cities which at the height of their glory instilled in their citizens a sense of greatness. But as the people of Sodom and Gomorrah learned when brimstone and fire rained down on them a world can vanish in a flash.

What the Dead Sea Scrolls and Gnostic Gospels reveal is the diversity of belief and practice in first-century Judaism and Christianity, respectively, when the forces were gathering that led to the destruction of the Second Temple in Jerusalem. History tends to gloss over the complexities of an era, the textures central to literature. The secret sayings of the Savior, for example, which transform him into a wilder figure than we know:

> Jesus said to them,
> "When you make the two into one,
> when you make the inner like the outer
>   and the outer like the inner,
>   and the upper like the lower,
> when you make male and female into a single
>   one,
>   so that the male will not be male
>   and the female will not be female,
> when you make eyes replacing an eye,

> a hand replacing a hand,
> a foot replacing a foot,
> and an image replacing an image,
> then you will enter the kingdom."

This reads like a poem, and indeed these secret sayings re-turn us to the source of poetry, which distills what is best in human thought, insofar as we can hear it, whether it is dictated by God or by the language. How one image replaces another will be revealed perhaps only in the kingdom, for here below we repeatedly confront the limits of our knowledge. Thus when Jesus asks his disciples to tell him what he is like Peter replies that he is a just angel, Matthew calls him a wise philosopher, and Thomas cannot say—which turns out to be the right an-swer. Jesus takes Thomas aside to tell him three things, which he does not reveal to the others, lest they stone him. Nor do we learn what these secrets are, for God is beyond all categories of knowledge. This recognition is what gives the Gospel its hid-den power: it is just the tip of an iceberg.

What did Thomas learn in India? "Jesus said, 'If you bring forth what is within you, what you bring forth will save you. If you do not bring forth what is within you, what you do not bring forth will destroy you.'" How to bring that forth before it destroys us? This is what poets pray to know in the dark nights of their souls. "For there is nothing hidden that will not be re-vealed," Jesus said. I am thinking that we waged a senseless war in Iraq, committing all manner of evil deeds, for which there has yet to be a reckoning. But these secret teachings make plain that sooner or later the truth will out.

"Ablutions on the banks of the Dead Seas," Perse wrote. And what better place to purify oneself for an encounter with the divine—or for the next stage of the journey, wherever it may lead? Every year, thousands of people come to the Dead Sea to perform ablutions, religious and secular, and as I drift closer to shore I hear a babble of languages from the bathers—German and Hebrew, French and English—which sound like prayers.

Ritual purifications are integral to most religions, and in the Abrahamic tradition they help the faithful to seek God. From the Jewish *mikveh* to the Christian sacrament of baptism to the Islamic act of washing called *wudu*, ceremonies were devised to prepare the faithful for the divine. To approach the godhead demands a turning toward what lies beyond what we can know: a form of purification which bears a family resemblance to the state of readiness a poet feels before the blank page. For poetic truth is of a similar order to the revelations central to Judaism, Christianity, and Islam: each offers a vision of the world unto itself, which exists both in and out of time—the "eternal present," as Octavio Paz defined it. Hearing poetry recited in settings that brim with religious meaning and historical memory makes me think that what poets and divines glimpse after long preparation holds for all of us, at every moment of our lives: the necessity, in the words of the prophet Zechariah, to "love truth and peace."

Near the water is a pit of mud said to be good for the skin, from which the Indian poet emerges, an untouchable Buddhist smeared from head to toe. He wades awkwardly into the sea, beating his chest, joking that he is a new Hindu god who will take his place among the three hundred thousand other gods in his country. The laughter is general as he scrubs the mud off his arms and legs. He jokes some more, and then, without thinking, bends over to cup his hands in the water, washes his face, and shrieks, "My eyes! My eyes!"

Silence falls over the sea in which nothing lives. The poet stands helplessly in the shallow water, reaching for somebody to guide him to the beach, where there is a hose to rinse his eyes. I am nearest to him, and though it takes some effort to get myself upright, bobbing forward, pushing my hands down through the heavy water as if to propel myself into the air, eventually I come to a standing position, with my feet some distance above the seafloor, and begin to paddle in his direction, protecting my eyes. It is slow going, it was so pleasant floating on my back, if I do not hurry he may go blind.

What choice do I have but to take his hand?

Selected Bibliography

Ali, Taha Muhammad. *Never Mind: Twenty Poems and a Story.* Translated by Peter Cole, Yahya Hijazi, and Gabriel Levin. Jerusalem: Ibis Editions, 2000.

The Al Qaeda Reader. Edited and translated by Raymond Ibrahim. New York: Broadway Books, 2007.

Andaya, Barbara Watson and Leonard Y. Andaya. *A History of Malaysia.* 2nd ed. Houndmills, England: Palgrave Macmillan, 2001.

Armstrong, Karen. *Buddha.* New York: Viking Press, 2001.

———. *Islam: A Short History.* New York: Modern Library, 2000.

———. *Jerusalem: One City, Three Faiths.* New York: Alfred A. Knopf, 1996.

Beaton, Roderick. *George Seferis: Waiting for the Angel: A Biography.* New Haven, CT: Yale University Press, 2003.

Blackburn, Simon. *Plato's Republic: A Biography.* New York: Atlantic Books, 2007.

Borges, Jorge Luis. *Selected Non-Fictions.* Edited by Eliot
Weinberger. Translated by Esther Allen, Suzanne Jill
Levine, and Eliot Weinberger. New York: Penguin Books,
1999.

Bowra, Maurice. *The Romantic Imagination.* Cambridge, MA:
Harvard University Press, 1950.

Brandon, James R. *Theatre in Southeast Asia.* Cambridge,
MA: Harvard University Press, 1967.

Burgess, Anthony. *The Long Day Wanes: A Malayan Trilogy.*
New York: W. W. Norton, 1992.

———. *Little Wilson and Big God, Being the First Part of
the Confessions of Anthony Burgess.* London: William
Heinemann, 1987.

Calvino, Italo. *Invisible Cities.* Translated by William Weaver.
New York: Harcourt Brace, 1974.

Catherwood, Christopher. *A Brief History of the Middle East.*
New York: Carroll & Graf, 2006.

Chin, Annping. *Confucius: A Life of Thought and Politics.* New
York: Scribner Books, 2007.

Chua, Amy. *Day of Empire: How Hyperpowers Rise to Global
Dominance—and Why They Fall.* New York: Doubleday,
2007.

Coll, Steve. *Ghost Wars: The Secret History of the CIA,
Afghanistan, and bin Laden, from the Soviet Invasion to
September 10, 2001.* New York: Penguin Books, 2004.

The Complete Dead Sea Scrolls in English, rev. ed. Translated by Geza Vermes. New York: Penguin Books, 2004.

Conrad, Joseph. *Almayer's Folly: A Story of an Eastern River.* New York: Modern Library, 2002.

———. *The Eastern Stories.* New Delhi: Penguin Books India, 2000.

Danner, Mark. *Torture and Truth: America, Abu Ghraib, and the War on Terror.* New York: New York Review Books, 2004.

Eliade, Mircea. *Shamanism: Archaic Techniques of Ecstasy.* Princeton, NJ: Princeton University Press, 1964.

The Essential Confucius: The Heart of Confucius' Teachings in Authentic I Ching *Order.* Translated by Thomas Cleary. New York: HarperCollins, 1992.

Fisk, Robert. *The Great War for Civilisation: The Conquest of the Middle East.* London: Fourth Estate, 2005.

———. *Pity the Nation: The Abduction of Lebanon.* New York: Nation Books, 2002.

Galand, René. *Saint-John Perse.* New York: Twayne Publishers, 1972.

Goldhill, Simon. *The Temple of Jerusalem.* London: Profile Books, 2004.

Goldsmith, Jack. *The Terror Presidency: Law and Judgment Inside the Bush Administration.* New York: W. W. Norton, 2007.

Gourevitch, Philip and Errol Morris. *Standard Operating Procedure.* New York: Penguin Press, 2008.

Greene, Graham. *Ways of Escape.* Toronto: Lester & Orpen Dennys, 1980.

Hersh, Seymour M. *Chain of Command: The Road from 9/11 to Abu Ghraib.* New York: HarperCollins, 2004.

Hill, Geoffrey. *A Treatise of Civil Power.* New Haven, CT: Yale University Press, 2008.

Hobsbawm, Eric. *On Empire: America, War, and Global Supremacy.* New York: Pantheon Books, 2008.

Horry, Ruth N. *Paul Claudel and Saint-John Perse: Parallels and Contrasts.* Chapel Hill, NC: University of North Carolina Press, 1971.

Horsley, Richard A. and Neil Asher Silberman. *The Message and the Kingdom: How Jesus and Paul Ignited a Revolution and Transformed the Ancient World.* New York: Grosset & Dunlap, 1997.

Hsieh, Yvonne Y. *Victor Segalen's Literary Encounter with China: Chinese Moulds, Western Thoughts.* Toronto: University of Toronto Press, 1988.

Human Rights Watch. *Civilian Pawns: Laws of War Violations and the Use of Weapons on the Israel-Lebanon Border.* New York: Human Rights Watch Report, May 1996.

――――. *Getting Away with Torture? Command Responsibility for the U.S. Abuse of Detainees.* New York: Human Rights Watch Report, April, 2005.

――――. *In the Name of Security: Counterterrorism and Human Rights Abuse Under Malaysia's Internal Security Act.* New York: Human Rights Watch Report, May 2004.

Ibrahim, Khalil. *A Continued Dialogue.* Kuala Lumpur: National Art Gallery, 2004.

Iyer, Pico. *The Open Road: The Global Journey of the Fourteenth Dalai Lama.* New York: Alfred A. Knopf, 2008.

Kafka, Franz. *The Great Wall of China: Stories and Reflections.* Translated by Willa and Edwin Muir. New York: Schocken Books, 1970.

Kassir, Samir. *Being Arab.* Translated by Will Hobson. London: Verso Books, 2006.

Kenner, Hugh. *The Pound Era.* Berkeley, CA: University of California Press, 1971.

Knodel, Arthur. *Saint-John Perse: A Study of His Poetry.* Edinburgh: Edinburgh University Press, 1966.

Laderman, Carol. *Taming the Wind of Desire: Psychology, Medicine, and Aesthetics in Malay Shamanistic Performance.* Berkeley, CA: University of California Press, 1991.

Léger, Alexis St. Léger. *A Selection of Works for an Understanding of World Affairs Since 1914.* Washington: The Library of Congress, 1943.

Little, Marie-Noëlle, ed. *The Poet and the Diplomat: The Correspondence of Dag Hammarskjöld and Alexis Leger.* Translated by Marie-Noëlle Little and William C. Parker. Syracuse, NY: Syracuse University Press, 2001.

Little, Roger. *The Shaping of Modern French Poetry: Reflections on Unrhymed Poetic Form, 1840–1990.* Manchester: Carcanet Press, 1996.

Maalouf, Amin. *The Crusades Through Arab Eyes.* Translated by Jon Rothschild. New York: Schocken Books, 1984.

Mango, Cyril. *Byzantium: The Empire of the New Rome.* London: Weidenfeld & Nicolson, 1980.

Man, John. *Genghis Khan: Life, Death, and Resurrection.* London: Bantam Books, 2004.

———. *Kublai Khan: The Mongol King Who Remade China.* London: Bantam Books, 2006.

Marcus, Amy Dockser. *Jerusalem 1913: The Origins of the Arab-Israeli Conflict.* New York: Viking Press, 2007.

Marshall, Robert. *Storm from the East: From Genghis Khan to Khubilai Khan.* Berkeley, CA: University of California Press, 1993.

Mayer, Jane. *The Dark Side: The Inside Story of How the War on Terror Turned into a War on American Ideals.* New York: Doubleday, 2008.

Merton, Thomas. *The Asian Journal of Thomas Merton.* Edited by Naomi Burton, Patrick Hart, and James Laughlin. New York: New Directions, 1973.

———. *Conjectures of a Guilty Bystander.* Garden City, NY: Doubleday, 1966.

———. *Merton & Sufism: The Untold Story, a Complete Compendium.* Edited by Rob Baker and Gray Henry. Louisville, KY: Fons Vitae, 2005.

———. *Thoughts on the East.* New York: New Directions, 1995.

———. *Zen and the Birds of Appetite.* New York: New Directions, 1968.

Merwin, W. S. *The Rain in the Trees.* New York: Alfred A. Knopf, 1988.

Miłosz, Czesław. *New and Collected Poems, 1931–2001.* New York: HarperCollins, 2001.

Mott, Michael. *The Seven Mountains of Thomas Merton.* Boston: Houghton Mifflin, 1984.

Murray, Nicholas. *Kafka*. London: Little, Brown and Company, 2004.

Naipul, V. S. *Among the Believers: An Islamic Journey*. New York: Alfred A. Knopf, 1981.

———. *Beyond Belief: Islamic Excursions Among the Converted Peoples*. New York: Random House, 1998.

The National Commission on Terrorist Attacks Upon the United States. *The 9/11 Commission Report*. New York: W. W. Norton, 2004.

Oren, Michael B. *Six Days of War: June 1967 and the Making of the Modern Middle East*. New York: Random House, 2002.

———. *Power, Faith, and Fantasy: America in the Middle East, 1776 to the Present*. New York: W. W. Norton, 2007.

Ostrovsky, Erika. *Under the Sign of Ambiguity: Saint-John Perse/Alexis Leger*. New York: New York University Press, 1985.

Pagis, Dan. *The Selected Poetry of Dan Pagis*. Translated by Stephen Mitchell. Berkeley, CA: University of California Press, 1996.

Pagels, Elaine. *The Gnostic Gosepls*. New York: Random House, 1979.

———. *Beyond Belief: The Secret Gospel of Thomas*. New York: Random House, 2003.

Paz, Octavio. *Itinerary: An Intellectual History.* Translated by Jason Wilson. New York: Harcourt, 1999.

———. *The Other Voice: Essays on Modern Poetry.* Translated by Helen Lane. New York: Harcourt, 1990.

———. *The Siren and the Seashell and Other Essays on Poets and Poetry.* Translated by Lysander Kemp and Margaret Sayers Peden. Austin, TX: University of Texas Press, 1976.

Perkins, David, ed. *English Romantic Writers.* New York: Harcourt, 1967.

Perse, Saint-John. *Collected Poems.* Translated by W. H. Auden, Hugh Chisholm, Denis Devlin, T. S. Eliot, Robert Fitzgerald, Wallace Fowlie, Richard Howard, and Louise Varèse. Princeton, NJ: Princeton University Press, 1971.

———. *Letters.* Translated and edited by Arthur J. Knodel. Princeton, NJ: Princeton University Press, 1979.

———. *Song for an Equinox.* Translated by Richard Howard. Princeton, NJ: Princeton University Press, 1977.

Plato. *The Portable Plato.* Edited by Scott Buchanan. New York: Viking Press, 1976.

Pound, Ezra. *The Pisan Cantos.* Edited by Richard Sieburth. New York: New Directions, 2003.

Qian, Zhaoming, ed. *Ezra Pound and China.* Ann Arbor, MI: University of Michigan Press, 2003.

Rich, Frank. *The Greatest Story Ever Sold: The Decline and Fall of Truth from 9/11 to Katrina.* New York: Penguin Books, 2006.

Ricks, Thomas E. *Fiasco: The American Military Adventure in Iraq.* New York: Penguin Press, 2006.

Rigolot, Carol. *Forged Genealogies: Saint-John Perse's Conversations with Culture.* Chapel Hill, NC: University of North Carolina Press, 2001.

Rong, Jiang. *Wolf Totem.* Translated by Howard Goldblatt. New York: Penguin Press, 2008.

Sambhava, Padma. *The Tibetan Book of the Dead: Liberation through Understanding in the Between.* Translated by Robert A. F. Thurman. New York: Bantam Books, 1994.

Sands, Philippe. *Torture Team: Rumsfeld's Memo and the Betrayal of American Values.* New York: Palgrave Macmillan, 2008.

The Secret Teachings of Jesus: Four Gnostic Gospels. Translated by Marvin W. Meyer. New York: Random House, 1984.

Segalen, Victor. *Essay on Exoticism: An Aesthetics of Diversity.* Translated and edited by Yaël Rachel Schlick. Durham, NC: Duke University Press, 2002.

———. *Stèles.* Translated and annotated by Timothy Billings and Christopher Bush. Middletown, CT: Wesleyan University Press, 2007.

———. *Stèles.* Translated by Michael Taylor. Santa Monica, CA: Lapis Press, 1987.

Segev, Tom. *1967: Israel, the War, and the Year that Transformed the Middle East.* Translated by Jessica Cohen. New York: Henry Holt and Company, 2007.

Seferis, George. *Collected Poems.* Translated, edited, and introduced by Edmund Keeley and Philip Sherrard. Princeton, NJ: Princeton University Press, 1995.

———. *A Levant Journal.* Translated, edited, and introduced by Roderick Beaton. Jerusalem: Ibis Editions, 2007.

———. *A Poet's Journal: Days of 1945–1951.* Translated by Athan Anagnostopoulos. Cambridge, MA: Harvard University Press, 1974.

Shanks, Hershel. *The Mystery and Meaning of the Dead Sea Scrolls.* New York: Random House, 1998.

Shehadeh, Raja. *Palestinian Walks: Notes on a Vanishing Landscape.* London: Profile Books, 2007.

Sherry, Norman. *The Life of Graham Greene, Volume II: 1939–1955.* New York: Penguin Books, 1995.

Silberman, Neil Asher. *The Hidden Scrolls: Christianity, Judaism and the War for the Dead Sea Scrolls.* New York: G. P. Putnam's Sons, 1994.

Smith, Huston. *Islam: A Concise Introduction.* San Francisco: HarperCollins, 2001.

Smith, Huston. *The World's Religions: Our Great Wisdom Traditions.* New York: HarperCollins, 1991.

Spence, Jonathan D. *The Chan's Great Continent: China in Western Minds.* New York: W. W. Norton, 1998.

Suskind, Ron. *The One Percent Doctrine: Deep Inside America's Pursuit of Its Enemies Since 9/11.* New York: Simon & Schuster, 2006.

Viorst, Milton. *Storm from the East: The Struggle Between the Arab World and the Christian West.* New York: Modern Library, 2007.

Waterfield, Robin. *Xenophon's Retreat: Greece, Persia, and the End of the Golden Age.* London: Faber and Faber, 2006.

Weatherford, Jack. *Genghis Khan and the Making of the Modern World.* New York: Crown Books, 2004.

Weinberger, Eliot. *An Elemental Thing.* New York: New Directions, 2007.

———, ed. *The New Directions Anthology of Classical Chinese Poetry.* New York: New Directions, 2003.

Whitfield, Roderick, Susan Whitfield, and Neville Agnew. *Cave Temples of Mogao: Art and History on the Silk Road.* Los Angeles: The Getty Conservation Institute, 2000.

Wisława Szymborska. *Poems New and Collected, 1957–1997* Translated by Stanisław Barańczak and Clare Cavanagh. New York: Harcourt, 1998.

Wright, Lawrence. *The Looming Tower: al-Qaeda and the Road to 9/11*. New York: Alfred A. Knopf, 2006.

Xenophon. *The Persian Expedition*. Translated by Rex Warner. New York: Penguin, 1972.

Xingjian, Gao. *The Case for Literature*. Translated by Mabel Lee. New Haven, CT: Yale University Press, 2007.

Acknowledgments

Many thanks to my traveling companions and others who helped at home and along the way: Amira and Munir Akash, Daniel Alarcón, Archbishop Chrysostomos, Gun-Aajav Ayurzana, Columbia Barossa, Niu Baoguo, Kelly Bedeian, Rustom Bharucha, Kevin Bowen, Jeffrey and Elizabeth Carson, Mundakundu Chinnaswamy, Peter Cole and Adina Hoffman, Michael Collier, Xi Chuan, Olena Kalytiak Davis, Nataša Durovićova, Hualing Engle, Tony Eprile, Hugh Ferrer, Pauline Fan, Thomas Gavin and Susan Holahan, Ted Genoways, Rosellen Gowdy, Michael Hogan, Iman Humaydan, Sahar Issa, Khalid Jaafar, John Keller, Eddin Khoo, Anthea King, Jane Hirshfield, Susan Johnson and Ann Rhomberg, Kathy Lavezzo and Harry Stecopoulos, Lola Lopes, Sally Mason, John Matthias, Jeanne McCulloch, Askold Melnyczuk, Wang Meng, Charles and Suzanne Merrill, Amir Or and Tziona Sahami, John Pack, John Peck, William Reisinger, Phil Alden Robinson, Sandy Rouse, Barry and Grace Sanders, Melissa Schiek, Nihad Sirees, Tom Sleigh, David Skorton, Jill Staggs, Rob Sutcliff, Downing Thomas, Anastassis Vistonitis, Stephen Vlastos, Derek Willard, Artemis Zenetou, and the diplomats and their staffs, at various American embassies and consulates, who prefer to remain nameless.

I am very grateful to my editor, Daniel Slager, who encouraged me to conceive of this book in the largest possible terms, and to my agent, Sloan Harris, who has the patience of Job. Dedicating this book to him is a small way to thank him for his guidance, kindness, and unflagging support through the years.

Special thanks to Anne McPeak, whose brilliant copy editing not only saved me many errors but inspired me to see my work anew, and to Allison Wigen, who shepherded my manuscript through production with uncommon grace and understanding.

I am indebted to Bruce Rogers and his staff for providing me with space and time in which to work at the Hermitage Artist Retreat, and to the editors of *The Notre Dame Review* and *The Virginia Quarterly*, in which portions of this book appeared, in slightly different form.

Finally, I wish to thank my wife, Lisa, and my daughters, Hannah and Abigail, who endured my absences, brightened my returns, and made the writing of this book a joy.

CHRISTOPHER MERRILL is the author of four books of poetry, including *Watch Fire*, for which he received the Peter I. B. Lavan Younger Poets Award from the Academy of American Poets; four works of nonfiction: *The Grass of Another Country: A Journey Through the World of Soccer*, *The Old Bridge: The Third Balkan War and the Age of the Refugee*, *Only the Nails Remain: Scenes from the Balkan Wars*, and *Things of the Hidden God: Journey to the Holy Mountain*; and several books of translations and edited volumes, among them *The Forgotten Language: Contemporary Poets and Nature* and *From the Faraway Nearby: Georgia O'Keeffe as Icon*. His writings have been translated into twenty-five languages; his journalism appears in a variety of publications; his many honors include a knighthood in arts and letters from the French government. Director of the International Writing Program at the University of Iowa, he and his wife, violinist Lisa Gowdy-Merrill, are the parents of two daughters, Hannah and Abigail.

Milkweed Editions

Founded as a nonprofit organization in 1980, Milkweed Editions is an independent publisher. Our mission is to identify, nurture and publish transformative literature, and build an engaged community around it.

Join Us

In addition to revenue generated by the sales of books we publish, Milkweed Editions depends on the generosity of institutions and individuals like you. In an increasingly consolidated and bottom-line-driven publishing world, your support allows us to select and publish books on the basis of their literary quality and transformative potential. Please visit our Web site (www.milkweed.org) or contact us at (800) 520-6455 to learn more.

Milkweed Editions, a nonprofit publisher, gratefully acknowledges sustaining support from Amazon.com; Emilie and Henry Buchwald; the Bush Foundation; the Patrick and Aimee Butler Foundation; Timothy and Tara Clark; the Dougherty Family Foundation; Friesens; the General Mills Foundation; John and Joanne Gordon; Ellen Grace; William and Jeanne Grandy; the Jerome Foundation; the Lerner Foundation; Sanders and Tasha Marvin; the McKnight Foundation; Mid-Continent Engineering; the Minnesota State Arts Board, through an appropriation by the Minnesota State Legislature and a grant from the National Endowment for the Arts; Kelly Morrison and John Willoughby; the National Endowment for the Arts; the Navarre Corporation; Ann and Doug Ness; Jörg and Angie Pierach; the Carl and Eloise Pohlad Family Foundation; the RBC Foundation USA; the Target Foundation; the Travelers Foundation; Moira and John Turner; and Edward and Jenny Wahl.

amazon.com   Bush Foundation

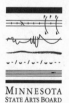

THE MᶜKNIGHT FOUNDATION

Interior design by Connie Kuhnz
Typeset in Warnock Pro
by BookMobile Design and Publishing Services
Printed on acid-free 100% postconsumer waste paper
by Friesens Corporation

ENVIRONMENTAL BENEFITS STATEMENT

Milkweed Editions saved the following resources by printing the pages of this book on chlorine free paper made with 100% post-consumer waste.

TREES	WATER	ENERGY	SOLID WASTE	GREENHOUSE GASES
40	18,410	16	1,167	4,082
FULLY GROWN	GALLONS	MILLION BTUs	POUNDS	POUNDS

Environmental impact estimates were made using the Environmental Paper Network Paper Calculator. For more information visit www.papercalculator.org.